Praise for *Getting China and India Right*

"*Getting China and India Right* is the only book to integrate the authors' insider perspective regarding both China and India with cutting-edge ideas on global strategy. Backed up by solid research, it is compelling and provocative. I agree entirely with Anil and Haiyan's central thesis that any Fortune 1000 company that does not develop a robust strategy for China and India risks not surviving as an independent entity by 2020. This book should serve as required reading for any CEO or senior executive who wants to see his or her company emerge or remain as one of the global leaders in its industry over the next ten years."

   —Ronnie C. Chan, chairman, Hang Lung Group, and vice-chairman, Asia
     Society

"Globalization has moved beyond trade, manufacturing, and R&D to a full globalization of the corporate brain, driven and enabled by new technologies that allow companies to operate and think globally. As the corporate brain goes global, the challenges become more complex and the opportunities more significant. This well-researched book crisply outlines the role of China and India in this new phase of globalization. It is an insightful guide to how companies can survive and succeed in the new era."

   —Wim Elfrink, executive vice-president, Cisco Services, and chief globalization
     officer, Cisco Systems

"Our own experience in the lodging industry makes it very clear that it is now impossible for any company to remain a global leader in its industry without a deep and sustained commitment to the world's two fastest growing economies—China and India. Timely, comprehensive, insightful, and richly documented, *Getting China and India Right* is a superb guide to understand the multi-faceted opportunities and challenges that these two economies present and how companies must rise up to them. Our senior leaders have benefited immensely from discussions with the authors. This book is essential reading for any CEO and his or her colleagues who are keen to engage with China and India on a sustained long-term basis."

   —Edwin D. Fuller, president and managing director, Marriott
     Lodging-International

"At a time when China and India present enormous opportunities and equally considerable risks, no global CEO, or any of his or her senior colleagues, can afford not to read this timely and insightful book. What makes this book particularly compelling and valuable is that it not only leverages the authors' insider perspectives on China and India but also brings cutting-edge ideas on global strategy to examine how the China-India phenomenon must reshape corporate strategies in general."

   —Jeffrey E. Garten, Juan Trippe Professor of International Trade, Finance, and
     Business, Yale School of Management, and former Undersecretary of Commerce
     for International Trade

"*Getting China and India Right* has a clear message to CEOs and senior executives of global companies. It is simply not enough to be just present in China or India. Anil and Haiyan convincingly point out that the global players of the future must have a robust China and India strategy that goes well beyond the traditional outsourcing and low-cost manufacturing model. Their arguments will inspire every global CEO to re-examine their current approach to the dynamic market opportunities and challenges in China and India. An outstanding book, highly readable, full of facts and analysis, and inspirational."

    —William V. Hickey, CEO, Sealed Air Corporation

"*Getting China and India Right* offers an insightful view of two growth engines for the future. Rich with strategic advice as well as concrete examples, it is a must-read for CEOs of companies looking for global growth."

    —Edgar Hotard, chairman, Monitor Group China

"The new global shape of the beer industry vividly reinforces the core premise of Anil and Haiyan's highly readable book—it is almost impossible for any company to remain a global leader in its industry without treating big emerging markets such as China, India, and Latin America as core to its strategic agenda. *Getting China and India Right* is the best source of insight available for executives who want not only to understand the multifaceted opportunities and challenges that these two giants present but also to figure out what these developments mean for the company's global strategy. The authors of this book are among the world's masters on the subject of global strategy in the new age of China and India. We have benefited from their insights. If you were to read only one book on this subject this year, this should be it. A real tour de force."

    —Graham Mackay, CEO, SABMiller plc

"My global experience in the consulting and technology services industry resonates strongly with the central thesis of *Getting China and India Right*. As the multi-polar world continues to evolve, China and India will emerge as major economic hubs. The high-performing companies of tomorrow must pursue a deep and long-term engagement with these two societies on all fronts: the rapidly growing market opportunities, the potential for cost efficiency, the large and highly scalable talent pool, and some extremely capable and ambitious competitors. Anil and Haiyan are truly global individuals who also benefit from a deeply rooted understanding of India and China. They have written an insightful, compelling, forward-looking, and practical book. Their expertise in global strategy, coupled with their deep scholarship, makes this one of the most important books on how the rise of India and China must reshape corporate strategies."

    —Harsh Manglik, chairman, Accenture India

"*Getting China and India Right* is an incisive and well-researched book about the growing dominance of India and China in the global economy and its implications for corporate strategy. The authors' in-depth analysis is richly supported by substantiating facts, figures, and examples."

    —Narayana N.R. Murthy, chairman and chief mentor,
      Infosys Technologies Limited

"As the global economy becomes increasingly interdependent, industry leaders need to understand and embrace the trends that are driving and affecting their business today. *Getting China and India Right* is the best book by far to analyze how the rise of China and India will fundamentally reshape corporate strategies. It is thoroughly researched, insightful, and compelling. As someone who plans strategy all day, I see it as a must-read for any Fortune 1000 CEO."

   —Mark J. Penn, CEO, Burson Marsteller; author of *Microtrends;* and
      key advisor to Bill Clinton, Tony Blair, and Bill Gates

"This book draws out the strengths of the economies of China and India and offers a blueprint to companies on how to draw up strategies to best approach the two economies for the long term."

   —Ratan N. Tata, chairman, Tata Group

"Anil and Haiyan correctly observe that the mere fact that a large number of multinationals are present in India and China does not necessarily imply that they understand these economies well or that they have robust strategies to capture the market and resource opportunities there. In *Getting China and India Right*, the authors forcefully make the point that cracking these twin markets and leveraging the talent and innovation opportunities that they offer is critical to the survival of every company. Importantly, they build on this point to develop a strategic roadmap for action. The practical advice they offer, with illuminating anecdotes and evidence, makes this a compelling read."

   —Ravi Venkatesan, chairman, Microsoft India

"This book is very timely. It not only highlights the importance of China and India as two of the most potent emerging economies but also illuminates the growing dynamics between these two future powers in the changing global economy. While it is extremely well researched, it is also highly readable and very practical in putting forward guidelines for corporate action."

   —Kyung H. Yoon, vice-chairman, Heidrick & Struggles

"The world economic landscape is undergoing a fundamental transformation. This book provides very helpful insights about the role of China and India in driving this transformation and what these developments mean for global strategy. *Getting China and India Right* is must-reading for any multinational firm CEO who wants to see his or her firm succeed in the coming years."

   —Ming Zeng, executive vice president–strategy, Alibaba Group, and author of
      Dragons at Your Door

Getting China and India Right

Strategies for Leveraging the World's Fastest-Growing Economies for Global Advantage

Anil K. Gupta

Haiyan Wang

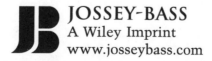

JOSSEY-BASS
A Wiley Imprint
www.josseybass.com

Published by Jossey-Bass
A Wiley Imprint
989 Market Street, San Francisco, CA 94103-1741—www.josseybass.com

Jossey-Bass books and products are available through most bookstores. To contact Jossey-Bass directly call our Customer Care Department within the U.S. at 800-956-7739, outside the U.S. at 317-572-3986, or fax 317-572-4002.

Jossey-Bass also publishes its books in a variety of electronic formats. Some content that appears in print may not be available in electronic books.

Library of Congress Cataloging-in-Publication Data
Gupta, Anil K.
    Getting China and India right : strategies for leveraging the
world's fastest-growing economies for global advantage / Anil K.
Gupta, Haiyan Wang.
        p.   cm.
    Includes bibliographical references and index.
    ISBN 978-0-470-28424-7 (cloth : alk. paper)   1. Marketing—China.
2. Marketing—India.   3. Globalization.   I. Wang, Haiyan.   II. Title.
    HF5415.12.C5G87   2009
    658'.0490951—dc22
                                                    2008046777

Printed in the United States of America
FIRST EDITION
HB Printing   10 9 8 7 6 5 4 3 2 1

Contents

Preface

The central premise underlying this book is that being present in China and India is not the same thing as getting China and India right.

Most CEOs and their senior colleagues are well aware that the world's economic center of gravity is shifting from the developed to the emerging economies, in particular China and India. Notwithstanding this general awareness, very few truly grasp the magnitude and pace of change and the multifaceted nature of the new reality. Fewer still have figured out what these developments mean for the future architecture of their company. Some of the most common mistakes are viewing China and India solely from the lens of offshoring and cost reduction, building marketing strategies that are centered around just the rich cities and the top 5 to 10 percent of the population, underestimating the ambitions and capabilities of emerging competitors, and treating these two countries as peripheral rather than core to their company's global strategy.

The rise of China and India is a game-changing phenomenon. Given the size and rapid growth of these two economies, a suboptimal strategy for China and India is no longer a matter of merely leaving some money on the table. Many of today's Western giants that do not have solid strategies for China and India will face severe threats to their very existence in as little as ten years, as competitors that *are* making the most of China and India mark these companies with a bull's eye for annihilation or acquisition. Putting in place the right strategies, which we outline in this book, is crucial to leveraging these economies for global advantage.

A 2006 report by the American Chamber of Commerce in Shanghai reported that 65 percent of its member companies were profitable and that nearly one-third of these had profit levels equal to or higher than in other countries. At first blush, these data may suggest that multinational companies are finally beginning to get their China (and similarly India) strategy right. But based on our analysis of and interviews with managers in over a hundred companies, we question the validity of any such conclusion. As a recent report by the IBM Institute for Business Value on MNC strategies in China noted, "Although a small, but growing, number of companies are tapping the mass market, the majority of MNCs still rely on premium-end products in the top cities for the bulk of their revenues and profits."[1]

Pursuing a premium-end niche strategy may be an easy way to show attractive profit margins from the China and India operations and keep headquarters executives happy. We contend, however, that focusing exclusively on profit margins as the measure of success runs a serious risk of leading to misplaced priorities. Pursuing market opportunities in China and India is like entering a large and rapidly growing new line of business. If you just skim the surface, it will appear as if you are doing well. However, what you may not know is that you have a rather small and declining market share and that you are setting yourself up for being pushed aside. Established multinationals face a particularly acute competitive threat from new global players from within China and India that have radically different capabilities, radically different mindsets, and radically different notions of speed—combined with easy access to global capital and global talent. As the China president for one of the world's largest multinationals noted to us, "Ten years from now, there will be fewer successful multinational corporations in China than you see today. Headquarters executives in many companies are simply unaware that they are being squeezed into a narrow corner."

In Chapter One, we develop the central idea that China and India are the only two countries in the world that simultaneously constitute four stories rolled into one, each of them with the potential to be game changing in its own right: (1) China and India as megamarkets for almost every product and service, (2) China and India as platforms to dramatically reduce a company's global cost structure, (3) China and India as platforms to significantly boost a company's global technology and innovation base, and (4) China and India as the springboards for the emergence of a new breed of fearsome global competitors. Many countries feature one or two of these stories, but other than China and India, no other features all four. Building robust strategies for China and India requires that the company address each of these four stories head-on.

In Chapter Two, we contend that the time for debating whether to pursue China or India is over and that the right question to ask is how best to pursue both China and India rather than which one. We begin by highlighting the important similarities and differences between China and India, as well as the rapidly growing trade and investment linkages between them. Building on this analysis, we outline the four types of strategic benefits that a company can derive by pursuing a China+India strategy: leverage the scale of both China and India; leverage the complementary strengths of China and India; transfer learning from one market to the other, thereby accelerating the pace of success in both markets; and leverage dual presence to reduce risks.

In Chapter Three, we analyze the structure of the market opportunities in China and India and discuss how a company should position itself to capture the hearts, minds, and wallets of the consumers in these two countries. We argue that unless a company operates in niche products and services, it should go wide and deep, pursuing a multisegment strategy. At the top end of the income spectrum, customers have high buying power and are likely to prefer global products and services. Thus, companies are unlikely to face much pressure for local adaptation of their products and services except for cultural reasons. The middle income segment constitutes the mass market. For most products and services, this is also the fastest-growing market in each country and can be ignored only at great peril to the company's future. This segment is often characterized by brutal competition, low pricing power, and low margins. In order to win here, a company will generally need to develop local products and services that are designed to be low cost. At the lower end of the income spectrum, a company is unlikely to generate much revenue. However, given high growth rates, this is the segment with the greatest possibilities for innovation. Every smart company should engage with this segment seriously, aim to break even, and view it as a learning laboratory for the discovery of new business models.

Chapter Four deals with the outbound part of the China and India story: how a company can use China and India as global platforms. We focus on three opportunities: cost arbitrage, intellectual arbitrage, and business model innovation. Realizing these opportunities requires a company to work on many fronts: managing internal politics; conducting a disaggregated value chain analysis to decide exactly which activities should be located in China, which in India, and which in other countries; deciding whether to set up the company's own operations or rely on outsourcing; building the necessary local capabilities; and then deploying the local capabilities globally without losing control of the value chain.

Chapter Five examines in detail the forces that are propelling the rapid emergence of global champions from China and India. We also compare the relative strengths and weaknesses of the Chinese dragons and the Indian tigers in relation to each other. Building on this analysis, we advance a multipronged strategy for multinational corporations to not only defend themselves but also compete with the dragons and tigers on the world stage: attack the new champions within their home markets and thus neutralize their home court advantage; consider joining forces with the dragons and tigers; pursue an integrated China+India strategy, thereby leveraging the combined scale and resources of both economies; and aggressively defend your existing competitive position outside China and India since defending an existing position is far easier than trying to regain lost ground.

Chapter Six looks at the human resource challenges that companies must overcome in their quest to win within China and India and leverage the strengths of these two countries for global advantage. Notwithstanding their billion-plus populations and the world's two largest pools of college graduates every year, China and India suffer from an acute shortage of professional staff such as seasoned managers and people with specialized skills (for example, accountants in China and software developers in India). As such, most companies, foreign and domestic, find themselves engaged in a perpetual war for talent. In this chapter, we begin by looking at why there exists this scarcity in the midst of plenty in China and India. We then put forward guidelines about what a company can do to increase its odds at winning the ongoing brutal war for talent.

In Chapter Seven, we pull together the conclusions from our analysis and outline what the features of a global enterprise must be if it is to emerge as one of the winners ten years from now. We argue that the magnitude and pace of change, as well as the multifaceted nature of the new reality, demands that senior leaders rethink some of their central assumptions in crafting global strategy, rethink what must be the drivers and processes to create innovations over the next ten years, rethink how the company must be organized and managed, and, above all, strive with full vigor to globalize the corporate mindset.

We conclude by noting that the successful global corporation of tomorrow will be one that figures out how to take advantage of three realities: the rapid growth of emerging markets and the increasing multipolarity of the world economy; enduring cultural, political, and economic differences across countries and regions; and the rapidly growing integration of national economies. Organizationally it will be managed as a globally integrated enterprise rather than as a federation of regional or national fiefdoms. And it will be led by business leaders who have global mindsets and are masters at building bridges rather than moats.

December 2008

Anil K. Gupta
Haiyan Wang
Bethesda, Maryland
New Delhi, India
Shanghai, China

Acknowledgments

Writing this book has been a personal as well as professional journey for both of us. We (Anil and Haiyan) were born and grew up in India and China, respectively. We had our early education in our native lands and started our professional careers there. Each of us has also made the United States home for over fifteen years. During this period, we have conducted extensive research on strategy and globalization and worked in advisory capacities for a large number of companies in many parts of the world, especially North America, Europe, and Asia. This book is a product of the accumulated learning that we acquired through countless interactions with professional colleagues and clients, combined with fresh research. We owe a debt to all of them.

Given the constraints of space, it is impossible for us to acknowledge each of the individuals who played a critical role in either encouraging us to undertake this project or in educating us about China and India. We would, however, like to identify some of the people who have played a particularly central role. We start with our parents (Charan Dass and Chandra Prabha Gupta in the case of Anil and Wang Yi and Chen ZongRong in the case of Haiyan). Having witnessed the transformation of India and China up close, they encouraged us to write a book that will help the world understand that the rise of these two countries is a back-to-the-future story and not a new phenomenon. Vijay Govindarajan (VG), Anil's classmate at Harvard and close friend and coauthor for over twenty-five years, played an important role in motivating us to get this project off the ground by reinforcing our conclusion that most multinational corporations have little more than a superficial understanding of China and India and that we have something valuable to say. David Wang and Mei Xu, Haiyan's brother and sister-in-law, played an equally important role in persuading her that when you believe in something, it is better to just do it rather than spend too much time debating the pros and cons. As successful entrepreneurs who have leveraged the U.S.-China corridor to create a rapidly growing enterprise, they have shared their insights about the do's and don'ts of leveraging China for global advantage. Other close friends who provided encouragement in the early stages of developing this book include our mutual friends Paresh Shah and Prashanth Boccassam (PV), entrepreneurs extraordinaire who know how to capitalize on the complementary strengths of the United States, India, and Europe to create and deliver valuable products and services.

Kathe Sweeney, senior editor at Jossey-Bass, has been a central player in helping us launch this project and in pushing us to get it completed without too much delay. Along with *The Quest for Global Dominance*, this is the second book project on which we have collaborated with Kathe. Given her role as senior editor for one of the world's leading publishers, her enthusiasm and guidance have been particularly important in bringing this project to fruition.

Our parents, VG, David, Mei, Paresh, PV, Kathe, and the large number of friends, colleagues, and clients: thank you all for giving us your time, friendship, care, and the benefit of your insights. Although we alone are responsible for the deficiencies that remain, we hope that you will be proud of the final product.

Getting China and India Right

1

CHINA AND INDIA-FOUR STORIES ROLLED INTO ONE

> The debate about whether Asia will once again
> dominate the global economy—as it did for two
> millennia before the industrial revolution in
> 18th-century Britain and the rise of the US—is
> over. The 21st century will be the age of Asia's
> return to economic pre-eminence.[1]
>
> —*Victor Mallet*, Financial Times, 2008

The first decade of the twenty-first century will go down as representing a strategic inflection point in the global economic landscape. For the first time in almost two hundred years, it is in this decade that, in terms of gross domestic product (GDP), the emerging economies will catch up with and race ahead of the developed ones—a trend that is likely to get added impetus as a result of the financial crisis presently engulfing many of the world's economies. China and India, the biggest contributors to world economic growth, are the flag bearers of this transformation.

Starkly put, China and India are changing the rules of the global game. They are two of the world's ten largest and the two fastest-growing economies. Thus, they account for the two biggest growth opportunities for almost every product or service, be it candy, cars, or computers. They are two of the world's poorest economies in terms of per capita income. Thus, they offer some of the lowest wage rates for blue- and white-collar work—wage rates that can have a transformational effect on competitive advantage. They are the world's two largest producers of science and engineering graduates. Thus, they present an opportunity to radically expand a company's intellectual capabilities without a proportionate increase in cost structure. And finally, they are the breeding grounds for a new cohort of ambitious, aggressive, and fast-moving global champions. Thus, they represent a competitive threat to established multinationals that is potentially far more severe than was ever the case from Toyota, Sony, Samsung, or LG.

The central thesis of this book is that any Fortune 1000 company that is not busy figuring out how to leverage the rise of China and India to transform the entire company runs a serious risk of not being around as an independent entity within ten to fifteen years from now. If you doubt the validity of this thesis, just look at how the structure of even the most basic and relatively low-tech industries has changed over the past twenty years. In 1987, Mittal Steel was just a tiny steel producer in Indonesia. Today, as ArcelorMittal, it is the world's steel behemoth, bigger than the next three players combined. In 1987, Cemex was a midsized cement producer in Mexico. Today it is one of the three largest building materials companies in the world. In 1987, South African Breweries was a domestic beer company confined to its homeland due to the antiapartheid sanctions imposed by the rest of the world. Today it is one of the world's three largest beer companies. Look ahead now, and factor in the sheer size and growth rates of China and India, the globalization of capital markets, and the rapid diffusion of technology. There can be little doubt that, over the next ten years, the magnitude and pace of change in every industry will be bigger and faster than over the past twenty.

As the history of most industries tells us, strategic inflection points are particularly dangerous times for incumbent firms. Consider the survival rates of incumbents in the computing industry after the shift from mainframes to minicomputers, from minicomputers to PCs, and from isolated PCs to the Internet. Such turning points require nonlinear transformations in core beliefs and core business models. A small number of established players—IBM under Lou Gerstner and Sam Palmisano and Apple under Steve Jobs—are able to engineer the needed transformation and come out fitter and stronger. These companies have cultures that thrive on change and are lucky to have leaders with a propensity to look at today from the lens of tomorrow. Most companies, however, deal with strategic inflection points by getting trapped in a vicious cycle. Their leaders look at tomorrow from the lens of today. Thus, they are either blind to the change or see it as a peripheral phenomenon. By the time they wake up, it is too late. Remember the case of Digital Equipment, the world's second largest computer company in the late 1970s. In 1977, Digital's founder and CEO, Ken Olsen, observed, "There is no reason for any individuals to have a computer in their home."[2] By 1998 Digital Equipment had vanished, acquired by PC maker Compaq.

Given the transformational impact of China and India, the world economy, and thus every industry in it, is at a similar strategic inflection point today. The leaders of every large company must choose, by design or by default, between two clear options: Do we want to be like Nokia, which has vowed to dominate not just every corner of the rich markets such as London and Manhattan but also every corner of the poorest markets such as the villages of Xinjiang province in China and Uttar Pradesh in India? Or do we want to be like Motorola, whose former CEO had declared that one of the linchpins of his strategy to save the company was to deemphasize the "low-margin" emerging markets?[3] Do we want to be like Accenture, which decided to grab the tiger by the tail and embarked on the growth of its India-based global delivery capabilities from five hundred people in 2002 to over thirty-five thousand people in 2007? Or do we want to be like BearingPoint whose former CEO stated publicly in 2005 that "we do not plan to engage in [a] rapid expansion" of the company's delivery capabilities in China and India?[4] If you belong in the first category of leaders, we invite you to read on. If you doubt our central thesis, we wish you the best of luck and hope that we will have the opportunity to compare notes in 2020.

The goal of this book is to provide business leaders with a strategic road map for capturing the growth, efficiency, talent, and innovation opportunities offered by China and India. We discuss how a company can leverage its global capabilities to discover, create, and win the market opportunities there. We examine how a company can leverage the talent and innovation opportunities from within these two countries to transform itself globally. And we look at how a company can effectively battle with the emerging dragons and tigers from these new epicenters of the world economy.

In this first chapter, we begin the journey by looking at the factors that are driving the reemergence of China and India, outlining the four game-changing realities that define the strategic importance of today's China and today's India, uncovering the challenges that make it extremely hard for many companies to deal with the new global reality, and laying out the tasks that await business leaders who want to drive the change rather than be blindsided over the next ten years.

Back to the Future: The Reemergence of China and India

The starting point for understanding the rise of China and India is to look at this phenomenon as a case of renaissance, of rebirth. Other than economic historians, few people know that for much of the past two thousand years, China and India were the two largest and, by the standards of those times, among the most scientifically and technologically advanced societies in the world.[5] China invented paper, gunpowder, and the compass, among other things. In turn, India brought to the world abstract mathematical concepts such as the number zero, negative numbers, decimals, and fractions. As recently as 1820, China and India together accounted for almost 50 percent of the world's

Table 1.1 China and India: A Look Back (Percentage of World GDP)

	United States plus Other Western Offshoots	Europe	China	India
1000	0.7%	13.4%	22.7%	28.9%
1500	0.5	23.9	25.0	24.5
1700	0.2	29.7	22.3	24.4
1820	1.9	32.3	32.9	16.0
1913	21.7	46.6	8.9	7.6
1950	30.6	39.3	4.5	4.2

Source: A. Maddison, *The World Economy: Historical Statistics* (Paris: OECD, 2003).

GDP (see Table 1.1). Barely a hundred years later, the tables had turned: by the early twentieth century, China and India added up to only about 15 percent of the world's GDP. By 1950, the giants had become pygmies, accounting for less than 10 percent of the world economy, even after adjusting for purchasing power parity.

What happened? The industrial revolution of the nineteenth century that made first Europe and then America rich passed China and India by. When the British became India's de facto rulers in the late eighteenth century, India's per capita income was roughly the same as Britain's. However, given a significantly bigger population, India's was a much larger economy. Unfortunately for India, the British had the benefit of good timing. India's emperor was weak, and the country was politically divided. This created an opportune time for a smart foreign ruler who knew how to colonize India and use its resources to fuel its own industrial development. China's was a somewhat similar story of internal fractions, a weak emperor, and control by foreign powers. The First Opium War of 1840 pitted China, whose emperor had recently issued an edict banning the addictive drug, against Britain, which wanted to continue its opium trade. China lost and was forced to cede Hong Kong to Britain and sovereignty over various other occupied "concessions" to foreign powers, including the United States, France, Russia, Germany, and Japan.

What is happening now in both China and India is the delayed industrial and technological revolution. Technology and capital move much faster now than they did two centuries ago. Thus, it is not surprising that economic growth that took one hundred years to make Europe and America rich may now take only twenty to thirty years. The evidence regarding the much faster pace of economic growth induced by the current wave of industrial and technological revolution is already in. In the nineteenth century, it took Germany, Britain, and America fifty years of industrial revolution to double their per capita incomes. China and India are now doing so in around ten.

Table 1.2 provides data on the size of the world's twelve largest economies as of 2005–2006 and their growth rates since 1990. Several observations are in order. First, the ranks of the twelve largest economies include four emerging countries: Brazil, Russia, India, and China (or, as Goldman Sachs famously coined them, BRIC for short). Second, economic growth in the BRIC countries vastly outpaces that in the rich countries. This is why most analysts predict that the BRIC economies will rapidly start overtaking the developed ones in the next twenty years.[6] Third, even among the BRIC countries, China and India are not just the two largest but also by far the two fastest-growing economies. Thus, they are likely to move up the ranks at a faster pace than other countries. Fourth, the population size of China and India is several times larger than that of any other country. As a result, their growth will have a much greater impact on the world economy than was the case with the rise of Japan or could be with the rise of Russia and Brazil.

Because of rising costs, it is very hard for a country to keep delivering rapid economic growth once its per capita income achieves parity with that of the other rich countries. Since Japan's population is about 40 percent that of the United States,

Table 1.2 World's Twelve Largest Economies by GDP

Country	2005 GDP ($ billions)	GDP Growth Rate (%)			2005 Population (millions)	2005 GDP/ Capita ($)
		1990–2000	2000–2005	2005–2006		
United States	$12,417	3.5%	2.6%	3.3%	296	$41,530
Japan	4,534	1.1	1.4	2.2	128	35,420
Germany	2,795	1.8	0.7	2.8	82	34,090
China	2,234	10.6	9.6	10.7	1305	1,700
United Kingdom	2,199	2.7	2.4	2.8	60	36,650
France	2,127	1.9	1.5	2.0	61	34,870
Italy	1,763	1.5	0.6	1.9	57	29,830
Spain	1,125	2.7	3.1	3.9	43	25,570
Canada	1,114	3.1	2.5	2.8	32	33,760
India	806	6.0	7.0	9.2	1095	726
Brazil	796	2.9	2.2	3.7	186	4,260
Russia	764	–4.7	6.2	6.7	143	5,380

Source: World Bank, *World Development Indicators 2007* (Washington, D.C.: World Bank, 2007).

its economy had to peak at a size well below that of the United States. Short of unimaginably catastrophic mismanagement of the U.S. economy, there is almost no way that Japan's economy could become the largest in the world. Consequently, as Japan grew, it joined the rich people's club but did not transform the world's economic structure. In contrast, China's per capita income has to reach only about one-quarter that of the United States for its economy to become the world's largest. Even then, China will still have a few more decades of rapid growth in front of it. Similar arguments apply to the case of India. To sum up, unlike Japan, both China and India will almost certainly overtake the U.S. economy and, in the process, fundamentally transform the world's economic structure.

Tables 1.3 and 1.4 provide projections regarding the structure of the world economy over the next forty years. These projections are based on generally conservative assumptions. Recent growth rates in all four BRIC countries have been faster than the original projections. Considering also the robustness of the underlying econometric models, we regard these

Table 1.3 Projected World Economic Structure (Percentage of World GDP)

	2004	2025	2050
United States	28%	27%	26%
European Union	34	25	15
Japan	12	7	4
China	4	15	28
India	2	5	17
Other countries	20	21	10

Note: During 2005, 2006, and 2007, the Chinese and Indian economies grew at a much faster rate than predicted. This acceleration has led most observers to make upward revisions in the projected size of these two economies in 2025 and 2050.

Source: "Reshaping the World Economy," *BusinessWeek*, Aug. 22, 2005.

Table 1.4 Rise of the BRIC Economies: When Each BRIC Country's GDP Is Projected to Exceed That of the G6

	Italy	France and the United Kingdom	Germany	Japan	United States
China	2004	2005	2008	2013[a]	2035[a]
India	2012[a]	2015[a]	2020[a]	2025[a]	2040–2045[a]
Russia	2020[a]	2030[a]	2035–2040[a]		
Brazil	2025–2030[a]	2035[a]	2040[a]		

Sources: D. Wilson and R. Purushothaman, "Dreaming with BRICs: The Path to 2050," Goldman Sachs Global Economics Paper No. 99, Oct. 2003; T. Poddar and Eva Yi, "India's Rising Growth Potential," Goldman Sachs Global Economics Paper No. 152, Jan. 2007.

[a]These are approximate years.

long-term projections as credible. To abstract from and summarize these projections, we can think of the world economy in 2050 as consisting of four major economic blocks—China, India, the United States, and the European Union—each accounting for about 15 to 25 percent of world GDP, with all other countries accounting for the remaining 15 to 25 percent. The decision makers in China and India are well aware of these projections. As they look at the history of the past two thousand years and the fact that the delayed industrial and technological revolution is propelling current growth, they believe firmly that the rise of their countries is inevitable and that it is their destiny to be superpowers again.

Four Stories Rolled into One

China and India pack a particularly powerful punch because each of these two countries represents four stories rolled into one, all playing out simultaneously:

1. *Megamarkets.* As fast-growing megamarkets, they provide some of the largest growth opportunities for every product or service.

2. *Cost-efficiency platforms*. As countries with some of the lowest wage rates, they have the potential to dramatically reduce a company's global cost structure.

3. *Innovation platforms*. As the producers of the largest annual pools of scientists and engineers in the world, they can enable a quantum leap in a company's technological and innovation capabilities.

4. *Launching pads for new global competitors*. As the home base of large, rapidly growing, and very capable companies that are eager to play on the global stage, they are becoming the springboards for the emergence of a new breed of fearsome global competitors.

Many countries feature one or two of these stories, but other than China and India, none features all four. Each one of these stories would have compelling strategic implications for almost any large company. The fact that China and India feature all four simultaneously makes these two countries central to the future of most companies.

Rapidly Growing Megamarkets

Within any country, the size of the market for any particular product or service (shampoo, clothing, fast food, cars, tractors, computers, mobile phones—you name it) depends on a number of factors: population size, buying power, demographics, cultural norms and habits, geography, stage of economic development, and others. Consider two of the most important factors: population size and buying power. Between them, China and India currently account for 40 percent of the world's population, about 10 percent of the world's GDP, and about 20 percent of the growth in the world's GDP. As these numbers suggest, China and India already account for between 10 to 40 percent of the global demand for most products and services. Furthermore, in line with GDP growth rates, demand is growing at an annual rate of about 10 percent in real terms. Factor in currency appreciation, and these numbers translate into even higher growth rates in U.S. dollar terms. Given the long-term economic projections set out in Tables 1.3 and 1.4, there is good reason to anticipate that by 2040 to 2050, China and India together may account for 40 percent of the world's market for almost every product or service.

Consider these illustrative examples of the large market that China and India currently represent:

- In 2007, China's car market became the second largest in the world. Between 2015 and 2020, it is likely to become the world's largest. At that time, India's car market is likely to be the third largest after China and the United States. According to Goldman Sachs, the total number of cars on the roads in China and India could rise from 30 million in 2005 to 750 million by 2040.[7]

- In 2007, China and India were, respectively, the first and second largest markets for Nokia Corporation. At the end of 2007, the estimated number of mobile subscribers was over 500 million in China and over 200 million in India. Each country was still adding over 6 million new subscribers every month.

- Wal-Mart executives have noted that China and, over a longer term, India, may be the only countries where they can build a revenue base as large as that in the United States.

- Between 2007 and 2020, airlines in China and India are projected to be the two largest buyers of commercial airplanes from Boeing and Airbus.

- In China, total investment banking revenues from activities related to equity and debt markets, mergers and acquisitions, and loans grew from $328 million in 2003 to $1.6 billion in 2006 and $2.2 billion in 2007. The figures for India were $146 million in 2003, $685 million in 2006, and $1 billion in 2007.[8]

- India is currently the primary battleground for Hewlett-Packard, Dell, and Lenovo in their fight for global dominance in the PC industry. H-P and Dell have commanding market shares in Europe and the United States, and Lenovo has a commanding market share in China. India represents a rapidly growing open field. Whichever of these companies establishes a dominant position within India will be able to leverage scale in two or three of the world's megamarkets to achieve global dominance.

- According to analysis by McKinsey & Company, even after discounting for delays and discontinued projects, India is likely to see an investment of about $750 billion in infrastructure between 2007 and 2015. The implications for companies such as Caterpillar, GE, ABB, and Jacobs Engineering that provide equipment, financing, and services for infrastructure are enormous. By way of example, McKinsey predicts that the size of the Indian market for earth-moving and construction equipment alone will grow over fivefold, from $2.3 billion in 2007 to $12 billion to $13 billion by 2015.[9] These are large numbers and will make a material difference to the growth rates, and hence stock prices, of whichever companies have the capabilities to capture these market opportunities. GE earned $1 billion in revenues from India in 2006 and appears well on its way to achieve a targeted $8 billion in revenue by 2010, only four years later.

Given the current and potential market size of China and India, it should be clear that a suboptimal China and India strategy is no longer a matter of merely leaving some money on the table. Any medium to large company that does not develop well-thought-out strategies to capture the growth opportunities in China and India could face severe threats to its very existence in a relatively short period of time. If you are not leveraging the market opportunities that China and India represent, rest assured that somebody else is. That somebody could be your well-known archrival. It is equally likely, however, that that somebody could be a new home-grown competitor from within China or India that will be able to scale up rapidly and build economic and organizational muscle to either annihilate or acquire your company.

Platforms for Global Cost Reduction

The potential of China and India to serve as platforms for cost reduction is perhaps the best known of the four compelling stories. What is less well known, however, is that with each passing year, the need to leverage China and India as cost-efficiency platforms is changing from a discretionary option into a strategic imperative. We start first with some comparative data on blue- and white-collar wages.

Table 1.5 compares the average hourly compensation (including benefits) for production workers in China, India, and several other countries. As these and other data indicate, although some countries (for example, Indonesia, Vietnam, and Bangladesh) have an even lower cost base, China and India continue to provide some of the lowest labor costs in the world. Our own field interviews during mid-2007 confirm that even in relatively high-cost locations within each country (such as the Suzhou Industrial Park near Shanghai and the province of Haryana near New Delhi), the total cost of blue-collar workers runs at about a dollar an hour in China and India. Labor costs in the countryside are even lower. In comparison, hourly labor costs exceed three dollars in Brazil, four dollars in Hungary, eighteen dollars in the United Kingdom, and over twenty dollars in both Japan and the United States. In short, the cost of

Table 1.5 Labor Cost Comparisons (Average Hourly Compensation Including Benefits for Production Workers)

	2003	2009 (Projected)
Indonesia	$0.30	$0.70
China	0.80	1.27
India	1.12	1.68
Russia	1.50	2.38
Mexico	2.45	3.28
Poland	2.70	3.83
Brazil	2.75	3.90
Hungary	3.53	5.30
South Korea	9.99	13.01
United Kingdom	17.87	20.14
Japan	20.68	22.61
United States	21.86	25.34
Germany	30.60	34.46

Sources: Economist Intelligence Unit, Euromonitor, U.S. Department of Labor, and Boston Consulting Group.

production workers in China and India remains a tiny fraction of that in the developed countries. It is also considerably less than the figure in even many of the emerging economies of Central Europe and Latin America.

Large cost differences between China and India on one side and the developed economies on the other exist also in white-collar jobs. In mid-2007, the total annual compensation (including benefits) for software engineers just out of college in India was about five thousand dollars, and the national average for all software professionals was around fifteen thousand dollars.[10] Compensation levels in China were only slightly higher. In mid-2007, a fresh engineer with an offer to join a manufacturing company in Shanghai could expect to receive about three thousand renminbi per month plus benefits, or a total annual compensation (including benefits) of about six to seven thousand dollars. To sum up, despite significant salary jumps in recent years as well as currency appreciation in both the yuan and the rupee, the cost of engineering talent in China and India remains at around 10 to 15 percent of that in the developed countries.

Given these large cost differences, delays in tapping China and India as cost-efficiency platforms are becoming increasingly risky. Both of these countries are wide open to foreign direct investment. Thus, if you are not tapping the cost base of China and India, the likelihood is high that your archrival is. You can also take it as a given that one or more low-cost competitors from within these two countries is busy planning an attack in your established markets. If you do not have a competitive cost structure, you will face a two-pronged challenge: lower profit margins as well as a lower market share. As your volumes shrink, the loss of scale economies will worsen your cost position. The resulting downward spiral will mean reduced cash flows, a weakening of stock price, and an inevitable change in management. The new CEO will have little choice other than an accelerated but belated push of the cost base to China or India, or both. In the worst-case scenario, your company will become a sitting duck for your savvier and more proactive competitors.

Accenture and Black & Decker provide excellent examples of companies that saw the potential writing on the wall and took steps to tap India and China for radical cost reduction. We discuss each of these cases in turn.

Accenture is one of the world's largest management consulting, technology services, and outsourcing companies. Table 1.6 compares key financial statistics for Accenture and Electronic Data Systems, two of the largest U.S.-based consulting and information technology (IT) services companies, with those for Infosys and Wipro Technologies, two of their largest India-based competitors.

As the data in Table 1.6 indicate, there is a vast gulf in the profit margins of the two Western multinationals versus their Indian counterparts. As much younger companies, Infosys and

Table 1.6 Comparative Financial Data on Selected Consulting and IT Services Companies

Company (Ticker Symbol)	Headquarters	Revenues[a] (billions)	Profit Margins (%)[a]	Net Income[a] (billions)	Market Capitalization[b] (billions)
Accenture (ACN)	United States	$22.4	5.99%	$1.34	$21.7
Electronic Data Systems (EDS)	United States	22.0	3.38	0.76	11.2
Infosys Technologies (INFY)	India	3.6	27.82	1.01	25.4
Wipro Technologies (WIT)	India	4.4	18.18	0.79	21.8

Source: www.finance.yahoo.com.

[a]Trailing twelve months as of Dec. 24, 2007.

[b]Market capitalization as of Dec. 24, 2007.

Wipro have significantly smaller revenues than Accenture and EDS. Yet they have significantly higher profit margins, roughly similar net income figures, and larger stock market capitalizations. These figures also indicate that should they choose to do so, the Indian companies have considerable economic power to acquire one or more of the established multinationals such as Capgemini, BearingPoint, or Computer Sciences Corporation, all of them smaller than Accenture and EDS. Clearly the global IT services industry is in the middle of a structural change.

Accenture was one of the early movers in recognizing this shift. Its leaders moved to increase the size of its India-based delivery capabilities from fewer than five hundred people in 2002 to more than thirty-five thousand in 2007—over 20 percent of the company's entire global staff. Even a first-cut analysis indicates that the impact of this strategic move has been enormous. Assuming a cost difference of at least $30,000 per employee between the United States and India, if Accenture were to hire all of these people in the United States or Western Europe, its cost structure would be higher by more than $1 billion, an unsustainable amount. In short, without the buildup in India, Accenture would be either a much less profitable or a much slower-growing company. Either of these scenarios would have had serious repercussions for the viability of the company (and its executive leadership).

Consider now the case of Black & Decker. With 2006 revenues of $6.4 billion, it is the largest U.S.-based company in power tools, home improvement products, and fastening systems. The bulk of the company's sales take place through major retail chains such as Home Depot and Lowe's, which exercise considerable economic power over their suppliers. The exercise of such power is both direct (demands for price reductions) and indirect (sales of their own private label brands that compete directly with the suppliers' brands). Black & Decker's major competitors are Makita from Japan, Bosch from Germany, and Techtronic Industries (TTI) from Hong Kong. TTI, a relatively recent entrant, appears to be the most unsettling of these competitors. With the bulk of its manufacturing operations based in China, TTI has one of the industry's lowest cost structures. It also is a rapidly growing player, whose 2006 revenues of $2.8 billion were more than double the figure for 2002. In recent years, TTI has been on a major spree to acquire well-recognized brands as well as cultivate marketing alliances; its products are now sold under its own as well as private label brands such as Milwaukee, Ryobi, Ridgid, and AEG. With a low-cost base on the one hand and well-recognized brands on the other, TTI appears to have a strong potential to change the global structure of the power tools industry over the next five to ten years. Black & Decker has taken notice and shifted large proportions of its own manufacturing operations to China. In a relatively mature industry where large retail chains exercise huge power, it is hard to imagine how Black & Decker could continue to remain a viable player without this major shift in cost base to China.

Platforms for Innovation

The third compelling story that China and India represent pertains to their potential to dramatically boost a company's global technology and innovation base. This potential is rooted in two opportunities. The first opportunity pertains to the large, well-trained, and low-cost pool of scientific and engineering talent within China and India that is eager for challenge, career advancement, and more and better creature comforts. Leveraging this talent pool can dramatically extend the R&D capabilities of most companies. The second opportunity pertains to the innovation demanded by the unique needs of the Chinese and Indian markets such as low buying power, energy and raw material scarcity, environmental degradation, large populations, and high population densities. Designing new products, services, and even entire business models to cater to these unique needs can yield innovations that can serve as cutting-edge sources of competitive advantage not just in other emerging economies but also back home in the developed economies.

Consider first the pool of available scientific and engineering talent within China and India. In 2005, the estimated number of people who received master's and Ph.D. degrees in engineering, technology, and computer science was about sixty thousand for the United States, about seventy-five thousand for China, and about sixty thousand for India.[11] Furthermore, over 50 percent of the Ph.D. degrees in engineering awarded in the United States were earned by foreign nationals. Among these, students from China and India constituted the dominant foreign groups, and a significant proportion of these chose to return to their home countries. In short, the pool of available research and development talent in China and India is among the largest in the world, growing rapidly, and with a relatively low cost. A company that can tap into this talent effectively and efficiently can boost the productivity of its R&D expenditures by several multiples. GE's John F. Welch Technology Centre in Bangalore and

Microsoft's research center in Beijing (Microsoft Research Asia) illustrate the potential of China and India to extend the intellectual capabilities of even the largest companies on the planet.

Inaugurated in Bangalore in September 2000, the John F. Welch Technology Centre has already become the largest of GE's four global research centers (the other locations are upstate New York, Shanghai, and Munich). Each of these multidisciplinary centers reports to the head of GE Research and works on corporatewide technology initiatives. With a staff of over three thousand scientists, 60 percent with master's and Ph.D. degrees, the Bangalore center is not merely the largest research center within GE but also one of the largest research centers of any company worldwide. The reason this center exists has little to do with cost. The real value lies in the fact that it can hire large numbers of highly trained people in arcane subspecialties (such as computational fluid dynamics), something that would be nearly impossible in almost any other country. The net result is a significant expansion in the size and capabilities of GE's research staff and thus a significant boost to the company's ability to differentiate its products and services and avoid having to compete on prices. As a global research center, most of the projects that Bangalore-based teams work on address business needs not just in India but also for GE worldwide. Some of the recent examples include a major part of the design work for GE engines that power Boeing's Dreamliner aircraft, a redesign of washing machines for the U.S. market so that they may use only one-third to one-half the amount of water without any reduction in cleaning effectiveness, and design of the locomotive for China's recently launched high-altitude rail service in Tibet. Given its central role and despite its short history, the John F. Welch Centre is already the source for over 10 percent of all patents filed by GE Global Research with the U.S. Patent and Trademark Office.

Microsoft Research Asia (MSRA), founded in Beijing in 1998, is Microsoft's largest research center outside its corporate headquarters in Redmond, Washington. It has an ideal location—within Beijing's ZhongGuanCun Science Park and near two of the best universities in China (Peking University and Tsinghua University). As Dr. Yong Rui, head of strategy for the center, commented to us in a mid-2007 interview, "If you throw a stone here, chances are pretty high that you'll hit a Ph.D." With a staff of over three hundred researchers and engineers (some of the best and brightest in China), MSRA has emerged as Microsoft's global center of excellence for a number of technology programs critical to the company's future. Illustrative examples include the development of a next-generation user interface that would allow users to interact with computers using speech, gestures, and expressions; next-generation multimedia technologies; and next-generation Web search and data mining technologies. MSRA has already emerged as one of the largest China-based filers of patents with the U.S. Patent and Trademark Office. In 2004, MIT's *Technology Review* named the Beijing center as one of the world's hottest computer labs and noted that it was "a key part of Microsoft's effort to ensure its global future through research."[12]

Consider now the potential for innovation offered by a company's decision to invent new products, services, and business models to serve the unique needs of Chinese and Indian markets. Given low per capita incomes, the vast majority of the inhabitants in China and India cannot afford to buy cars that cost twenty thousand dollars, PCs that cost a thousand dollars, or cell phone services that cost ten cents a minute. This is true not just in business-to-consumer (B2C) contexts but also in many business-to-business (B2B) contexts. The market for hospital equipment such as CT scanners and MRI machines provides an example. Yes, a growing number of well-financed hospitals in the major cities can afford to buy the same equipment as can be found at hospitals such as Massachusetts General or Johns Hopkins. However, think about the potential market that can be unleashed if companies such as GE and Siemens could develop imaging machines that are high caliber in terms of core functionality, cost a fraction of their existing high-end models, but may lack many of the sophisticated yet nonessential features.

Low buying power is only one feature of what makes the Chinese and Indian markets unique. Consider also the scarcity of water, shortage of space, dependence on energy imports, and ongoing environmental degradation. In an integrated global economy (and the fact that we live on a small planet), these are challenges not just for China and India but for the entire world. These challenges are also economic opportunities. As we noted, China and India possess vast and relatively low-cost scientific and engineering capabilities. Companies that can leverage these resources (on top of the existing global R&D network and historical stock of technical knowledge) to address the unique needs of China and India have the potential to emerge as the globally dominant players of tomorrow.

Jeffrey Immelt, GE's CEO, has termed this new perspective on globalization as "in country, for the world." As he elaborates, "[Look at] water. There's a shortage everywhere, even in places like California and Florida. Some systems we're working on in the Middle East, India, and China are trying to do water desalination at $0.001 per milliliter, which is an off-the-charts low cost. We'll never hit that in the U.S. But we'll hit it someplace outside. And the second we do, a huge market is going to open up inside as well."[13]

Springboards for the Emergence of Fearsome New Competitors

The fourth compelling story that China and India represent pertains to their role as breeding grounds for fearsome new competitors. Unlike the emergence of global players such as Toyota, Sony, Samsung, and Hyundai from Japan and South Korea between 1970 and 2000, the more recent emergence of global champions from China and India is taking place at a much faster and more fearsome pace. Virtually all Japanese and Korean giants grew organically. In contrast, the globalization of Indian and Chinese companies already shows signs of being much more acquisitions driven. Capital markets, both public and private, are significantly more global today than they were two decades ago. Thus, globalizing companies from China and India can access equity and debt capital from global capital markets much more freely and easily than was possible twenty years ago. Also, Chinese and Indian companies now have easy access to global investment banks as well as global consulting firms, most of them with well-staffed offices in both countries. Finally, the large size of Chinese and Indian economies means that many domestic companies from these two countries are able to accumulate global scale before venturing abroad.

Illustrative examples of emerging global champions from China across a diverse set of industries include Huawei Technologies, Lenovo, Haier Group, and Chery Automobile.

- Huawei is China's leading telecommunications equipment company and perhaps the toughest long-term competitor to Cisco Systems. It reported 2007 sales of $16 billion, a 45 percent growth over 2006. Huawei derived over 60 percent and a growing proportion of these revenues from customers outside China in developing as well as developed economies.

- Lenovo is China's leading company in personal computers. Its 2005 acquisition of IBM Corporation's PC business made it the third largest PC company in the world behind Hewlett-Packard and Dell. Lenovo's official global headquarters is in North Carolina, its American CEO (William Amelio) lives in and works out of Singapore, and its chief marketing officer (Deepak Advani) is an Indian-American.

- Haier Group is China's leading home appliance manufacturer with a growing manufacturing and market presence and market share in the United States, Europe, India, and other countries. In 2005, Haier made an aborted acquisition attempt to buy the U.S.-based Maytag Corporation. With revenues exceeding $14 billion in 2006, Haier was the fourth largest white goods manufacturer in the world. In 2008, after GE announced its intention to sell or spin off the home appliance business, Haier had emerged as one of the keenest potential bidders.

- Chery Automobile is China's fourth largest domestic auto company, and the most ambitious and global of them all. It was founded in 1997. By 2007, it had already produced and sold over 1 million cars. Chery's 2007 sales of 380,000 cars represented an increase of 25 percent over the previous year. Exports accounted for over 30 percent of the company's unit sales. In 2007, Chery announced a global strategic alliance with Chrysler Corporation to manufacture small cars that would be sold by Chrysler under the Dodge brand.

Illustrative examples of emerging global champions from India across a diverse set of industries include Infosys, Tata Steel, Bharat Forge, and Suzlon:

- Infosys is one of India's home-grown giants in information technology. Founded in 1981, Infosys became a Nasdaq-listed company in 1999. By the end of 2007, it had a market capitalization of over $25 billion and twelve-month trailing revenues of $3.6 billion, and it was growing at over 40 percent per year. In mid-2007, rumors circulated that Infosys had considered a bid for France-headquartered Capgemini, a company three times bigger in terms of revenues but with a market capitalization of only $10 billion.
- Founded in 1907, Tata Steel is Asia's first and India's largest private sector steel company. Tata Steel was widely regarded as one of the world's lowest cost steel producers.

In early 2007, Tata Steel acquired the Anglo-Dutch steel giant Corus for $11 billion, a company three times its size. After this acquisition, Tata Steel became the sixth largest steel company in the world.

- Bharat Forge was India's leading and one of the world's largest manufacturers of forgings, such as parts for engines, axles, and similar automotive subsystems. Its revenues for fiscal 2006–2007 exceeded $1 billion, representing a 38 percent growth over the previous year. Bharat Forge operated across Europe, North America, and Asia. Between 2003 and 2007, it acquired two companies in Germany, one in Sweden and one in the United States. Bharat Forge also held a majority stake in a Changchun-based joint venture with First Auto Works, one of China's biggest car companies.

- Founded in 1995, Suzlon Energy was the world's fifth largest (and Asia's and India's leading) manufacturer of wind turbines. Suzlon's 2006–2007 revenues were $2 billion, representing a 100 percent growth over the previous year. In mid-2007, Suzlon acquired Germany's REpower Systems at a price exceeding 1.3 billion euros.

The rapid growth and global ambitions of the emerging dragons and tigers from China and India significantly escalate the urgency with which established multinationals must begin to consider the rise of these two countries as game-changing rather than peripheral developments. In 2000, there were very few companies from China and India in the ranks of the world's top 500 companies by sales revenue. By 2008, this number had grown to 36. Could it be that, by 2020, over 150 of the world's 500 largest companies will be based in China and India? Not unlikely. If we are even partially correct in our projections, it will be a very different world. Yet the vast majority of today's business leaders appear to be unprepared for the challenges (and the opportunities) that lie ahead.

Challenges for Multinationals

Adapting to changes in the external environment is always an ordeal for incumbent organizations. It becomes particularly challenging when the external changes are not just nonlinear but also occurring at a rapid pace. This is the case with the rise of China and India. While the challenges are both external and internal, the latter can be particularly damaging to a company's future prospects. External challenges impinge on all players in the industry. However, a company's ability (or lack of it) to deal with internal challenges is what determines whether it will exploit these changes and thrive or be buried by them. We discuss first the external and then the internal challenges.

External Challenges

We discuss below some of the major strategic challenges (as distinct from operational ones such as widespread corruption) that China and India pose for multinational companies.

Vast and Diverse Societies. Some of the common strategic challenges that cut across both China and India pertain to the vastness, the diversity, the internal complexity, and the multilayered political structure in each country. Each country is large not just in terms of population but also geographically. China's surface area is as large as that of the United States. India's is smaller but still larger than that of the European Monetary Union. In short, both China and India could be viewed as continents rather than just countries. As a direct result, both countries also feature very high levels of internal diversity along multiple dimensions: economic wealth, language, culture, and, particularly in the case of India, religion. This vastness and diversity make it especially hard for managers from other countries to develop a good understanding of these countries without a significant commitment of time and effort, including on-the-ground immersion.

Take internal disparity in wealth. China and India have some of the highest levels of income inequalities in the world, a situation that is worsening over time. According to estimates by *Forbes* magazine, in early 2008, forty-two Chinese citizens had a net worth exceeding $1 billion. Many of our Chinese informers believe that the actual number of billionaires in China is much larger. The number of billionaires in India was estimated to be fifty-three, also among the world's top five. It is sad but true that China and India boasted not just these very large levels of personal wealth but also two of the largest numbers of the really poor people in the world. China's Gini coefficient (a measure of income inequality within the country) rose from .41 in 1993 to .47 in 2004. The figures for India were .33 in 1993 and .36 in 2004.[14] This vast disparity in wealth means that the behavior of consumers in Shanghai or Mumbai tells us little about the behavior of hundreds of millions of other Chinese and Indians who live in poorer towns and villages and yet whose combined buying power is very large and growing rapidly.

Consider language and cultural diversity. Even if we leave aside minority languages (such as Tibetan, Mongolian, Miao, and Tai), China's languages include many vastly different dialects (such as Mandarin and Cantonese). In India, linguistic diversity is even greater, with twenty-two officially recognized national languages. Relative to the United States or Europe, China and India also feature greater cultural and religious diversity. Given the ongoing liberalization of religious practice within the country, China has a rapidly growing number of Buddhists, and the estimated number of Chinese Muslims is greater than 20 million. India has an estimated 140 million Muslims, followed by a sizable minority of Christians, Sikhs, Buddhists, Jains, and followers of other faiths. The strategic implication of this multidimensional diversity is that developing a single homogeneous strategy for China or India will rarely be optimal or even barely satisfactory.

Politically too, China and India represent a complex structure. Of course, given India's democratic system, it is all too common that the central government may be composed of uneasy alliances between coalition partners and that the ruling parties in various states may be different from that (or those) at the center. However, even in seemingly monolithic China, political power is distributed widely—across various ministries at the center that do not always see eye to eye, and across the provinces, counties, and cities, where the governing premise for centuries has been that "the mountains are high and the emperor is far away." Thus, in both China and India, a company may find that an agreement with one arm or one level of government does not necessarily mean that it will not run afoul of some other branch or level of government.

Rapid Pace of Change. Aside from the fact that China and India are very different from the developed countries as well as vast and diverse, another factor that makes it difficult for managers to understand them well is that they are changing rapidly. Thus, as with the Internet, yesterday's knowledge may well be obsolete today. As an illustrative example, consider the importance of foreign direct investment (FDI) to China's future growth. In 2005, China received $79 billion in FDI, the highest of any country in the world. Yet if you consider that China has accumulated foreign exchange reserves of over $1.5 trillion and domestic savings of over $2 trillion, it is obvious that there is no longer any shortage of capital within China. Thus, corporate strategies that assume that the Chinese government still places high importance on FDI may well be based on obsolete knowledge.

Given their recent emergence as major economic powers, governments in both China and India are still trying to figure out the best policies for economic growth, social harmony, protecting the environment, protecting the country's national sovereignty, as well as the nature and extent of their country's integration with the rest of the world. Also, given rapid development, many of the policies run a high likelihood of change within short time spans. This may happen either because of a change in the ruling party (as in the case of India) or leaders (as in the case of China) or because the objective circumstances today are vastly different from those of five years ago.

More Global and More Demanding Capital Markets. Given the ability of most investors to move capital with the click of a button, capital markets have globalized more rapidly and to a much greater extent than the markets for any other commodity, including products, services, technology, and labor. Thus, we now have a growing disconnect between where a company's products and services are produced, where its employees are located, and where its shareholders may sit. For historical reasons and because its corporate headquarters is located in Helsinki, we may think of Nokia as a Finnish company. Yet it is not unlikely that on any given day, the bulk of its shares may be owned by investors from other countries. Assuming that these investors are rational, we should expect that they will care about only one outcome, the return on their investment, and will allocate capital to where it can yield the highest gains. Not surprisingly, the average tenure of corporate CEOs has declined steadily over the past ten years. There is no reason for us to expect that shareholders will become less demanding over the next ten.

In such a context, leaders of existing multinationals do not have the luxury of time. Given the vastly greater growth rates as well as appreciating currencies in both India and China, the economic clout of companies based in these two countries is rising rapidly. The reverse is true of many established multinationals in the developed countries.

Other Unique Difficulties. Aside from common strategic challenges that bedevil both China and India, each country also offers its unique difficulties. In China, some of the most important challenges pertain to the entrenched dominance of state-owned enterprises in many sectors of the economy, growing economic nationalism, media that are expected to serve national policy rather than be objective or neutral and a legal system that is still being developed after its decimation during the Cultural Revolution. In India, some of the unique challenges pertain to a still quite poor infrastructure, bureaucratic red tape, and potential for unexpected opposition from local politicians, nongovernmental organizations, and local media that may be sympathetic to the latter.

Internal Challenges

In developing robust strategies for China and India, many established companies face not just external challenges but also internal challenges rooted in cognitive insularity, legacy mindsets, and, on occasion, just plain hubris. We describe each of these in turn.

Cognitive Insularity. The legendary Jack Welch, GE's former CEO, has long lamented the cognitive insularity of many CEOs of large companies. Instead of exposing themselves directly to the ground-level reality on the shop floor, in the labs, and in the marketplace, they spend far too much time in the comforts of their offices and home towns. The net result is that they rule their companies through filtered reports and abstract numbers. Isolated from direct observation, they render themselves incapable of making decisions that are guided not just by numbers but also by gut-level judgment. In short, they become bureaucrats who can keep the current business running rather than what they should be: entrepreneurs who seek new opportunities and in the process transform the company.

In a world that is becoming increasingly multipolar at a rapid pace, cognitive insularity can be dangerous. We do not suggest that most CEOs do not read the daily newspapers and thus are somehow unaware of the rise of China and India. However, we do believe that most CEOs and their direct reports have little more than superficial knowledge of the magnitude, pace, and nature of change occurring in the global economy. There is a difference between superficial awareness and comprehensive up-to-date knowledge. It is differences such as these that explain why the former CEO of BearingPoint, the IT services company, decided to set up global delivery centers in India and China but then went on to conclude that there was no urgent need to scale up these capabilities. They also explain why the former CEO of Motorola viewed the low-margin emerging markets as lower-priority markets for the company.

Unfortunately, cognitive insularity appears to be a widespread problem not confined to just some isolated cases. A recent article in *Economist* aptly titled "All Mouth and No Trousers" reported the results of a survey by the Boston Consulting Group.[15] According to the BCG study of several large Western firms, even though an estimated 34 percent of the potential market for these firms was in Asia, this region accounted for only 14 percent of sales, 7 percent of employees, 5 percent of assets, 3 percent of R&D, and only 2 percent of the top two hundred executives.

Legacy Mindsets. It is an interesting and oft-repeated story that Harry Warner, the founder of Warner Bros., the Hollywood studio, remarked in 1927: "Who the hell wants to hear actors talk." We find this story interesting not because it portrays Warner as irrational but because it shows him as very rational yet trapped into a legacy mindset. In the heyday of silent films, actors needed to look good. Whether they had good voices was irrelevant. Not surprisingly, most of them had terrible voices. Given this reality, Warner was indeed right in wondering why anybody would want to hear actors talk. However, what he overlooked was that a new business model might emerge whereby actors would be hired not just for their looks but also for their voices.

In the context of today's global reality, we find that many CEOs are similarly trapped in legacy mindsets. Consider the case of a U.S.-based power tools company. This company has two highly successful brands in Western markets, a lower-priced brand (call it Alpha) targeted at do-it-yourself consumers and a higher-priced brand (call it Beta) targeted at professionals such as plumbers, electricians, and carpenters. Although this company has a large offshore manufacturing base in China, its sales and market share within China itself are minuscule—despite the fact that during 2007, urban construction in China exceeded that in the rest of the world combined. Our discussions with some of the current and former executives of this company lead us to believe that they may be trapped in a legacy mindset. Given low labor costs, there is not much of a do-it-yourself market in China. Thus, there is no market for Alpha. Moreover, Chinese plumbers, electricians, and carpenters cannot afford the price that the company charges for its higher-end brand. Hence, there is no market for Beta. In short, the conclusion has been that China does not offer much of a market opportunity for the company's products and brands!

Given the starkly different realities of the markets in China and India, companies need to stop thinking of themselves as portfolios of legacy products, legacy services, legacy brands, or legacy business models. Instead, they need to think of themselves as portfolios of capabilities that can be deployed to create new products, new services, new brands, and even new business models which target the mega-opportunities that China and India offer. If the power tools company discussed above were to think in these terms, it might see that China offers a major market opportunity to introduce a new third brand (call it Gamma). The products and services under this new brand might encompass newly designed and much cheaper professional tools tailored for the smaller pocketbooks and smaller hands of China's professionals.

Hubris. *Hubris* refers to exaggerated self-pride. Given the vast gulf in the per capita buying power of the ordinary consumer in China or India (and the substandard infrastructure that exists in much of India), it is easy for senior executives from developed countries to get caught up in surface-level appearances and to look down on the capabilities (and ego) of potential customers, business partners, suppliers, or even employees in China or India. Consider, for example, the comments of Chrysler's CEO in 2000 after a visit to India, "Call me when you've built some roads."[16] As we noted earlier, the probability is very high that barely fifteen years later, by 2015, India may be the third largest car market in the world after China and the United States.

Instead of hubris, what leaders need is a clear understanding of the new challenges as well as the new opportunities. Yes, in per capita terms, China and India are still very poor economies and will be so even in 2050. At the same time, this poverty, when combined with steely ambition, the world's largest pools of scientists and engineers, and access to global capital markets, makes China and India hotbeds for some of the world's cutting edge innovations. The perspective of Carlos Tavares, chief product strategist and the number two executive at Nissan Motor Co. behind CEO Carlos Ghosn, stands in stark contrast to that of Chrysler's former CEO. Although there have been reports of some internal resistance, Tavares is pushing ahead determinedly to make India one of the company's global small car hubs. As he notes, "Any time you need to achieve a cost breakthrough, people will tell you that it's not possible."[17]

The Task Ahead

The rest of the book is devoted to the action implications of the tectonic shifts discussed in this chapter. Each of the six chapters that follow focuses on one important action domain.

Think China and India, Not China or India

In Chapter Two, we start from the notion that it is a waste of time and energy to debate whether a company should focus on

China or India. Any company that downplays the importance of either country is courting trouble. There are at least four reasons that we argue strongly in favor of an integrated China+India mindset. First, although China is ahead of India by about ten to fifteen years, each of these two economies is well on its way to becoming one of the world's four or five largest markets for virtually every product or service. Thus, overlooking either market implies forgoing many of the important benefits associated with larger scale: cost efficiencies, market power, and revenue growth. Second, while Chinese and Indian economies will exhibit a remarkable degree of convergence over the next twenty years, in the short to medium term, they offer complementary strengths (China in manufacturing and India in services) that a smart global company can profitably exploit. Third, notwithstanding important differences, China and India also have massive similarities. An integrated China+India strategy allows the multinational corporation to transfer learning from China to India and from India to China, thereby accelerating the pace of the company's success in both markets. Fourth, an integrated China+India strategy enables the global enterprise to reduce political, economic, and intellectual property risks associated with operating in just China or just India.

Megamarkets and Microcustomers: Fighting for Local Market Dominance

In Chapter Three, we examine how a company should position itself to capture the hearts, minds, and wallets of customers in China and India. We argue that unless a company operates in niche products and services, it should go wide and deep, pursuing a multisegment strategy. At the top end of the income spectrum, customers have high buying power and are likely to prefer global products and services. Thus, companies are unlikely to face much pressure for local adaptation of their products and services except for cultural reasons. The middle income segment constitutes the mass market. For most products and services, this is also the fastest-growing market in each country and can be ignored only at great peril to the company's future. This segment is often characterized by brutal competition, low pricing power, and low margins. In order to win here, a company will generally need to develop local products and services that are designed to be low cost. At the lower end of the income spectrum, a company is unlikely to generate much revenue. However, given high growth rates, this is the segment with the greatest possibilities for innovation. Every smart company should engage with this segment seriously, aim to break even, and view it as a learning laboratory for the discovery of new business models.

Leveraging China and India for Global Advantage

Chapter Four deals with the outbound part of the China-India story: how a company can use China and India as global platforms. We focus on three opportunities: cost arbitrage, intellectual arbitrage, and business model innovation. Realizing these opportunities requires a company to work on many fronts: managing internal politics; conducting a disaggregated value chain analysis to decide exactly which activities should be located in China, which in India, and which in other countries; deciding whether to set up the company's own operations or rely on outsourcing; building the necessary local capabilities; and then deploying the local capabilities globally without losing control of the value chain.

Competing with Dragons and Tigers on the World Stage

Chapter Five examines in detail the forces that are propelling the rapid emergence of global champions from China and India. We also compare the relative strengths and weaknesses of the Chinese and Indian globalizers vis-á-vis each other. Building on this analysis, we advance a multipronged strategy for current multinationals to not only defend themselves but also compete with these dragons and tigers on the world stage. First, a company should attack the new champions within their home markets by taking the battle for markets within China and India seriously. Second, it should neutralize the new champions' supply-side advantage by also tapping fully into the cost efficiency and innovation opportunities offered by China and India. Third, a company should pursue an integrated China+India strategy. A company from outside China and India will often find it easier to pursue an integrated multi-country strategy than would be the case with emerging players from within either of these two countries.

Winning the War for Talent: Dealing with Scarcity in the Midst of Plenty

Chapter Six looks at the human resource challenges that companies must overcome in their quest to win within China and India and to leverage the strengths of these two countries for global advantage. Notwithstanding their billion-plus populations and the world's two largest pools of college graduates every year, China and India suffer from an acute shortage of professional staff, such as seasoned managers and people with specialized skills (accountants in China and software developers in India, for example). As such, most companies, foreign and domestic, find themselves engaged in a perpetual war for talent.

In an environment such as this, you have no choice but to be market competitive in terms of compensation. However, you do have the ability to increase the odds that the turnover of professional staff in your company would be around 5 percent rather than 50 percent. This depends directly on your firm's ability to build proprietary competitive advantages in the local labor market. How might you build such competitive advantages?

- *Invest in building a visible and positive profile in the local media and on local campuses.* A stronger corporate brand breeds pride in and loyalty to your company. Some related issues to think about are: How often does the corporate CEO visit China and India? How often are he or she and the local country manager interviewed by the local media? How often do local managers visit targeted local campuses, give talks, and serve as guest professors?

- *Offer career opportunities in the company's global network outside the employee's home country.* This is one area where the multinational firm may have a distinct advantage over many domestic companies.

- *Invest in building an emotional bond between employees and your company.* In general, the family plays a bigger role in China, India, and other Asian countries than in the West. Do you, for example, send congratulatory notes to the employee's spouse (or parents) for a job well done? Do you invest in family get-togethers and other social events that foster pride in your company and the transformation of your work units into social communities?

In addition, smart companies increasingly recruit from colleges in not just the tier 1 (the largest and most developed) cities but also tier 2 and even tier 3 cities, where salaries are cheaper and turnover lower. However, ensuring that staff hired in tier 2 and 3 cities and campuses would be as productive as those hired in tier 1 locations requires investment in the establishment of local in-company training centers (or corporate universities).

Global Enterprise 2020

In the final chapter, we pull together the conclusions from our analysis and outline what the features of a global enterprise must be if it is to emerge as one of the winners ten years from now. We argue that the magnitude and pace of change, as well as the multifaceted nature of the new reality, demand that senior leaders rethink some of their central assumptions in crafting global strategy, rethink what must be the drivers and processes to create innovations over the next ten years, rethink how the company must be organized and managed, and above all strive with full vigor to globalize the corporate mindset.

The successful global corporation of tomorrow will be one that figures out how to take advantage of three realities: the rapid growth of emerging markets and the increasing multipolarity of the world economy; enduring cultural, political, and economic differences across countries and regions; and the rapidly growing integration of national economies. Organizationally it will be managed as a globally integrated enterprise rather than as a federation of regional or national fiefdoms. And it will be led by business leaders who have global mindsets and are masters at building bridges rather than moats.

2

THINK CHINA AND INDIA, NOT CHINA OR INDIA

> When someone brings China and India together, it
> will be a big story.[1]
> —*Shiv Nadar, chairman and CEO, HCL Technologies*

Surprising as it may seem, far too many companies still spend considerable time and energy debating whether to focus on China or India. The question is certainly important enough that in their popular series in *BusinessWeek*, Jack Welch and Suzy Welch devoted an entire column to the topic "choosing China or India."[2]

Our central thesis in this chapter is that for most Fortune 1000 companies, the time for this debate is over. The right question to ask is how best to pursue both China and India rather than which one. A company can derive several benefits from an integrated China+India strategy. It can capture the scale benefits from going after two (rather than just one) of the largest and fastest-growing markets in the world. It can leverage the complementary strengths of both countries. It can transfer learnings from one market to the other, thereby accelerating the pace of success in both. And it can use presence in both countries to reduce the level of overall risk associated with operating in just one of them. In short, a smart company can use a China+India strategy to align itself with the rapidly growing economic integration between the two countries.

China and India: Cousins, Not Twins

We begin with an overview of the major similarities and differences between China and India.

Vast Sizes and Populations

At 9.6 million square kilometers, China's surface area is virtually identical to that of the United States. At 3.3 million square kilometers, India is a smaller country. Nonetheless, it is still almost as large as the twenty-seven-country European Union (EU), which has a surface area of just over 4 million square kilometers. In terms of population, China at 1.3 billion and India at 1.1 billion are less far apart. Also, both are much larger than either the United States (299 million people) or the EU (493 million people). In essence, both China and India are continents. These numbers also tell us that despite their large surface areas, China and India have very high population densities: China (135 people per square kilometer) and India (333 people per square kilometer) versus the United States (31 people per square kilometer) and the EU (123 people per square kilometer). Not surprisingly, China and India already account for four of the ten largest megacities in the world.

I = C − 12: Rapid Economic Growth and China's Twelve-Year Lead

As the two fastest-growing economies in the world, China and India are growing rapidly in absolute as well as relative terms. However, China's rapid growth started several years earlier than India's. And even today, China continues to grow somewhat faster than India. In 1980, China and India had roughly the same, albeit very low, per capita incomes. Since then, China's economy has grown to become almost three times as large as that of India. Deng Xiao Ping kick-started the economic revolution in China around 1979. In contrast, India started on the path of domestic liberalization and global integration in 1991, fully twelve years later. That twelve-year gap remains alive and well today. According to our analysis, the simple equation $I = C - 12$ captures a vast proportion of the economic differences between India and China today.

Most of the key economic indicators for India in 2006–2007 look strikingly similar to the figures for China in 1994–1995. Similarly, projecting ahead, if you take India's GDP for 2007 and compound it at an 8 percent annual growth rate, it turns out that India's GDP in 2020 should be the same as China's GDP in 2007. Might India be ready to host the summer Olympics in 2020 in as impressive a fashion as China did in 2008? We deem such a scenario highly likely.

India's Demographic Dividend

The median age of India's population is 24.3 years as compared with 32.6 years for China. Because of the one-child policy, China's population is not only eight years older than that of India, it is also aging faster. As a result, China's dependency ratio is on the rise, whereas that of India is declining. Given this demographic dividend, most analysts expect that from around 2020 onward, India's economic growth is likely to exceed that of China.[3] Looking at the inevitable aging of the population, a common refrain among China's policymakers is, "China must get rich before it gets old."

Manufacturing Sector

In 2006, manufacturing accounted for 47 percent of China's GDP but only 28 percent of India's. Taking into account China's much higher GDP, this implies that China's manufacturing sector ($1.2 trillion in 2006) is five times as large as that of India ($251 billion in 2006). China's lead over India in the manufacturing sector is formidable. It rests on several sources of comparative advantage: larger scale at the plant level, greater experience, significantly better infrastructure, and more compliant labor. China has been a manufacturing and export powerhouse since the early 1990s. The manufacturing revolution in India, now in full swing, started only around 2005.

Services Sector

In 2006, services accounted for 41 percent of China's GDP but 55 percent of India's. In particular, India is far ahead of China in software services as well as most other types of services that can be delivered remotely by information technology. Examples of the latter range from low-end commodity services (such as call centers) to high-end knowledge-intensive services (such as software development, chip design, market research, marketing analytics, legal research, securities analysis, drug discovery services, and so forth). India's lead over China in these types of IT-enabled services rests on several sources of comparative advantage: native fluency in the English language, economies of scale, over twenty years of experience in serving global customers, incorporation of Toyota-like process discipline and rigor into the creation and delivery of services, and deep domain knowledge of key customer industries. Including foreign multinationals such as IBM and Accenture, almost ten IT services companies have an India-based professional staff numbering over fifty thousand each. In contrast, in China, the largest IT services company has a staff of only around ten thousand.

Infrastructure

China's physical infrastructure (such as highways and paved roads, rail lines devoted to goods transport, seaports, and airports) is significantly more developed than India's.[4] This is due in part to more effective policymaking and implementation in China and in part to the fact that China started to invest heavily in infrastructure in the mid-1990s, something that India is beginning to do only now. Between 1998 and 2005, China spent 8.2 percent of GDP on hard infrastructure as contrasted with India's 4 percent. Indian policymakers appear to have finally realized the huge constraints that weak infrastructure puts on the development of the country's manufacturing sector and exports. Working on a strategy of public-private partnership, a new five-year plan that commenced in 2007 is intended to double annual investments in infrastructure.

Foreign Direct Investment

Over the past ten years, China has attracted about ten times as much foreign direct investment (FDI) as has India.[5] The following are some of the major reasons for this difference: until recently, major tax breaks given by the Chinese government to foreign-invested enterprises,[6] the attraction of a larger domestic market within China, much better infrastructure, and more compliant labor. In 2005, China attracted a net inflow of over $75 billion in FDI as compared with only $6.6 billion for India. However, the pace of FDI inflow into India has started to gather steam. Inbound FDI in India was about $16 billion in 2006 and about $25 billion in 2007; the projected figures for 2008 are $40 billion.

Energy Scarcity

As large, rapidly growing economies, China and India share the same challenges with respect to energy shortages. In 2006, China consumed 7.4 million barrels of oil per day and imported about 50 percent of it. India consumed 2.6 million barrels per day, with imports supplying almost 69 percent of this need.[7] Over the coming decade, the situation is likely to get worse. Governments, companies, and people in both countries are responding to this situation in roughly similar ways. Both governments are on an active hunt to secure access to energy resources outside their borders, especially in Africa. At the same time, both societies have dramatically increased their reliance on renewable (nonfossil) energy sources such as wind, solar, and nuclear. In 2007, China and India were already among the world's top four countries in terms of installed wind power capacity. Excluding electricity and heat trade, China and India already derive 15 and 40 percent, respectively, of their energy from renewables, as compared with less than 5 percent for the United States. Also, China and India generate only 2.3 percent and 2.6 percent, respectively, of their electricity from nuclear power. Compare these figures with those for the United States (19.4 percent), Japan (30 percent), Germany (31.8 percent), and France (78.1 percent). It is clear that China and India will have to dramatically increase their reliance on nuclear power over the next two decades.

Environmental Degradation

China and India also share similar environmental challenges, for example, emissions of carbon dioxide. In 2005, China and India were among the five largest emitters of energy-related carbon dioxide into the atmosphere, the other three being the United States, Russia, and Japan. Yet on a per capita basis, China's emissions at 3.92 tons per capita and India's at 1.09 tons per capita were a small fraction of the figures for the United States (19.4 tons per capita) and Japan (9.4 tons per capita).[8] Herein lies the challenge for both China and India as well as the developed countries. Since carbon dioxide emissions affect all of humanity and global warming has reached alarming proportions, it is unimaginable that China and India can continue to focus solely on per capita figures. At the same time, it also is unthinkable that they will forgo future economic growth for the sake of the environment. Such a situation offers both enormous challenges as well as opportunities: challenges for the governments in terms of how to come to an agreement regarding cuts in emissions that would be fair to all parties, rich as well as poor, and opportunities for corporations that see the writing on the wall and go full blast to make their products and services radically more efficient on both fronts: energy use and environmental impact.

Health and Primary Education

China ranks ahead of India in health and primary education. The 2006–2007 Global Competitiveness Report by the World Economic Forum ranks China at number 55 and India at number 93 (out of a total of 125 countries) on measures of health and primary education. According to the World Bank's data for 2005, life expectancy at birth in China was 71.8 years versus that for India at 63.5 years. The estimated adult literacy rate in China is 91 percent, whereas that in India is 61 percent.

Innovation Drivers

The 2006–2007 Global Competitiveness Report ranks India ahead of China in higher education and training (number 49 versus number 77). Historically, India has placed much greater emphasis on tertiary education, whereas China's emphasis has been much stronger on primary and secondary education. However, recent policy changes in both countries are leading toward a convergence over the next twenty years. The Global Competitiveness Report also ranks India ahead of China in technological readiness (number 55 versus number 75), business sophistication (number 25 versus number 65), innovation (number 26 versus number 46), and company operations and strategy (number 25 versus number 69). Unlike China's economic isolation between 1949 and 1979, India's economy always remained integrated with the global economy. Thus, Indian managers have had much longer exposure to Western management thought. Also, India started establishing elite business schools in the 1960s, a process that China did not embark on until the late 1990s.

Political Institutions

It is no secret that China and India differ greatly in the structure of their political institutions. China's is a command-and-control economy. Senior political leaders are appointed by the Communist Party of China, and the media are expected to help implement national policies. In contrast, India is a free-wheeling democracy modeled after that of the United Kingdom. Political leaders are elected by the citizens, and the media remain free from government censorship. It is important to note, however, that China's political system is far from monolithic. It is already the reality today, and will become increasingly so in the coming years, that different ministries and bureaus within China may have serious policy disagreements with each other. Similarly, policy disagreements (if not officially, then in terms of de facto implementation) are becoming increasingly common between the central government and those at the provincial and local levels.

Social Culture

But for differences in language and food, most Indians would feel quite at home within a Chinese family and vice versa. In both cultures, caring for the family (in particular, children) is paramount. Both societies place equally high value on education and saving for the future. They are also like-minded on the importance of face, that is, respecting the dignity of others—in particular peers, superiors, and elders. Thus, in both cultures, people feel equally uncomfortable in saying "no" outright. Notwithstanding these enormous similarities, the Chinese and Indian cultures do differ in at least one important respect. Given the centrality of religious beliefs in India, its culture is far more spiritual than that of China. Given the lack (or weakness) of religious beliefs in China, its culture is far more pragmatic than that of India.

Summing up, we see the Chinese and Indian societies and economies as akin to cousins rather than either twins or total strangers. Although there are important differences, the similarities between the two are also large.

Growing Economic Integration Between China and India

But for a brief border war in 1962 and the subsequent tensions that keep rearing periodically, China and India have enjoyed a mutually harmonious relationship going back at least two thousand years. The ties that brought China and India together were religious and intellectual, as well as economic. As illustrative examples, consider the following. Buddhism was founded in India around the fifth century B.C.E. and then made its way into China. In the eighth century, an Indian scientist was appointed by China as the president of its Board of Astronomy. And the famous fifteenth-century Chinese admiral Zheng He (who reportedly had a more impressive fleet than that of Christopher Columbus) visited India often and played an important role in expanding trade links between the two countries.

In modern times, the period from 1949 to 2000 could be seen as the dark ages, an era of almost complete economic isolation between the two countries. Bilateral trade and investment came to a halt and was essentially insignificant. The current decade, however, has seen a near-complete transformation of the economic relationship between China and India. The primary driver of this transformation has been the fact that starting in the 1990s, both countries have become increasingly outward looking in their economic policies and thus embraced a deepening of their economy's integration with the rest of the world. Importantly too, both China and India are now fellow members of the World Trade Organization.

Table 2.1 tracks the growth of China-India bilateral trade since 2000. It is clear that the economies of China and India are becoming rapidly intertwined. In the current decade, trade between the two countries has grown twice as fast (about

Table 2.1 Growth of China-India Trade

Year	Bilateral Trade Between China and India ($billions)	Percentage Growth
2000	$2.9	47%
2001	3.6	23
2002	4.9	38
2003	7.6	54
2004	13.6	79
2005	18.7	38
2006	24.9	33
2007	36.0	45

Source: Abstracted from data obtained by the authors from the Ministry of Commerce, People's Republic of China.

50 percent annually) as each country's trade with the rest of the world (about 23 to 24 percent annually).

Few people outside China and India are aware that by the end of 2007, China had become India's number one trading partner. From China's side, India is now one of its top ten trading partners. Also, China's trade with India is growing far more rapidly than its trade with the other nine. Thus, India is rapidly becoming an increasingly important trading partner for China too.

Our computations indicate that after adjusting for partner GDP (bilateral trade divided by the trading partner's GDP), India's trade with China is greater than that with Japan, the United States, or the entire world. After similar adjustments, China's trade with India is only slightly below that with Japan, the United States, or the entire world.

Even if the growth rate in India-China trade slows to 25 percent annually from the current rate of about 50 percent, bilateral trade between them will be almost $75 billion in 2010 and $225 billion in 2015—as large as China-U.S. trade just three years ago. These are very large numbers. Political and business leaders need to start getting ready now for this radically different world.

Trade is only one of the two major economic ties that bind nations. The other is investment. We predict that the invest-ment links between India and China are likely to grow even faster than trade links. This would be an important development because investment links imply much deeper integration than trade links. At present, investment links between the two coun-tries are relatively modest. Haier in home appliances, Huawei in telecommunications equipment, and Lenovo in PCs have a significant presence in India. Similarly, some Indian companies such as Bharat Forge in auto components, Suzlon in wind tur-bines, and Tata Consulting and Infosys in IT services are build-ing a presence in China. These types of greenfield investments will continue to grow. However, the quantum leap will happen as some of the bigger companies from India and China acquire third-country companies that already have a large presence in the other country.

Consider, for example, Tata Motors's recent acquisition of Jaguar and Land Rover from Ford Motor Company. Given Jaguar and Land Rover's positions in the Chinese market, Tata Motors now finds itself with almost $2 billion in revenues from China. This is a large number and will have a significant impact on the centrality that Tata Motors accords to the Chinese mar-ket. Also, given Tata Group's trend-setter status in India, its strategic moves and mindset shifts are likely to have spillover effects on the rest of Indian industry.

Obviously it is hard to predict who will buy whom over the coming years. However, it is certain that over the next five to ten years, the world will see a growing number of foreign acqui-sitions by Indian and Chinese companies. As these acquisitions materialize, it is inevitable that investment linkages between India and China will grow rapidly.

To sum up, the rapid and multifaceted growth in economic integration between India and China will have profound impli-cations for political and business leaders. The world is watch-ing the rise of China and India with fascination. However, most people do not realize that the implications of tighter economic links between the two could be even more profound.

We now discuss the details of how a combined China+India strategy can benefit multinational enterprises with a presence in both countries.

Strategic Implication 1: Leverage the Scale of Both China and India

The first major benefit from a combined China+India strategy is that the company can capture the compelling growth opportunities, as well as the associated scale efficiencies, offered by a committed pursuit of the markets in both countries.

Consider the case of the PC industry. Worldwide PC shipments grew about 12 percent from 239 million units in 2006 to 268 million units in 2007. At a growth rate of about 5 percent, the U.S. market is largely mature. The biggest growth opportunities lie in China and India, where PC shipments are growing at over 20 percent annually. It appears quite likely that China will emerge as the world's largest PC market by around 2013 and India the second largest by around 2020. Stephen J. Felice, Dell's senior vice president for Asia-Pacific, has observed: "India is Dell's largest-growing country in the world . . . [with] 50% to 70% year-on-year growth in the foreseeable future."[9] As the major PC vendors (HP, Dell, Acer, and Lenovo) look at these trends, it is clear that none of them can hope to remain (or emerge) the global leader without a committed pursuit of PC buyers in both China and India.

The importance of leadership in the Indian market appears particularly crucial for Lenovo, the dominant player in China (35 percent market share in 2007) but relatively weak globally (7.5 percent market share in 2007). Among the major markets outside China, India is not only the fastest growing but, as a relatively young market, also the most fluid in terms of Lenovo's (or any of the other big players') ability to shift market shares.

In the United States and Europe, which are more established and relatively more mature, it is a much tougher challenge for Lenovo to steal market share from the larger incumbents. Not surprisingly, Lenovo sees India as a major plank in its strategy for global dominance. In one of its key moves, on January 1, 2006, the company restructured its global operations from four regions to five. Prior to the restructuring, the four regions were the Americas; Europe, Middle East, and Africa; Asia-Pacific excluding China; and China. After the restructuring, India was carved out of Asia-Pacific to be managed as a region in its own right.[10]

A combined China+India market strategy becomes even more important when major elements of the cost structure are subject to significant economies of scale and the profit margins are likely to be razor thin. This is increasingly the case for ultra-low-cost products targeted at the middle- and low-income segments of emerging markets. Take the case of the EC280, a new desktop Dell introduced in March 2007 for first-time buyers in emerging markets.[11] EC280 is a compact machine that occupies one-eighth the space of a regular desktop. It uses a low-end Intel microprocessor and comes loaded with Microsoft Windows. In 2007, the starting retail price for the complete machine including monitor was about $335. If you consider the fact that novice buyers would be buying this desktop from a retail store rather than online (thus necessitating a margin for the retailer), it is clear that the profit margins for Dell on this machine must be very slim. Such a product strategy can be economically viable only if Dell can leverage sales of this machine not only across the vast market in China but also that in India, as well as other major emerging markets such as Brazil.

The global battle between Cisco Systems and Huawei Technologies also provides an interesting example of the criticality of pursuing a combined China+India market strategy. Headquartered in China, Huawei is one of Cisco's toughest challengers on the global stage (see Figure 2.1 for a comparison

Figure 2.1 Revenues for Cisco and Huawei, 2003-2007 (billions of dollars)

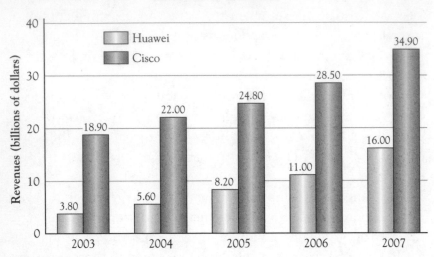

of the revenue figures for Cisco and Huawei over the last five years).

Huawei's competitive advantage rests heavily on cost leadership and derives primarily from the fact that the bulk of its R&D and manufacturing operations are based in China. Huawei's cost competitiveness has made it particularly attractive to customers in emerging markets. In fact, in 2007, Huawei derived 72 percent of its revenues from markets outside China, largely in emerging economies. According to media reports, as well as our own interviews with telecom operators in India, Huawei has publicly stated that one of its strategic goals is to become India's number one supplier of telecom infrastructure equipment.[12] The implications for Cisco are clear: it must regard Huawei as a serious competitor and build a counter-strategy that rests on at least three legs: ongoing sustenance of technological advantage over Huawei, a drastic reduction in cost structure to reduce or eliminate Huawei's cost advantage, and an attack on Huawei in both of its key strategic markets: China and India.

Strategic Implication 2:
Leverage the Complementary Strengths
of China and India

While Chinese and Indian economies will exhibit a remarkable degree of convergence over the next twenty years, in the near term, they offer complementary strengths that a smart global company can profitably exploit. China is much stronger than India in physical infrastructure and manufacturing efficiency. India is much stronger than China in software development, IT-enabled services, and many types of analytical and knowledge-intensive tasks such as legal research, finance and accounting, and advertising.

China's advantage over India in most areas of manufacturing is well known. As we noted earlier, China's manufacturing sector is currently five times as large as that of India. Thus, in many industries, Chinese manufacturers have a significant scale advantage over their Indian counterparts. In the manufacturing sector, they also enjoy other advantages, such as a significantly better logistics infrastructure (roads, railways, and ports), significantly greater experience at responding effectively and efficiently to the needs of foreign customers, and a more compliant labor force. It should be noted that as of late 2007 and early 2008, labor costs, especially in southern China, were on a steep climb due to a combination of tougher labor laws and an appreciating currency. Notwithstanding these developments, in most industries, China's manufacturing sector remains (and, for several years, is likely to remain) well ahead of India's.

In reverse, India's lead over China in IT services is equally well known. India's IT services sector is more than five times as large as that of China. Also, paralleling China's comparative advantage in manufacturing, India's lead in IT services rests on multiple factors: a very strong export orientation, extensive experience at remote delivery of IT services to global clients, highly developed process rigor, in-depth knowledge of specific industries, and fluency in the English language.

IBM Corporation provides a near-perfect example of how to leverage the complementary manufacturing versus IT services capabilities of China and India. IBM has built its largest procurement center outside the United States in Shenzhen, China. Sourcing from Asian (primarily China-based) suppliers accounts for about 30 percent of the company's $40 billion annual procurement budget. On October 1, 2006, IBM even relocated its chief procurement officer, John Paterson, to China. As Paterson noted in his letter to the company's suppliers, "This [move] places us closer to the core of the technology supply chain which is important, not only for IBM's own internal needs, but increasingly for the needs of external clients whose supply chains we are managing via our Procurement services offering. As IBM's business offerings continue to grow, we must develop a deeper supply chain in the region to provide services and human resource skills to clients both within Asia and around the world."[13]

In contrast to IBM's heavy reliance on China for hardware procurement, the company has made India the global center for the delivery of IT services. At the end of 2007, IBM employed over seventy thousand IT professionals in India—about 20 percent of its global workforce and four times its staff size in China. The vast majority of the India-based staff was being deployed to serve the needs of IBM's global clients. In short, IBM Corporation had made China one of its most important global hubs for hardware procurement and India one of its most important global hubs for the delivery of IT services.

The complementary strengths of China and India extend beyond manufacturing and IT services. China's chemical industry (particularly specialty chemicals) is significantly more advanced than India's. Also, certain types of pharmaceutical raw materials are available more abundantly and at lower cost in China than in India. Thus, many Indian pharmaceutical companies rely on China as one of their primary suppliers of pharmaceutical ingredients.

In turn, India is emerging as an important source of specialized talent (finance, accounting, and global marketing) for many Chinese companies as well as the Chinese units of major multinationals. To quote Andrew Tsui, chairman of southern China for Korn/Ferry International, an executive search firm, "Through the MNC executive circuit, Indian executives have good exposure to modern management principles, are exposed to the challenges of emerging markets and can communicate well in English."[14] Shenzhen-headquartered Huawei Technologies is one example of a Chinese company that has begun to use Indian executives to crack open English-speaking markets.

Another nontraditional area where India is emerging as a complement to China is the country's highly developed skills in creating ads for diverse markets. Paralleling similar moves by other global agencies, in mid-2007, Interpublic Group PLC announced the launch of a twenty-four-hour production studio in India whose creative staff would work alongside colleagues in New York and London to create ads for global accounts. The roots of India's comparative advantage in advertising lie in the country's individualism (which fosters creativity) and the world's highest degree of linguistic and religious diversity (which fosters skills at creating ads that can work across diverse languages, religions, and cultures with minimal adaptation). In a telling example of a Chinese company that is keenly aware of the complementary strengths of China and India, Lenovo centralized its global advertising activities to a hub in Bangalore in mid-2007. The new hub is responsible for the creation of Lenovo's ads for the entire global market (with the notable exception of China). While Lenovo will leverage India's strengths for global advertising, it will continue to leverage China's strengths for low-cost manufacturing.

Strategic Implication 3:
Transfer Learning from One Market to the Other

The combination of enormous similarities yet important differences between China and India offers considerable opportunities for multinational corporations with operations in both countries to transfer learning from one to the other. Were the two markets to be radically different, there would be severe limits on the relevance or the transferability of ideas across them. And were the two to be virtually identical, there would be little to learn from each other. Thus, the similarity-difference ratio between China and India provides major opportunities for multinational corporations to benefit from the mutual transfer of lessons from their operations in the two countries. Such knowledge transfer can benefit companies by reducing the likelihood of costly errors and accelerating the ramp-up to successful operations.

Business and political leaders in both countries are well aware of the potential for mutual learning. Consider, for example, the following excerpt from an article titled, "Dalian: China's Bangalore," in *China International Business*:

> In terms of software exports, Dalian places third among Chinese cities, behind Shanghai and Beijing. But significantly, it is the city currently placing the most emphasis on software, with the aim of making it Dalian's central industry. The local government, citing the example of Bangalore, known as the Silicon Valley of India, is doing its best to promote the development of the industry. . . . "Developing the software industry is the best choice for us,' says Xia Deren, who has been mayor of Dalian since 2003.[15]

Look now at the following observation by Anand G. Mahindra, CEO of India's $6 billion revenue Mahindra Group:

> China is the best thing that happened to India. Now we can say to the politicians, "Look, this is our competition, this is what they're doing. Why aren't we?" It's something to whip up our competitiveness. China is the benchmark. . . . For a country that invented yoga, the science of stretching, we just didn't stretch ourselves.[16]

A combined China+India strategy can provide a company opportunities for knowledge sharing in virtually all elements of the value chain. We identify two of the most important areas.

First, we look at market development and go-to-market strategies. The fact that China's economy is twelve to fifteen years ahead of India's provides many companies with a significant opportunity to leverage the lessons from China to fine-tune their strategies for the Indian market at a faster pace. China's PC industry, for example, is almost four times as large as India's. Aside from size, however, the Chinese and Indian markets share many common features: extremely rapid growth, large proportions of first-time buyers, the need to reach customers not just in tier 1 markets but also tiers 2 to 4 and even smaller markets, the importance of selling through the retail channel, very low buying power, low penetration of credit cards, and a need for local language software.

Although the two markets are not identical, many important features of business models can be shared across both markets, and Lenovo is attempting to do so in a systematic way. William J. Amelio, Lenovo's president and chief executive, had this to say:

> One of the first things we [did] was to say, let's figure what the essence is of the China model and then can we employ it somewhere else? India was a great first choice. Essentially we had a 167-page manifesto. We had the team figure out how to distil that down to five salient points that we could then implement in any country. And then we put together a Swat team that understood the essence of that and was able to go into the country and implement. We've been highly successful in India.[17]

The PC industry is just one of hundreds of business areas where companies can transfer lessons from China to India (and vice versa) in order to reduce the time needed to hone their strategies for both markets.

The second important area is frugal designs for products, services, and solutions. China and India are unique among the major economies in that they are both rich and poor at the same time. Both have market sizes that are almost as large as, and growing faster than, the rich countries of western Europe. Both also have rapidly growing numbers of very affluent people. Importantly, however, the vast majority of the population in both countries is extremely poor by Western standards. Per capita income in China is one-twentieth and in India one-fortieth of that in the United States.

Thus, unless a company sells high-end niche products such as Louis Vuitton bags or Porsche cars, it has little choice but to invent products, services, and solutions that can be sold at ultralow prices while still yielding satisfactory profit margins. There is no need for a company to engage in such frugal innovation separately for China and India. A frugal design that works in one market should generally need only minor adaptations for the other. FonePlus, a prototype product developed by Microsoft China in mid-2007, is a cell phone with a built-in Windows operating system that, when connected to a TV and keyboard, can morph into a low-end computer. Microsoft views FonePlus as a multicountry product that could have as big a market in India as in China.[18]

The notion of frugal designs that will work across both China and India can be generalized to include products and services that are frugal in terms of raw material use and impact on the external environment. Given their rapid growth rates and vast populations, China and India have already emerged as two of the biggest contributors to the scarcity of virtually all commodities (including crude oil) as well as degradation of the environment. Admittedly, on a per capita basis, oil consumption in China and India is a small fraction of that in the developed countries. However, given the large populations, the absolute numbers become very large. The same is true for carbon dioxide emissions from China and India: they are small in per capita terms but huge in absolute terms.

It seems unlikely that either China or India will abandon rapid economic growth for the sake of the broader humanity.

At the same time, it also is impossible to imagine how they can continue to suck in ever larger quantities of raw materials and spew out ever larger quantities of harmful emissions. The solution to this dilemma must (and will) lie in new products and services that are designed to be ultraefficient in terms of raw material use and impact on the external environment and yet extremely cheap in terms of total cost. An example is the MAC 400, an electrocardiogram unit being developed by GE at the John F. Welch Technology Centre in Bangalore. This machine is smaller than an average laptop, works on battery power, and can be handled by a medical representative rather than a doctor.[19] The market for this machine should be as large in China as in India, not to speak of other emerging markets such as Brazil and Indonesia.

Strategic Implication 4:
Leverage Dual Presence to Reduce Risks

The fourth major benefit that a combined China+India strategy can yield pertains to the potential for risk reduction offered by dual presence. The opportunities for risk reduction exist in at least three areas.

First, dual presence can reduce exposure to political risk. Given rapid changes in their economies, governments in both China and India are still trying to figure out whether and how to differentiate between domestic and foreign enterprises and what types of policies to adopt for each category of firms. Also, as illustrated by China's new enterprise income tax law (which became effective on January 1, 2008, and eliminates the tax advantages that foreign enterprises had historically enjoyed over domestic ones) and a new antimonopoly law (which became effective on August 1, 2008, and may put new restrictions on acquisitions within China by foreign firms), future changes in public policy need not necessarily favor foreign enterprises. In the case of India, policy uncertainties also derive from the fact that the government is often ruled by a coalition of widely disparate partners and that the incumbents almost always lose in the next election. A multinational enterprise with a dual presence in both China and India is likely to be exposed to a lower level of total risk as compared to one with presence in just China or just India.

Second, dual presence can reduce exposure to economic risks such as currency fluctuations and shifting labor costs. Over the twelve months from early 2007 to early 2008, manufacturing costs in southern China (especially in labor-intensive industries such as shoes) increased by as much as 40 percent due to a variety of factors: a rapid increase in the cost of raw materials and energy; a new labor law that protects workers' rights more stringently than before; growing economic opportunities in central and western China, which have made migrant workers less willing to move to the coast; elimination of preferential tax policies for foreign companies; and a growing national emphasis on cleaner industries. Thus, increasing numbers of companies with manufacturing presence on China's east coast have begun to explore relocating to inland China or India and Vietnam. A recent study by the American Chamber of Commerce in Shanghai noted that over half of foreign manufacturers in China believe that the mainland is beginning to lose its manufacturing advantage over India and Vietnam.[20]

Finally, dual presence in China and India can reduce a company's exposure to intellectual property risk. A way to realize this benefit is by disaggregating and distributing core R&D and core component production across China and India as well as other countries. Consider the case of a European manufacturer that sells machinery to construction contractors. Burned by the experience of seeing its former Chinese partner produce copycat versions of an earlier model, this company has consolidated the production of some subsystems in India and others in China, while keeping assembly operations localized within each country. Such an approach permits the company to benefit from the low manufacturing costs in each country. At the same time, it reduces the extent to which the totality of the company's design blueprints and manufacturing processes are exposed to local partners or job-hopping local employees.

Conclusion

Notwithstanding a certain degree of economic rivalry and unresolved political tensions between China and India (as between China and Japan, and China and the United States), we deem it inevitable that economic ties between the two countries will continue to grow and become increasingly significant in absolute terms. By 2025, it is highly probable that China-India economic ties (through trade, investments, and technology linkages) may be among the five to ten most important bilateral relationships in the world. The rising dragons and tigers from China and India will be one set of beneficiaries from this trend. However, to the extent that multinational enterprises from outside China and India (such as Cisco, GE, IBM, or Nokia) are likely to be less directly affected by the occasional political tensions between the two countries, the potential benefits from a combined China+India strategy are likely to be even greater for these third-country multinationals.

3

MEGAMARKETS AND MICROCUSTOMERS

Fighting for Local Market Dominance

> eBay may be a shark in the ocean, but I am a
> crocodile in the Yangtze River. If we fight in the
> ocean, we lose—but if we fight in the river, we win.
> *Jack Ma, chairman and CEO, Alibaba Group*[1]

Founded in 1995, eBay has been one of the major success stories of the Internet age. Meg Whitman, who was recruited as the company's CEO in early 1998, is widely hailed as the architect who built eBay from before its initial public offering to a market capitalization of over $40 billion at the time of her retirement in March 2008.

Whitman was well aware of China's potential to emerge as the largest Internet market in the world. She noted to security analysts in 2005, "Share of e-commerce in China is likely to be the defining measure of success on the net."[2] She made sure that eBay was an early entrant into China. The company did so by spending $30 million in March 2002 to acquire a one-third stake in EachNet, China's equivalent of eBay. EachNet had been founded in 1999 by Tan Haiyin and Shao Yibo, two Harvard M.B.A.s who intended to emulate eBay's success in China by adapting the eBay model to some of the unique features of the Chinese market such as payment systems, demographics, and consumer behavior. In the initial years, EachNet proved to be a roaring success. In June 2003, at the time of eBay's decision to acquire complete ownership of EachNet, its market share in China was 85 percent.

Yet by the end of 2006, eBay's dreams in China appeared to be on the verge of collapse. The company's nemesis was TaoBao, an auction site launched by China's Alibaba Group in May 2003. By early 2006, TaoBao had emerged as the leading customer-to-customer and business-to-customer auction site in China. In December 2006, eBay decided to pull back from China, shut down its local Web site, and become a 49 percent owner in a new operation, TOM EachNet, run by TOM Online, a China-based portal and wireless operator.

EBay is just one of a countless number of companies for which there exists a wide gulf between the potential of the vast market opportunities in China and India and the extent to which the company has been able to realize the potential. Toyota is now the largest auto company in the world, yet its market share in both China and India is tiny and well below that of the leading players. Black & Decker is the number one power tools company in the United States and one of the leading competitors in Europe. Yet its market share in both China and India, the hotbeds of new construction, is minuscule. *BusinessWeek* is the largest weekly business magazine in the United States with a circulation of nearly 1 million copies every week. Yet in India, it is almost nowhere compared with the top three local business magazines, each with a circulation of around 500,000.

Companies face many external and internal challenges in capturing market opportunities in China and India. External challenges pertain to the fact that for most products and services, these markets are very different from those in the developed countries, present extremely low buying power on a per capita basis, are internally diverse and complex, can be brutally competitive, and in some industries pose regulatory hurdles. Internal challenges pertain to the tendency on the part of many companies to see the market opportunities in China and India as mere extensions of those in their home markets. Such companies demonstrate a strong proclivity to replicate their home country products, services, and business models in these markets instead of being open to inventing new approaches from the ground up. In extreme, albeit rare, cases, a company's leaders may even be blind to the magnitude of market potential in China or India, or both. Take the case of AT&T Wireless. In 1995, AT&T partnered with India's Tata and Birla groups to set up Idea Cellular, a mobile operator, each party acquiring a one-third stake. In October 2004, AT&T Wireless merged with Cingular. In July 2005, Cingular sold its stake in Idea to the other two partners for about $250 million. Barely three years later, India had emerged as the second largest mobile market in the world; if Cingular had not sold its stake, it would be worth about $3 billion in 2008. Cingular, now renamed AT&T Wireless, is once again looking for a (much more expensive) way to get back into India.

In this chapter, we analyze the structure of the market opportunities in China and India and lay out the strategic guidelines that can improve the odds of success in these two vast, rapidly growing, and dynamic markets.

Vast, Diverse, and Dynamic: Market Opportunities in China and India

For any business, there can be no substitute for undertaking one's own investigation into the size and structure of the market opportunities in China and India. The answers obviously vary across industries. Broadly, however, three observations are likely to be pertinent. As of 2008, China and India together account for approximately 10 percent of the world's GDP, 20 percent of the annual growth in the world's GDP, and 40 percent of the world's population. Thus, depending on the specific drivers of demand for an industry's products and services, it is very likely that as of 2008, the combined market size in China and India falls somewhere between 10 and 40 percent of global demand. Furthermore, as these economies continue to grow at a rate three times faster than that of the developed economies, it is all but certain that by the middle of this century, China and India together will account for nearly 40 percent of the global demand for almost every product or service.

In this section, we discuss some of the salient details regarding the vast, diverse, and dynamic nature of market opportunities in China and India.

Large Size and Rapid Growth

China and India are not just two of the largest but also two of the fastest-growing economies in the world. Based on estimates by McKinsey Global Institute, Table 3.1 summarizes the projected levels of aggregate private consumption in these two countries by 2025. Falling in the midrange of projections by other analysts such as Goldman Sachs and HSBC, these data assume a compounded annual growth rate (CAGR) of between

Table 3.1 Aggregate Private Consumption in China and India (billions of real 2000 dollars)

	2005	2025	2025 Versus 2005	CAGR (%)
China	$710	$3,265	4.6x	7.9%
India	370	1,521	4.1	7.3

Note: By 2025, China's consumption figures are projected to be over twice as large as those for Germany ($1,511 billion in 2000 dollars) and almost as large as those for Japan ($3,718 billion in 2000 dollars). India's consumption figures are projected to be larger than those for Germany but about half as large as those for Japan or China.

Source: Abstracted from McKinsey Global Institute, *From "Made in China" to "Sold in China": The Rise of the Chinese Urban Consumer*, Nov. 2006; McKinsey Global Institute, *The "Bird of Gold": The Rise of India's Consumer Market*, May 2007.

7 and 8 percent for both economies. Applying these growth projections to the actual data for 2005 (and assuming much lower growth rates in the developed economies) leads to the conclusion that by 2025, the total size of aggregate private consumption in China would be twice as large as that in Germany, almost as large as that in Japan, and on a path to catch up with the United States by 2035 to 2040.

India is starting from a base about half as large as that of China. Thus, by 2025, India's market size will still be only about half that of China. Nonetheless, aggregate private consumption in India is expected to be larger than that of Germany, making India's the fourth or fifth largest market in the world for most products and services.

Building on these aggregate projections, Table 3.2 summarizes the expected growth rates for selected categories of consumer goods and services. As discretionary incomes rise, the growth in expenditures is likely to be particularly steep in areas

Table 3.2 Projected Real Annual Growth Rates for Consumer Goods and Services In China and India, 2005-2025

	CAGR, 2005–2025 (%)	
Category	China	India
Health care	12.0%	10.8%
Housing and utilities	11.7	6.1
Transportation	10.3	8.3
Communication	9.8	13.4
Education and recreation	9.7	11.0
Personal products and services	8.1	9.2
Household products	7.0	6.9
Apparel	6.1	6.5

Source: Abstracted from McKinsey Global Institute, *From "Made in China" to "Sold in China": The Rise of the Chinese Urban Consumer*, Nov. 2006; McKinsey Global Institute, *The "Bird of Gold": The Rise of India's Consumer Market*, May 2007.

such as health care, communication, education and recreation, housing and utilities, and transportation.

Billionaires Versus Paupers

Aside from their large size and rapid growth, another important reality of the Chinese and Indian markets is the extremely high levels of disparity in incomes and wealth between the haves and have-nots:

- According to recent data by the Asian Development Bank, between 1993 and 2004, the Gini coefficient of inequality increased from 0.41 to 0.47 in China and from 0.33 to 0.36 in India. In comparison, for 2004, the Gini coefficient was 0.46 in the United States but only 0.31 in Japan and 0.28 in Germany.[3]

- According to *Forbes* magazine's 2008 list of the world's billionaires, China and India are now home to 42 and 53 billionaires, respectively. The only countries to have a larger number of billionaires are the United States (477), Russia (87), and Germany (59).[4]

- Thirty years of rapid growth in China, especially in the urban centers, have created a particularly sharp disparity between the rich and the poor. According to government estimates, the rural sector of China accounts for 54 percent of the country's population but only 8 percent of its GDP. The interpretation here is not that China's rural citizens have become poorer over the last thirty years. Instead, the reality is that economic growth in the urban centers has far outpaced that in the rural areas.

The Urban-Rural Divide

Tables 3.3 and 3.4 contain summary data on the cities, towns, and villages in China and India. These data highlight vividly

Table 3.3 Cities, Towns, and Villages in China, 2005

Category	Number	Average Population	Percentage of National Population	Percentage of National GDP
Tier 1 city	4	9.4 million	3%	13%
Tier 2 city	21	3.9 million	6	21
Tier 3 city	19	1.3 million	2	9
Tier 4 city	77	920,000	5	16
Tier 5 city	209	660,000	11	18
Tier 6 city	324	740,000	18	14
Rural village	NA	NA	54	8

Source: Abstracted from *China City Statistical Yearbook 2005*; and IBM Institute for Business Value, "Capture the New Market Frontiers: Unlocking the Untapped Mass Markets Within China," 2007.

Table 3.4 Cities, Towns, and Villages in India, 2005

Category	Number	Average Population	Percentage of National Population	Percentage of National Disposable Income
Tier 1 major city	8	More than 4 million	9%	18%
Tier 2 mainstream city	26	More than 1 million	4	6
Tier 3 climber city	33	More than 500,000	3	4
Tier 4 small town	5,094	Less than 100,000	14	18
Rural village	600,000	1,200	70	54

Source: Abstracted from McKinsey Global Institute, *The "Bird of Gold": The Rise of India's Consumer Market*, May 2007.

the large size of each country and, in the case of China, the very high degree of urbanization:

- Only 9 percent of China's population lives in the twenty-five cities categorized as tier 1 (think Shanghai or Beijing) or tier 2 (think Nanjing or Tianjin). Alternatively stated,

even if one were to visit every one of the twenty-five largest cities in China (let alone just the major hubs such as
Shanghai and Beijing), one would have barely scratched
the surface of the economic and social reality in this vast
country. Ninety-one percent of China's population (over 1.1
billion people, which is more than the entire population of
India) lives outside the twenty-five largest cities.

- Nearly 700 million Chinese live in rural communities. Their
  per capita income is a tiny fraction of that in the cities in
  tiers 1 through 4 and well below the national average.

- India is currently much less urbanized than China. Seventy
  percent of Indian citizens live in rural areas as compared
  with 54 percent in China. Furthermore, in India, only about
  sixty-seven cities have a population of over a half-million.
  In China, this number is almost ten times larger: above six
  hundred.

Rapid Growth of the Middle Class

Tables 3.5 and 3.6 summarize the breakdown of consumers in
China and India by income categories. These tables also contain projections about the expected growth rates of the categories over the next twenty years. Two major conclusions
emerge.

First, the number and buying power of the rich Chinese and
Indians will grow by vast amounts. By 2025, in real terms (net of
inflation), total consumption by rich citizens in both China and
India will be fourteen to sixteen times as large as that in 2005.
For many luxury products such as Louis Vuitton bags and Tag
Heuer watches, China is already one of the three largest markets in the world. Dassault, the jet manufacturer, sold five business jets in India in 2006 as compared with six in the previous
fourteen years. Compared with these numbers, the market in
2025 should be much larger.

Table 3.5 Growth of Private Consumption in China, 2005–2025

Category	Annual Household Income (Real 2000 RMB)[c]	Percentage of Urban Households in 2005	Percentage of Urban Households in 2025— Projected	Total Consumption (Billions of 2000 RMB) for 2005	Total Consumption (Billions of 2000 RMB) for 2025— Projected	Projected Size in 2025 Versus 2005
Global	Over 200,000	Less than 1%	2%	148	2,371	16.0×
Affluent	100,000–200,000	1	5	143	2,079	14.5
Upper aspirants[a]	40,000–100,000	4	61	370	12,235	33.1
Lower aspirants[a]	25,000–40,000	35	15	1,572	1,678	1.0
Urban poor	Below 25,000	59	16	1,371	838	0.6
Total urban population[b]	NA	100	100	3,704	19,201	5.2
Rural	In 2005, rural consumers accounted for 54 percent of national population but only 8 percent of national GDP

Sources: Abstracted from National Bureau of Statistics of China; *China City Statistical Yearbook 2005*; McKinsey Global Institute, *From "Made in China" to "Sold in China": The Rise of the Chinese Urban Consumer*, Nov. 2006; IBM Institute for Business Value, "Capture the New Market Frontiers: Unlocking the Untapped Mass Markets Within China," 2007.

[a]These two categories constitute the middle class (225 million people in 2005 and 704 million people in 2025).

[b]China's urban population is projected to expand from 572 million in 2005 to 926 million in 2025.

[c]In 2000, 1 US$ = 8.28 renminbi (RMB).

Table 3.6 Growth of Private Consumption in India, 2005–2025

Category	Annual Household Income (Real 2000 INR)[b]	Percentage of National Population in 2005	Percentage of National Population in 2025—Projected	Total Consumption (Trillions of 2000 INR) for 2005	Total Consumption (Trillions of 2000 INR) for 2025—Projected	Projected Size in 2025 Versus 2005
Global	Over 1 million	Below 1%	2	1	14	14×
Strivers[a]	500,000–1 million	1	9	1	16	16
Seekers[a]	200,000–500,000	4	32	2	25	12
Aspirers	90,000–200,000	41	36	9	12	1.3
Deprived	Below 90,000	54	22	4	2	0.5
Total population	NA	100	100	17	70	4.1

Sources: Abstracted from National Council for Applied Economic Research, *The Great Indian Middle Class*, 2004; McKinsey Global Institute, *The "Bird of Gold": The Rise of India's Consumer Market*. May 2007.

[a]These two categories constitute the middle class (50 million people in 2005 and 583 million in 2025).

[b]In 2000, 1 US$ = 45.70 Indian rupees (INR).

Notwithstanding the growing wealth of the rich citizens, the second conclusion is that in absolute terms, the biggest market growth will occur in the middle of the pyramid as vast numbers of today's poor become richer and migrate up. Although there is no consensus definition of what constitutes the middle class, going by the numbers in Tables 3.5 and 3.6, by 2025, each of these two countries will see an additional 500 million people migrate up from the ranks of the poor into the middle income segments. Between 2005 and 2025 in China, real annual consumption by the middle-income segments is expected to grow by 11.9 trillion renminbi (in 2000 renminbi) as compared with 4.2 trillion renminbi for the affluent and richer segments. In India, real annual consumption by the middle-income segments is expected to grow by 38 trillion Indian rupees (in 2000 Indian rupees) as compared with 13 trillion Indian rupees for the rich segments.

Megamarkets But Microcustomers

Given the large size of the markets in China and India, and the glitter of downtown Shanghai, downtown Beijing, and downtown Mumbai, it is easy to forget that the average buying power of most consumers in China and India is very low. This is true not just in the countryside but also in urban areas, even in tier 1 cities such as Beijing and New Delhi.

Consider the hard facts. At market exchange rates, the estimated per capita income in 2007 was just twenty-five hundred dollars in China and a mere thousand dollars in India. Our own field interviews in mid-2008 indicate that even in places such as downtown Beijing, the total annual compensation of a twenty-four-year-old lab technician with a bachelor's degree working in the local subsidiary of a U.S.-based biotech company was only about six thousand dollars, or one-tenth of the figure for a similar employee in the United States. The data for India are roughly similar. In summary, perhaps the best way to view the market realities in China and India is to think of them in terms of megamarkets and microcustomers.

Business leaders need to remember that just as midtown Manhattan and central London do not represent, even remotely, the buying power of the average family in the United States or United Kingdom, this is true also of midtown Shanghai in relation to the rest of China and midtown Mumbai in relation to the rest of India. The bulk of the market reality lies well outside the luxury hotels where the visiting multinational executive is likely to stay. This is true even in the tier 1 cities. Once you go outside the top tier cities, it becomes visibly clear to the naked eye.

Fighting for Local Market Dominance

In this section, we outline the strategy guidelines that companies need to follow in order to capture market opportunities in China and India.

Start with a Defensible Beachhead

The notion of starting with a beachhead is particularly relevant for a company that has yet to enter China or India. Given the growing speed with which relatively young enterprises can now unseat long-established ones, even among the world's five hundred or thousand largest companies, there will always be a sizable proportion for which global expansion, including entry into China and India, will be a fresh question. How to enter China or India, or both, will also remain a fresh question for newly formed business units within established enterprises. Finally, consider the large number of companies within China or India that are growing rapidly and considering global expansion. Thus, companies from China will increasingly face the question of how to enter India, just as companies from India will increasingly face the question of how to enter China.

Each of these two markets, China and India, is too big, too complex, and too diverse for a broad-brush attack. Entering either or both of these markets with all product lines targeted at all relevant market segments guarantees that executives will be taking on too much complexity too soon. Also, a broad-brush attack does not allow the company to make smaller, less costly mistakes that it can learn from before expanding the scale and scope of market entry. In short, a broad-brush attack increases the risk of early failure, which can be debilitating on several fronts: psychological and political costs for the executives leading the charge into China or India, tarnished image in the home as well as host country media, and a significant increase in the costs of entry.

A much smarter approach is to identify and occupy a beachhead that offers the best potential for early success and can serve as a launching pad for deeper market penetration. A beachhead refers to a niche defined in terms of a product line, a customer segment, a geographical area, or some combination of these three. An ideal beachhead has low economic or political entry barriers, low risk of failure, and the ability to serve as a platform for subsequent migration to other desirable market segments. Consider the following examples.

McCormick & Co. is a U.S.-headquartered food products company that sells spices, seasonings, and flavors to two sets of customers: retail stores for ultimate sale to end consumers and industrial businesses such as fast food chains and other food processing companies. When McCormick entered China in the 1990s, it targeted Western fast food chains such as McDonald's as its initial beachhead segment. Since these companies were already McCormick's customers in other markets, selling to them in China was relatively easy. Also, the product specifications and quality requirements of these customers were almost identical to those in the United States, thereby eliminating the risk of a misalignment between the company's offerings and market needs. Finally, given McCormick's established relationships with these customers, there was minimal risk that the company would run into nasty contractual disputes or suffer from nonpayment of invoices. This beachhead strategy allowed McCormick to launch its China operations in a relatively low-risk manner. Over time, the company was able to capitalize on its initial manufacturing presence, a growing pool of local managers, and a rapidly growing knowledge of the broader Chinese market to diversify its customer (as well as product) base to include Chinese fast food chains, Chinese retailers, and Chinese food processing companies.

Another example is Germany-headquartered Metro Group, one of the world's largest retailers whose various businesses include a cash-and-carry wholesale business targeted at professional customers such as hotels, restaurants, caterers, and small retailers; hypermarkets and supermarkets; department stores; and online retailing. When Metro entered India in the early part of this decade, it chose cash-and-carry wholesale operations as its beachhead segment. The reasoning was simple: India's regulations did not permit foreign multibrand retailers to operate within the country. However, there were no such restrictions on business-to-business wholesaling. Thus, a cash-and-carry operation has permitted Metro to enter India years ahead of players such as Wal-Mart and Carrefour. It has built procurement capabilities, logistics systems, distribution centers, and market knowledge that could prove to be potent if the company were to enter the retail business more directly through franchisees or, if the regulations change, its own retail stores.

Pursue a Multisegment Strategy

We discussed the vast disparities in buying power that exist not only across Chinese and Indian cities, towns, and villages but even within the major cities. However, income is not the only dimension along which extreme diversity is a defining feature of

the societies in China and India. Given their large geographical size and vast populations, each country is almost like a con-
tinent. Thus, each also exhibits high diversity along multiple
dimensions: languages and dialects, climates, religions, and cultural proclivities, for example. Given this diversity, unless a
company makes niche products targeted at a very narrow customer base, such as Hugo Boss apparel or Ferrari sports cars,
market success in China and India is almost impossible without
finely segmenting the local market in each country, developing
a strategy tailored to the needs of each segment, and exploiting a strong position in one segment to enter and occupy one or
more adjacent segments.

Nokia serves as an excellent example of a company that has
benefited from a disciplined pursuit of a multisegment strategy.
Other than the United States, Nokia is a clear market leader
in all of the world's major markets: Europe, China, and India.
In early 2008, its global market share stood at over 40 percent,
larger than the combined market share of its three biggest competitors: Samsung, Motorola, and Sony Ericsson. Among the
many factors that explain Nokia's success, we view its multisegment strategy as one of the most important. Consider its strategy for India, where it has a well over 50 percent market share
in mobile phones. Its product offerings in India cover the entire
range from the high-end N- and E-series phones, which retail
for over a thousand dollars and are targeted at urban professionals, to the Nokia 1200, which retails for around thirty dollars
and is targeted at low-income customers, including vast numbers of urban and rural workers who work in physically rough
environments.

The 1200 model is designed to be dust- and splash-proof
with a rubberized keypad and antislip back cover, a bright flash-
light for emergency use in a country that suffers from too many
power outages, a time-tracking feature to help the user control the duration of each call, multiple phonebooks that make

sharing the phone easier, and an easy–to-use menu in multiple languages with calendars. Most of these features would be of little use to affluent professionals who never have to share their phones and who live and work in air-conditioned homes and offices supported by backup power generators. Nokia's multisegment strategy is reflected also in its choice of distribution channels. The high-end phones are marketed through Nokia's own concept stores; in contrast, the low-end phones are sold in approximately seventy thousand outlets through the length and breadth of India, including rural markets. Nokia derives many benefits from its multisegment strategy: a dominant market share; huge economies of scale in R&D, component sourcing, and production; and brand loyalty, which pays off handsomely as lower-income customers get richer and trade up to higher-priced phones.

Otis China is another good example of a multisegment strategy. Given the vast scale of urban construction in China, it is now the largest market for new elevators in the world. Not surprisingly, the market is also very diverse and varies along many dimensions, including use for passengers versus freight, building height, elevator speed, passenger capacity, elevator technology, and customer price sensitivity. Otis has wisely followed a strategy of covering virtually all segments. Focusing on only the high-end segments would not only have deprived Otis of major revenue opportunities but would also have left it vulnerable to serious competitiveness risks. Although the market for high-end elevators is very large, that for other types of elevators is even larger, given the ongoing urbanization of China. Leaving these middle- and lower-end opportunities to other players would have implied that Otis would deprive itself of the enormous and lifelong maintenance and service business that follows the installation of a new elevator. At least as important, it would have given Otis's competitors an opportunity to amass technological capabilities and scale that could be leveraged against Otis in its high-end niche. Otis uses different brand names to target different segments: Otis, Xizi Otis, Sigma, and Express. As is evident, some of the brands do not even use the name *Otis*. The different brands also use different and appropriately tailored sourcing, production, and marketing strategies.

Adidas in China provides an interesting example of a different type of multisegment strategy—one that is driven by the realization that even within the same local market, buyer preferences may differ based on cultural factors. The company has adopted a two-pronged retail strategy in China. One type of store emphasizes new designs that originate at Adidas's design center in Shanghai, tap into local creativity, and are tailored specifically to Asian bodies and tastes (for example, the rise of a pair of pants, how the shoulders fit, how funky the colors should be). The other type of store emphasizes the company's eighty-seven-year heritage and carries more global designs and products. The mall beneath the company's headquarters in Shanghai has one store of each type within the same building.[5] This type of a multisegment strategy not only enables Adidas to capture a larger portion of the market opportunity but also serves as a useful vehicle to develop deeper knowledge of the diverse and changing preferences of its customers in China.

Make Your Mantra "Market-Centric, Market-Centric, Market-Centric"

Whenever a company enters a new market, it must make fundamental decisions regarding the extent to which it will carry over its existing brand names, products and services, designs, and business models to the new market versus the extent to which it will engage in local adaptation or even outright innovation from the ground up. The choice can range from a near-complete replication of existing approaches at one end to a near-complete bottom-up innovation at the other. When the U.K.-based business newspaper *Financial Times* entered the U.S. market in the 1990s, it could have, at one extreme, chosen to merely reprint the U.K. edition and sell it in the United States. At the other extreme, it could have chosen to create an entirely new business publication with a new look and new brand name for the U.S. market. Instead of going with either of these two extremes, the publisher chose an intermediate approach. The brand name, the look and feel (such as the pink color of the paper and the type used), and much of the content remained identical. However, the U.S. edition has more in-depth coverage of U.S. news and gives greater prominence to that international news which would be of more relevance or interest to U.S. readers.

The same question (how much replication, how much adaptation, and how much innovation; see Table 3.7) applies to every company that must design or reassess its strategy for the China and India markets. Based on our analysis of and discussions with executives in over a hundred companies with operations in China and India, it is our contention that the vast majority of incumbents from the developed countries reflect naiveté in their strategies for these two markets. The roots of this naiveté lie in the history of companies' experience at globalization.

Until recently, for most multinational corporations (MNCs), globalization meant going to countries that could be classified as either *rich-and-rich* (large market size and high per capita incomes, as in the case of the United States, European countries, Japan, Canada, and Australia) or *poor-and-poor* (small market size and low per capita incomes, as in the case of virtually all developing countries). The rich-and-rich markets were not very different from the home market or from each other; thus, a strategy of replication or partial local adaptation would often suffice. The poor-and-poor markets were very different from the MNCs' home markets and quite small in size; as a result, there was little economic justification for undertaking the cost and effort of wholesale business model innovation. Since the cost of a suboptimal strategy for the poor-and-poor markets was fairly small, it made sense for the MNC to bring its developed country products

Table 3.7 How Much Adaptation? Alternative Strategies

Strategy for a New Market	Details	When Appropriate?	Examples
Replication	A near-complete replication of the company's business model in the new market: same brand names, same product and service concepts, same business model.	The key characteristics of the new market (such as buyer needs, buyer behavior, and buying power) are virtually identical to those of the current market.	Starbucks's strategy for Canada LVMH's strategy for China
Local adaptation	An adaptation of many secondary features of the company's business model to the unique needs of the local market; however, the core features of the business model remain unchanged.	The key characteristics of the new market are partially similar to but also partially different from those of the current market.	Disney's theme park in Hong Kong, which incorporates Chinese characters in addition to the traditional ones McDonald's strategy for India (the use of lamb instead of beef in hamburgers)
Bottom-up innovation	De novo creation of products, services, and business models (and often also brand and subbrand names) for the new market.	The economic as well as sociocultural characteristics of the new market are radically different from those of the current market.	AIG's microinsurance policies in India, which permit a customer to insure, say, a single cow Yum Brands's (the parent company of Pizza Hut, KFC, and Taco Bell) launch of East Dawning, a Chinese fast food chain, in Shanghai

and practices to the developing country market and be satisfied with skimming the top layer of the available economic pie.

The large size and rapid growth of China and India force MNCs to confront an entirely new reality for the first time: markets that are simultaneously *rich-and-poor*: very large in terms of market size but very poor in terms of per capita incomes and buying power. Yes, there is a market of affluent buyers at the top of the economic pyramid. However, the size of the market in the middle of the pyramid is even bigger and will become vastly larger over the next twenty years. Economically as well as culturally, the needs, the buying power, and the buyer behavior of this middle market are very different from those of the affluent buyers. Thus, attacking the China and India markets from a mindset of replication or even partial adaptation means that the company would be leaving the bulk of the market opportunity to other players. Domestic players from within China and India are likely to have a particularly strong advantage in capturing these middle and low-end markets. They understand these markets well, have a radically lower-cost structure, and, as local players, can respond speedily to the diverse and changing needs of these customers. Given the scale of these middle and low-end markets, it is inevitable that within a few years, these domestic players will have the size and capability to attack the established MNCs not just within China and India but also in the latter's home markets.

This is how ArcelorMittal, which started out as a small steel mill in Indonesia, has become the world's largest steel company; SABMiller, which started out as a South Africa–based domestic beer company, has become the world's largest brewer; and Cemex, which started out as a midsized cement producer in Mexico, has become one of the world's largest building products companies. Hundreds of such aspiring global champions are currently serving the middle and low-income markets in China and India. In short, in most industries, a China and/or India strategy that rests primarily on replication or even partial adaptation of home country products, services, and business models may be not merely suboptimal for established MNCs but also dangerous from the perspective of long-term survival.

As depicted in Table 3.8, *the implementation of a market-centric approach requires that corporate leaders see their company first and foremost as a portfolio of capabilities rather than as a portfolio of brands, products, and services.* Of course, existing brands and product and service concepts matter. However, a market-centric company views home country brands and product and service concepts merely as a subset of possible options that they could

Table 3.8 Home Country–Centric Versus Market-Centric Approaches to China and India Markets

	Home Country–Centric	Market-Centric
Starting point	Home country brands, products, services, and business models	Explicit as well as latent needs of customers in China and India
Key strategic questions	How large is the market in China and India for our products, services, and brands? How do we capture this market profitably?	How can we leverage our and our partners' existing and new capabilities to create products, services, and solutions to meet the targeted customers' needs? How can we create and develop the market while ensuring a sustainable return on investment for all stakeholders? How can we take these innovations to other emerging (or even developed) markets to capture economies of scale?
Organizational model	China and India operations run by a command-and-control approach from corporate headquarters	China and India operations viewed as global hubs that are integral parts of a geographically dispersed virtual headquarters

deploy in big, emerging markets such as China and India. For a market-centric company, the primary focus must be on figuring out what the market needs are and then developing and deploying its own and its business partners' capabilities to create products, services, and solutions that meet these needs at affordable prices and sustainable profit margins.

Yum Brands, the parent company of Pizza Hut, KFC, and Taco Bell, provides an interesting example of a market-centric approach. Sam Su, president of Yum's China operations, has adopted a market-centric approach at both levels: individual brands as well as the parent company. In the United States, for example, the Pizza Hut brand stands for fast food. However, pizza is a new and relatively more expensive food for Chinese consumers. Thus, Sam Su has made Pizza Hut outlets in China more upscale and fancier than in the United States. They are positioned as a sit-down casual dining experience for middle-income consumers rather than as fast and inexpensive food for people on the go. At the parent company level, Sam Su's approach is even more innovative. He has launched an entirely new brand of restaurants, East Dawning, currently being test-marketed in Shanghai and Beijing. East Dawning serves a carefully selected menu of Chinese dishes at reasonable prices. At the level of underlying capabilities, there is much that carries over from Yum's core businesses to East Dawning. However, at the level of the storefront brand, the store design, and the menu, East Dawning reflects ground-up innovation. It is easy to see that the market for Chinese food in China is much bigger than for Western fare such as pizza, fried chicken, and tacos.

As reflected in comments at the beginning of this chapter by Alibaba's Jack Ma about the dangers that a shark could face when battling a crocodile in the Yangtze River, eBay's problems in China are starkly indicative of the downside of forgetting to be market-centric, especially in a market such as China, which differs from Western markets not just economically and culturally but also in terms of language and political system. After acquiring complete control over EachNet in 2003, eBay was reported to have centralized the management of its China operations to such an extent that even decisions such as office expansion required corporate approval. eBay also decided to harmonize its customer-facing activities in China with those in the United States. As in the United States, it made the interface simple. However, local customers liked Web sites that were "loaded with information, links, graphics, banners, and multimedia" and thus regarded eBay EachNet's Web site as "too empty."[6] Ebay also did not permit direct interaction between a buyer and a seller until the sale had been completed. In contrast, TaoBao permitted the parties to contact each other and haggle over prices, a practice more consistent with Chinese customers' preferred approach. Compared with TaoBao, eBay was also late in incorporating an escrow into its online payment system. These are just some of the problems that eBay created for itself—problems that could have been avoided if it had been more market-centric.

Focus on Market Development, Not Just Market Share Development

Given the fast pace of economic development, millions of consumers in China and India each year buy their first cell phone, their first PC, their first washing machine, their first car, their first apartment, and, if they can afford to sit down and relax, their first glass of wine. Considering that in each country, over the next twenty years, 500 million citizens are likely to migrate up from the ranks of the poor to the middle class, this pace of new customer addition is unlikely to abate. A direct implication of this reality is that companies aiming for market leadership in China and India must focus at least as squarely on market development as they would on protecting and increasing their market share.

A company can play two types of complementary roles in the market development process. One role pertains to the ecosystem within which the company will operate within China and India. The question to ask here is, What can we do to make the entire ecosystem more robust (more productive, more efficient, higher value creating, and so forth)? The second role pertains to individuals who could potentially become your industry's customers and consumers. The question to ask here is, What can we do to help these individuals become more interested in buying our products and services and smarter at using them?

The German company Metro Cash & Carry's operations in India illustrate what we mean by ecosystem development. As a wholesale operation that sells to other businesses, such as hotels, restaurants, caterers, and small retailers, its development challenge is on the buy side rather than the sell side. In India, the supply chain from the farm to the end consumer suffers from many pathologies: as many as six to seven intermediaries, poor transport and roads, and ignorant farmers and other workers who handle the farm produce. As a result, an estimated 35 to 45 percent of farm produce rots and never makes it to the market. Not surprisingly, modernizing the supply chain has become one of Metro's major focus areas in India. The following are some of the many ways in which the company is attempting to develop the ecosystem in which it is embedded:

- Teaching farmers to stop watering the spinach the night before it is to be picked
- Teaching farmers to stop piling vegetables on the ground after they are picked since bacteria from the ground decrease shelf life
- Giving farmers plastic crates to enable the direct transfer of vegetables from the vines into the crates
- Teaching fishing crews how to cool fish by immediately gutting it and stuffing it with shaved ice to increase the shelf

life and enable Metro to create a market for fish in locations far from the coast

- Teaching shepherds to vaccinate their herds and treat them for sicknesses such as foot-and-mouth disease
- Cutting out middlemen by sending refrigerated trucks straight to the farms[7]

The result of these ecosystem development efforts has been an increase in farm productivity, an increase in farmers' compensation, and a more varied and fresher supply of produce at lower prices to Metro's own customers.

Caterpillar provides a vivid example of customer education by persuading customers in China to consider using its Cat 627G Wheel Tractor-Scraper. The normal approach in the earth-moving industry is to publish technical articles with statistics on productivity and efficiency in trade magazines. However, in a market such as China, it is still uncommon for construction companies to keep data on productivity and efficiency. In order to make its case in a manner that would hit home with key groups of customers, Caterpillar picked an existing project in Jilin province to convert 900,000 acres of wasteland into arable land. The company invited local contractors, landowners, government officials, and the media to a demonstration event featuring the new Cat machines. The event was able to make a persuasive case that use of these machines would cut the work schedule by five months, thereby enabling farmers to start earning a living that much sooner. Where technical data on productivity and efficiency might have fallen on deaf ears, being able to demonstrate that their machines could help farmers start making money five months ahead of schedule was a powerful message. The news, featuring the Cat machines, hit the local media and within a few days was picked up by the national CCTV network.[8]

Since the goal of market development is to help the market make the transition from one state to another, effectiveness at this task requires acute sensitivity to the peculiarities of the market's current state, a commitment to leading the market development efforts, and ingenuity in figuring out how to lubricate the transition. These ideas are illustrated well by the efforts of Future Group, India's largest retail conglomerate. As a company that is five times as big as its nearest competitor, Future Group and its units easily have a bigger stake in market development than in market share development. Market development in this context includes helping mostly lower-middle-income customers at the company's newly built supermarkets feel comfortable in an environment that looks utterly different from the hustle and bustle of small shops operating in crowded spaces. One of the mechanisms that the company uses to ease the transition is the creation of organized chaos. The company redesigned the stores and replaced wide and straight aisles with narrow and crooked ones. By design, this made the stores more congested, noisier, and more chaotic. As Kishore Biyani, the founder of Future Group, noted in an interview with the *Wall Street Journal*, "The shouting, the untidiness, the chaos is part of the design. . . . With long aisles, the customers never stopped. They kept on walking on and on so we had to create blockages. . . . Making it chaotic is not easy."[9]

Develop Ultra-Low-Cost Solutions

Except in the case of companies supplying only high-end niche products such as Hermès accessories or Audi cars, the imperative to develop ultra-low-cost solutions derives directly from the fact that the buying power of the middle- and low-income Chinese and Indian consumers is extremely low and, by the standards of the rich economies, will remain low for at least the next two decades. Even when China's GDP becomes the largest in the world (perhaps around 2030), its per capita income will still be less than one-fourth that in the United States. Thus, as a critical element of their multisegment strategy to become market leaders in China and India, companies must figure out how to develop and deliver ultra-low-cost products, services, and solutions.

It is crucial to remember that *while low labor costs play an important role in cost reduction, they are not the most important factor in the creation and delivery of ultra-low-cost solutions. The most important factor is smart design: of the entire business model, the end product or service, and the components.* Design decisions dictate the choice of activities, how the various activities will be performed, who will perform them, the magnitude of scale economies, the choice of materials, and operating, use, and maintenance costs, to name just a few of the factors that affect total cost. The importance of design as a major driver of cost was noted years ago in a study by the Defense Advanced Research Projects Agency, an arm of the U.S. government, which noted that "cost reduction opportunities decreased as products moved from concept to production. At the beginning of the conceptual design phase, 90 percent of the cost reduction opportunities remained, while at the start of production only 7 percent of these opportunities remained."[10]

The importance of business model design as the primary driver of cost is illustrated well by Bharti Airtel, India's largest mobile operator. Bharti Airtel offers nationwide cellular services at less than two cents per minute, perhaps the lowest in the world. Even China Mobile, the number one operator in China, has prices that are twice as high. Notwithstanding the low prices, Bharti Airtel has consistently delivered some of the highest profit margins in mobile telephony. One of the major factors in its ability to drive costs down has been an innovative business model whereby the company has outsourced two of the major components of its business system: provision of network capacity to Nokia Siemens Networks (NSN) and Ericsson and provision of end-to-end management services to IBM. NSN and Ericsson get paid not for selling the equipment but for providing network capacity; importantly, they are paid "only when the capacity is up and running and has been used by customers, thereby excluding payment for unused capacity at any point in time."[11] Regarding management services, Bharti Airtel has handed over complete responsibility for supplying, installing, and managing all hardware and software requirements to IBM. In turn, IBM is paid a share of Bharti Airtel's revenues.

These outsourcing agreements, the first of their kind in the global telecommunications industry, have transformed the relationship between the vendors and Bharti. Instead of the vendors wanting to stuff as much hardware and software as they possibly could into the Bharti system, they are now driven to minimize the total cost of the system and expand the system's delivery capacity while meeting the agreed service-level requirements. As experts in their domains, NSN, Ericsson, and IBM ought to be much smarter than Bharti in figuring out how to do so. These outsourcing arrangements have also eliminated large chunks of wasted time and effort spent in contract negotiations with the vendors every few months.

At the end of 2007, the number of cell phone subscribers in India stood at about 200 million. Over the next five years, this figure is expected to reach over 500 million. This growth can happen only if companies such as Bharti Airtel (and its competitors Reliance, Idea, and Vodafone) figure out how to extend mobile telephony to rural areas, where the distances are larger, infrastructure weaker, and income levels much lower than in urban India. As a way to address these challenges in a commercially viable manner, some of the experiments that the wireless operators and their equipment providers are working on include a small antenna that could be installed on the roof to serve a tiny village, antennae that are powered by solar and wind energy, towers that are made from light steel and have more efficient designs, and sharing of towers among competitors.[12] These innovations have little to do with thinking of low labor costs in India as the primary driver of the companies' ability to offer ultra-low-cost wireless services to the rapidly expanding pool of low-income customers.

Opportunities to offer ultra-low-cost solutions exist in virtually every sector of the Chinese and Indian economies: computing, Internet services, transportation, banking, health care, education, housing, hotels, recreation, and many others. In every one of these cases, *innovations in the business model, product or service designs, and component designs will be the most important driver of cost reduction, with low labor costs playing an important, albeit secondary, role*.

Position Your Company as a Partner to China and India

It should be clear by now that the market environment in China and India is such that a company that wants to achieve market leadership there must adopt a long-term perspective to its presence in and commitment to these two societies. These markets are not just very different but also physically distant from the developed economies of North America and Europe. Internally too, both markets are vast, highly diverse, and complex. Thus, except in rare cases, most companies will find that their existing knowledge about how to succeed in other markets teaches them little about how to succeed in China and India. If they want to aim for market leadership rather than merely skimming the cream at the top, they will need to engage in considerable learning from scratch. Also, given the rapid pace of change, much of this year's market knowledge is likely to become obsolete a year from now. Thus, companies have little choice but to build strong managerial capabilities on the ground and give these managers considerable autonomy to devise locally tailored market-facing solutions. These actions require that companies view China and India as long-term stories and as their permanent homes.

Other factors reinforce the importance of positioning a company as a partner to China and India. Given the importance of market development, companies need to make investments in understanding the ecosystem within which their Chinese and Indian operations will be embedded and in improving the productivity, efficiency, and value added by the ecosystem. The ecosystem will consist of business partners on all fronts: buy side, sell side, providers of complementary products and services, educational institutions, nongovernmental organizations, the media, and government and political entities at various levels. A company that does not come across as having a long-term commitment to the local economy is unlikely to be viewed as a trustworthy partner. Such a company will be confined to playing a secondary role after new market opportunities have already been developed, discovered, and captured by their more committed competitors.

Yet another factor that reinforces the need to view China and India as permanent homes is that in almost every sector of the economy, the market environment in these countries is extremely competitive. Whether it is cars, computers, cell phones, or hotels, every major company from every major economy in the world is eager to capture a share of the market opportunity. In addition, each country has dozens of local competitors that bring their own ambitions, local knowledge, and local capabilities to the marketplace. In such an environment, a company viewed as wavering in its commitment to the local economy is likely to find that it ranks low on the list of preferred employers by top talent and the list of preferred partners by other companies.

Suggesting that the company should position itself as a long-term partner to China and India does not imply that the company would necessarily have to incur major losses for several years before seeing a satisfactory return on investment. Depending on how effective a company has been at developing a beachhead strategy in the early years, how market-centric the company is, and how rapidly it can develop low-cost solutions to serve these markets, the economic returns can start flowing fairly early. B&Q, a chain of home improvement stores and a unit of the British retailer Kingfisher, entered China in 1998 and is now the market leader in the home improvement retail industry there. It turned profitable in 2003 and, according to the company's managers, has been improving its profit margins by about 1 percent a year.[13]

Given the long-term growth prospects of the Chinese and Indian markets, the goal must always be to focus on both the short and the long terms. No company can afford to go bankrupt while chasing distant prospects. At the same time, an excessively short-term orientation means either that the company will give up too soon or that it will end up as a marginal player pursuing a niche segment at the top. Either way, the company's long-term viability is likely to be in jeopardy.

Cisco Systems provides a good example of how a company can position itself as a long-term partner to India and China. In December 2006, Cisco created a second global headquarters (internally called Cisco East) in Bangalore and began relocating several of the most senior executives to India. Building on several China-focused announcements over the next year, in April 2008, John Chambers, the company's CEO, announced the next stage of the company's strategy for China. The new initiatives under this strategy included memoranda of understanding between Cisco and two of the major policymaking bodies in China: the National Development and Reform Commission (NDRC) and the Ministry of Commerce (MOFCOM).

The agreement with NDRC was aimed at broadening and deepening cooperation between Cisco and China "in the areas of manufacturing and service outsourcing, next-generation Internet, venture investment, training and development, as well as environmentally-focused research and development including energy efficiency, emission reduction and network-based green urban development." Every one of these areas is of significant and long-term importance to China and the Chinese government. In turn, the agreement with MOFCOM was aimed at helping MOFCOM "implement the Thousand-Hundred-Ten

Project for China's business process operations industry." Cisco announced that through this program, it would provide training to improve employees' skills in China's business process operations sector with the goal of transferring portions of its global business process services to China over the coming three to five years.[14]

Conclusion

A 2006 report by the American Chamber of Commerce in Shanghai reported that 65 percent of its member companies were profitable; of these, nearly one-third had profit levels equal to or higher than in other countries. At first blush, these data may suggest that multinational companies are finally beginning to get their China (and, by extension, perhaps also India) strategy right. But based on our field interviews with managers in and analysis of over a hundred companies, we question the validity of any such conclusion. As a more recent report by the IBM Institute for Business Value on MNC strategies in China noted, "Although a small, but growing, number of companies are tapping the mass market, the majority of MNCs still rely on premium-end products in the top cities for the bulk of their revenues and profits."[15]

It is easy to figure out how to keep headquarters executives happy by delivering reports that show attractive profit margins from operations in China and India. We believe, however, that focusing exclusively on profit margins as the measure of success runs a serious risk of leading to misplaced priorities. Pursuing market opportunities in China and India is like entering a large and rapidly growing new line of business. If you just skim the surface, it will appear as if you are doing well. However, what you may not know is that you have a rather small and declining market share and that you are setting yourself up for being pushed aside. Nevertheless, you cannot afford to go in blindly, bet the company on ill-conceived moves, and go down in flames.

What China and India require is a mindset of logical incremen-talism.[16] By this, we refer to a mindset where an overall strategic logic, as put forward in this chapter, guides your moves, and yet you operate with the fundamental premise that there is much about the future of China and India that you will discover over time as these societies evolve and become very different from what they are today.

4

LEVERAGING CHINA AND INDIA FOR GLOBAL ADVANTAGE

> In five to ten years from now, when we think of
> AMD, we will think of it as an Indian company, a
> Chinese company, and a North American company.
> The three regions will cover all the crucial areas,
> namely: Where the products come from, where the
> technologies are developed and where the most
> advanced markets exist.[1]
>
> *Dirk Meyer, president and chief operating officer, AMD*

The Qinghai-Tibet Railway, which started operations in July 2006, is the first time in history that the Tibet Autonomous Region has been connected by rail links with other parts of China. It is also the world's highest-plateau railroad running on the "roof of the world," with about 960 kilometers of the track located 4,000 meters above sea level, the highest point being 5,072 meters above sea level. GE supplied the locomotives for these trains. The bulk of the engineering work for these locomotives was done at the company's John F. Welch Technology Centre in Bangalore, India, with guidance from senior engineers in Erie, Pennsylvania.[2]

Like many of its other products and services, Apple's iPod transformed the music distribution business. It was also the first major product Apple introduced after the Macintosh and its various versions. Although Apple's CEO Steve Jobs and his colleagues led the overall design, the bulk of the work on the iPod was done in India and China. Apple outsourced the "brains" of the iPod (a microprocessor) to Portal Player, a Silicon Valley–based semiconductor company. Portal Player's engineers in Hyderabad, India, and Silicon Valley worked around the clock to design the chip. The chip itself was manufactured in Taiwan. The final assembly of the iPod took place in China.

In December 2007, GlaxoSmithKline, the U.K.-based pharmaceutical company, announced that it would invest over $100 million over the next twelve months to build a major neuroscience research center in Shanghai, China. Once up and running, the center would be responsible for virtually all of the company's research on neurodegenerative diseases. Explaining this decision, Moncef Slaoui, head of the company's R&D operations, noted, "For us, China is not about outsourcing and cheap labor. We don't want to give them the crumbs. It's about different science. We will link our fate to their fate. Within five to ten years, we will be moving from 'made in China' to 'discovered in China.'"[3]

In late 2007, Cessna Aircraft Company, a subsidiary of U.S.-headquartered Textron, announced that it will outsource the complete production of its Cessna 162 SkyCatcher model to China's Shenyang Aircraft Corp. Jack Pelton, Cessna's president, explained that without partnering with Shenyang, Cessna probably would not have started the SkyCatcher program. According to Lewis Campbell, Textron's chairman and chief executive, outsourcing to Shenyang would enable Cessna to sell the planes for about $109,500 each: $71,000 less than what it would if the planes were built at the company's factories in Kansas.[4]

As these examples illustrate, the comparative advantage of China and India has broadened considerably beyond cheap labor to also include leading-edge talent in some of the world's leading-edge industries, as well as home-grown innovation in technologies, products, processes, and even business models. In this chapter, we begin by outlining the potential opportunities for competitive advantage that China and India offer to any multinational enterprise. We then examine what the enterprise must do in order to convert the potential into reality.

A Look at the Opportunities

There are three primary dimensions along which China and India are becoming central to global competitive advantage for a rapidly growing number of companies across a wide range of industries: *cost arbitrage, talent arbitrage, and innovation.*

Each of the three sources of competitive advantage can be hugely important on its own. However, if they can be leveraged in tandem, the impact can be especially powerful. The biopharmaceuticals industry shows how. Industry estimates are that for every drug approved for sale by the U.S. Food and Drug Administration (FDA), the process begins with an analysis of 5,000 to 10,000 compounds. Of these, about 250 enter preclinical testing. Only 5 of these make it to clinical testing, from which 1 may finally pass all hurdles and get FDA approval. The process can take up to fifteen years and cost $1 billion. Consider now that both China and India produce five times as many chemists as the U.S. does at the bachelor's level and three times as many at the master's level. Furthermore, depending on qualifications and city location, this talent costs only about one-fifth to one-third of that in the United States. In short, for the same or lower R&D budget, a company such as AstraZeneca or Novartis can hire a much larger number of analysts in China and India and significantly accelerate the pace of drug discovery.

The other side of drug development is clinical testing. Given the large populations and low income levels in China and India, enrollment in clinical trials can be fast, easy, and highly efficient since a single site can recruit a much larger number of patients. Low income levels also imply that it can be relatively easy to find large numbers of treatment-naive patients (patients who have never undergone any treatment for the particular disease), thereby greatly reducing the likelihood that the results from clinical trials may be confounded by the effects of previous drugs and thus improving their reliability. On top of the speed and efficiency of patient recruitment, India (more so than China at present) also offers robust skills in clinical data management, which can further help reduce the time lag in making sense of the results from clinical testing. To sum up, the powerful combination of lower cost and a vast talent pool can be leveraged by a global pharmaceutical company to accelerate the pace of product innovation significantly.

The same logic applies to an increasing number of industries, from semiconductors to cars to medical diagnostics. AMD is a microprocessor company and archrival to Intel. Survival and success in this industry depends crucially, although not solely, on the scale, effectiveness, and efficiency of R&D activities. However, given brutal industry rivalry and losses over the past two years, AMD can ill afford to increase its R&D budget as a proportion of sales revenue. What it can do, however, is to try and get much more bang for its buck by increasing the scale of R&D operations in places such as China and India, where the size of the available talent pool is as large as or larger than in the United States or Europe and the costs much lower. We see this as one of the primary reasons that Dirk Meyer, the company's president, can convincing say that, with each passing year, his company will be not just an American company but will also become an Indian company and a Chinese company.

We now take a closer look at each of the three sources of competitive advantage.

Cost Arbitrage

Notwithstanding ongoing escalation in Chinese and Indian wages over the past several years, labor costs for most types of blue- and white-collar work in both countries remain well below those in the developed economies. Given that per capita income

Table 4.1 Labor Cost Comparisons, December 2007

	United States	China	India
U.S.-headquartered industrial goods manufacturer with factories in the United States (Midwest locations), China (tier 2 cities), and India (tier 2 cities):			
Blue-collar worker	More than $20/hour	$1.50–2.00/hour	$1.50–2.00/hour
Twenty-five-year-old production line supervisor (engineering degree plus three years' work experience)	$50,000–60,000/year	$6,000/year	$6,000/year
U.S.-headquartered telecommunications services company with engineering centers in the United States and India:			
Newly graduated software engineer with a bachelor's degree	$85,000/year	NA	$9,000/year
Software engineer with five years' experience	$105,000/year	NA	$22,000/year
Department manager (age thirty-five to forty-five years)	$150,000–200,000/year	NA	$45,000–75,000/year

Note: Estimated total costs, including benefits.

Source: Data from the authors' field interviews, December 2007–April 2008.

in China is about one-twentieth and in India about one-fortieth of that in the United States, this is exactly what we would expect. Table 4.1 provides illustrative data from two companies in our field research.

As a broad generalization, these as well as similar data from other companies lead to the following conclusions about the reality as of December 2007:

- For blue-collar work, costs in the United States are about fifteen to twenty times higher than in China or India.

- For junior engineers (age range twenty-two to twenty-five years), the United States is about nine or ten times more expensive than China or India.

- For more experienced engineers (age range twenty-seven to thirty years), the United States is about five times more expensive than China or India.

- For department heads (age range thirty-five to forty-five years), costs in the United States are about three times higher than in China or India.

- For senior executives (such as company president or other C-level executives) of similar-sized companies, cost differences between the United States, China, and India have narrowed considerably or even vanished entirely.

These cost differences provide considerable opportunities for cost arbitrage for most companies in most industries. It is precisely for these reasons that Sony has shifted virtually all production of consumer products from Japan to China and why IBM has transformed its services business into a heavily India-led global enterprise.

Talent Arbitrage

Measured in terms of the number of Nobel Prize winners and citation impact of published journal articles, the United States continues to reign supreme in terms of the quality and scale of the scientific research being performed within its universities. In the scientific fields, there is no living Nobel Prize winner who did his or her pioneering work at a university or laboratory

Table 4.2 Bachelor's Degree Graduates in Engineering, Computer Science, and Information Technology (in thousands)

	2000–2001	2001–2002	2002–2003	2003–2004	2004–2005
United States	114	121	134	137	134
China[a]	220	252	352	442	517
India	82	109	129	139	170

[a]China figures include short-cycle degrees, typically completed in two or three years.

Source: Abstracted from V. Wadhwa, G. Gereffi, B. Rissing, and R. Ong, "Where the Engineers Are," *Issues in Science and Technology*, National Academy of Sciences, Spring 2007.

in China or India. Although these two countries are getting stronger in pure scientific research, it will take at least ten years before they can have a notable impact on scientific knowledge.

Notwithstanding the salience of pure science, it is important to note, however, that more than 99 percent of the talent that powers economic development (at the country level) and competitive advantage (at the company level) is of the relatively more mundane kind, such as chemists, computer programmers, clinical research assistants, laboratory technicians, engineers, statisticians, financial analysts, and architects. For these types of skills, the quality of education at many colleges in China and India is not only comparable to that in the West but is getting better. These two countries also offer the advantages of scale and lower cost.

Table 4.2 provides data on the annual output of bachelor's degree holders in engineering, computer science, and information technology in the United States, China, and India.

As these data indicate, China and India already produce a larger number of engineering, computer science, and information technology graduates than the United States. Furthermore, enrollments in China and India are rising rapidly, while those in the United States are fairly stable. Thus, it is all but certain that the gap in the size of talent pool will increase rapidly over the next ten years. Similar trends are likely at the master's-degree level. The current output of master's-level graduates in computer science and engineering is about sixty thousand in each of the three countries. However, the numbers in China and India are rising, while those in the United States are flat.[5] China and India will also benefit from the growing proportion of foreign-trained scientists and engineers who are returning to their native lands.

The scale, quality, diversity, and cost of the available and growing talent pool in China and India offer significant opportunities to a global enterprise that knows how to leverage this talent for global advantage. Over the past ten years, an increasingly large number of companies have already figured out how to leverage Indian talent for activities such as call centers and data entry. In addition to these well-recognized opportunities, a whole spectrum of new opportunities is now emerging in more knowledge-intensive domains such as product and process R&D; analysis of complex financial deals and instruments; legal research to help a company deal with, say, patent or merger-related issues in American or European courts; mining of market research data to derive strategic implications; back-end engineering work on architectural projects; and conversion of books, annual reports, and technical manuals into digital formats so they can be accessed over devices such as a mobile phone or a personal digital assistant, to name just a few. Given that virtually all college-educated Indians have a very high level of fluency in the English language, India continues to enjoy a significant advantage over China in many of these tasks. Until China closes the language gap (which, in our judgment, will take at least ten years), its location advantage is likely to be primarily in research and development, where it leads India and where daily or frequent communication with peers and customers in other countries is generally not necessary.

Leveraging for Innovation

Given their vast talent pools, China and India are already playing an increasingly important role in technological and product

Table 4.3 Number of Patents Granted by the U.S. Patent and Trademark Office

	1994	2004	2007
All patents	113,704	181,320	182,930
U.S.-origin patents	64,345	94,129	93,691
Foreign-origin patents	49,359	87,191	89,239
China-origin patents	48	597	1,235
India-origin patents	28	376	578

Source: U.S. Patent and Trademark Office: http://www.uspto.gov/go/taf/cst_all.htm.

innovation. This is evident from Table 4.3 which contains trend data on the number of patents granted by the U.S. Patent and Trademark Office to all inventors, foreign inventors, and inventors based in China and India.

While the absolute numbers of patents granted by the U.S. Patent and Trademark Office to inventors based in China and India are small, note that the data pertain to patents granted rather than patent applications filed; the latter figures are almost certainly much larger. Also, the rate of growth in patents granted to China- and India-based inventors is very high. Thus, by 2015 to 2020, their share is likely to have grown significantly. It is clear that for any company whose competitive advantage depends significantly on R&D, ignoring China or India as locations for global R&D is likely to be a hazardous oversight.

The potential of China and India to serve as platforms for global innovation goes well beyond the availability of talent. These two countries face some of the world's toughest challenges as well as unique opportunities. Given the scarce supply and rising prices of raw materials and energy that is already evident, given also global warming, it will be utterly impossible for China and India to provide much better housing, much better food, much better transportation, much better education, and much better health care for their 2.4 billion citizens with today's technologies and business models.

Consider banking. About 70 percent of India's population lives in villages, and less than 5 percent of these have access to a bank branch. In short, in India today, about two-thirds of the population (nearly 700 million people) has no access to any bank of any type. It is hard to imagine that the solution will come in the form of brick-and-mortar branches of the sort that are common in much of the world today. Instead, the solution will almost certainly come in the form of extremely low-cost and ubiquitous mobile banking. Given current trends, it is a given that within three to four years, at least half of the adults in rural India will own a mobile phone and have access to mobile voice and data services. It is possible that India (and, similarly, China) will emerge as hotbeds of innovations in large-scale, secure, and extremely efficient mobile banking. Banks and telecommunications companies that see this opportunity and go after it may well end up leading the world in mobile banking solutions.

Procter & Gamble (P&G) provides another example of business model innovation with detergents in China. Not unlike Coca-Cola's syrup model (where the company supplies concentrate to local bottlers), P&G has started distributing high-value performance chemicals to local partners, which add the basic ingredients and packaging before distributing them to local retailers and consumers. The result is huge savings in transportation and energy costs, cheaper products for end consumers, and local jobs. Might this business model be transferable to other emerging markets, such as India, Southeast Asia, Latin America, and Africa? Absolutely. In fact, as consumers in developed economies start feeling the bite of higher raw material and energy costs, might some of the business models that originate from China and India have leading-edge relevance also for developed markets? As Alan Lafley, P&G's CEO notes, Asian firms are now "very innovative, especially with business models."[6]

Transportation provides another example. According to Goldman Sachs, the number of cars on the roads in China and India is likely to rise from about 30 million to 40 million today to about 750 million by 2040.[7] From the perspective of materials, energy, and emissions, growth at this scale is impossible if the technology in cars in 2040 is even remotely similar to that of today. There are only two possible solutions. One is that raw material and energy prices become prohibitively high and economic growth in these two countries comes to a screeching halt. The other (and the one that we bet on) is that China and India will become the hotbeds for breakthrough innovations in technologies, products, processes, and business models. Robert Lutz, head of product development for General Motors, is probably not off the mark when he notes that "cars powered by fuel cells (devices that use hydrogen to make electricity) are likely to take off in China before they do in the United States."[8]

Realizing the Opportunities

Leveraging China and India as hubs for global advantage requires making decisions and taking actions along several fronts:

- Undertaking an activity-by-activity analysis of the value chain in order to decide which specific set of activities should be based in China, which in India, and which in other countries: for example, IBM's decision to use India as the global hub for IT services and China as the global hub for procurement.

- For each activity that will be based in China or India, deciding whether to set up the company's own operations or rely on external vendors: for example, Apple's decision to rely on subcontract manufacturers for the assembly of iPods in China.

- Ensuring that the China- and India-based global hubs will be able to develop the required world-class capabilities and, where important, cost structures: for example, Microsoft's efforts to cultivate relationships with leading-edge computer science departments in China to help ensure that it is able to recruit the best and brightest graduates for its research center in Beijing.

- Ensuring that as the company's value chain becomes more disaggregated and geographically dispersed, it will have the required visibility into and control over the activities of various players so that standards of quality, ethical behavior, and other practices are upheld throughout the value chain: for example, Wal-Mart's efforts to ensure that its several hundred suppliers in China and India meet the company's quality requirements, behave ethically, and pursue ever-more environment-friendly policies.

- Building the integrating mechanisms that will enable the hubs in China and India to be responsive to the needs of the company's global operations and enable the output of these hubs to be deployed to subsidiaries and customers in other countries: for example, the structural and budgetary links between GE's research centers in Bangalore and Shanghai and its business divisions.

- Managing the evolution of China- and India-based hubs as these operations become larger, more experienced, and more mature, on the one hand, and as China and India become more expensive, on the other: for example, upgrading the status of internal or external manufacturers within China and India from purely manufacturing operations to design and manufacturing operations.

- Managing the intracorporate friction that may accompany the shift of resources and power from the company's existing hubs in developed countries to the new hubs in China and India.

Disaggregated Value Chain Analysis

The starting point in figuring out how to leverage China and India for global advantage is to decide which activities in the

Figure 4.1. Illustrative Example of the Value Chain in Biopharmaceuticals R&D

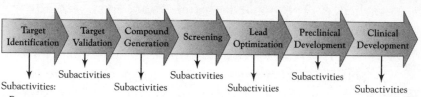

Target Identification | Target Validation | Compound Generation | Screening | Lead Optimization | Preclinical Development | Clinical Development

Subactivities   Subactivities   Subactivities   Subactivities

Subactivities: Subactivities   Subactivities   Subactivities

Subactivities:
- Proteomics
- Chemo-informatics
- Bioinformatics
- Expression profiling
- Gene sequencing
- DNA and RNA preparation
- mRNA library

value chain should be located within China or within India, or in both countries, and, in either case, at which locations within the country. Analytically, the way to arrive at the correct decisions is to undertake a disaggregated value chain analysis, which has three steps:[9]

1. Draw an end-to-end map of all of the activities and subactivities in the value chain, starting with suppliers at one end to customers at the other. The more finely grained the map is, the better the subsequent analyses are likely to be. Figure 4.1 provides an illustrative example of a typical value chain for the drug development stage in the biopharmaceuticals industry.[10]

2. For each activity or subactivity in the value chain, figure out the optimal architecture for the activity based on the following key criteria: quality and market responsiveness, total cost, and level of associated risk. We use the term *activity architecture* to refer to the following two decisions: number of locations and charter of each location. The four ideal

types of activity architecture are (1) global centralization in one location, (2) multiple but differentiated centers of excellence, (3) regional decentralization, and (4) country-level decentralization.

3. On an activity-by-activity basis, once you have clarity about the optimal architecture for the activity, make decisions about the optimal set of locations. With respect to China and India, the analysis should result in clear answers to the following questions:

- Which specific activities will not be performed within China or within India? For these activities, the company's operations within China and India will need to rely on peer subsidiaries in other countries.

- Which specific activities will be performed within China or India, or both, on a local-for-local basis?

- Which specific activities will be performed within China or India, or both, on a local-for-regional (for example, Asia-Pacific or all emerging markets) basis?

- Which specific activities will be performed within China or India, or both, on a local-for-global basis?

An important question regarding the global optimization of the value chain pertains to the extent of granularity in the analysis. At one extreme, granularity can be relatively coarse. An example would be a U.S.-headquartered toy manufacturer that centralizes all product development in the United States and all manufacturing in China. At the other extreme, the granularity can be much finer. A stark example of fine granularity is a U.S.-headquartered company that provides outsourced technical support services to its client companies. This company has created three operations centers: in Manila (Philippines), Bangalore (India), and Boca Raton (Florida). When a customer calls the U.S. toll-free number for technical support, the call is routed first to a level 1 analyst in Manila. If this analyst is unable to satisfy the customer, the call is rerouted to a more specialized but also more expensive level 2 analyst in Bangalore. If this also fails to solve the customer's problem, the call is then rerouted again to an even more highly skilled but very expensive level 3 analyst in Boca Raton. All of this multicountry routing takes place during the same call from the customer while maintaining a high degree of continuity in the conversation with him or her. A senior executive who is also a cofounder of the company explained that it would be impossible for his company to compete without this three-layered architecture. Costs for the skills that this company needs are the lowest in Manila and the highest in Florida. The goal is to maximize customer satisfaction at the lowest possible cost. Thus, it matters greatly as to what proportion of customer calls can be handled satisfactorily at level 1, what proportion gets transferred to level 2, and what proportion to level 3.

As an example of finely grained value chain disaggregation in the context of a physical goods business, consider the case of Li & Fung, a Hong Kong–based company. Li & Fung supplies over two thousand customers from a network of about ten thousand suppliers spread over forty countries. Fulfilling an apparel order from a U.S. customer can mean that the fabric is woven in China, the fasteners are sourced from South Korea, and the sewing is done in Guatemala.[11]

There are pros and cons to both coarse and finely grained disaggregation. Coarse disaggregation means that the complexity and the cost of coordination would be low, and there would be less risk of misalignment across complementary but geographically dispersed activities. At the same time, coarse disaggregation may lead to a less-than-complete optimization of location choices for the performance of the different activities. In contrast, finely grained disaggregation can lead to a more complete optimization of location choices but can also significantly increase complexity, raise the costs of coordination, and heighten the risk of misalignment. Thus, the final decision

Figure 4.2. Impact of Integration Capabilities on Ability to Optimize Location Choices

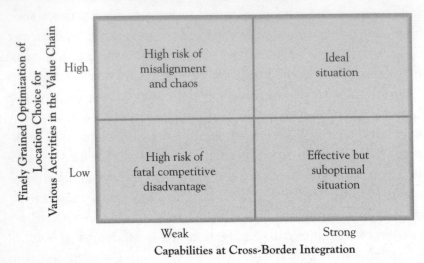

regarding the extent of granularity in value chain disaggregation must rest on how advanced the company's capabilities are at cross-border integration of the physical as well as the information supply chain.

In an era where communications as well as transportation technologies are advancing exponentially, we advocate that companies should overinvest in the development of multicountry integration capabilities (a topic we discuss later in this chapter). The stronger the integration capabilities are, the greater would be the extent to which the company can atomize the value chain and push harder in optimizing the choice of locations. Figure 4.2 depicts the relationship between integration capabilities and location optimization.

Give Primacy to Quality and Responsiveness. In deciding whether and how to use China and India (and, similarly, other locations) as platforms for global advantage, the first assessment screen must be whether the China- and India-based activities will meet or exceed your standards for quality and responsiveness. Clearly cost structure is important. However, cost minimization can never take precedence over quality and responsiveness. Quality of output from a research lab, a manufacturing base, or a call center depends not just on the capabilities of the talent available at the location, but also on the company's own actions to further develop these capabilities. It also depends on how the company organizes and manages these operations. Thus, in making location choices, the company must look at both: available capabilities at the various locations and what these capabilities could become after proactive actions to develop them further.

Ensuring that the China- or India-based operations are responsive to global needs also depends on several factors: training, cultivation of mutual understanding, communication links, supply chain links, and others. In the case of production and service centers, an increasingly effective approach to build responsiveness while maintaining a low-cost structure is to adopt a dual-shore policy: locate the global production and delivery center in India or China, but build a second production and delivery center physically proximate to the market. The proximate centers take care of unplanned rapid-turnaround demands from the customer, whereas the global centers take care of long lead time but planned customer needs. The dual-shore strategy originated with the leading India-based IT services companies, which derive over 90 percent of their revenues from outside India but locate over 90 percent of their staff in India. These companies faced intense pressures for customer responsiveness and invented the dual-shore mechanism as a strategic response.

The dual-shore approach is now being embraced also by companies that manufacture physical goods. A leading example is Bharat Forge, an auto components supplier headquartered in India. Bharat Forge supplies components to almost all of the major auto companies in India, Europe, the United States, and China. Through a combination of greenfield start-ups and acquisitions, the company owns eight plants: two in India, three in Germany, and one each in Sweden, Scotland, and the United States. It also has a joint venture in China with FAW, the largest auto company in that country. Bharat Forge's acquisition strategy has been driven explicitly by the goal of ensuring that it can supply all of a customer's needs from two plants: one based in India and one based close to the customer. This approach significantly reduces supply chain risks, makes the supply chain more responsive to customers' needs, and still enables the company to benefit heavily from a significantly lower cost structure in India.

Focus on Total Costs. In making decisions about whether to use India or China as global platforms for any particular activity, it is also important to look at total costs rather than just the cost differential between performing the operation in India or China versus elsewhere. While this may seem like an obvious statement, we have come across far too many companies that get carried away by superficial analysis and make wrong decisions that they regret later. At a macrolevel, total costs include the following five components:

- Cost of operations at the hub within China or India
- Cost of coordination between this hub and other entities within the global enterprise, as well as relevant external players such as customers, suppliers, and business partners
- Supply chain costs pertaining to both physical and information goods
- Costs of misalignment between complementary but geographically dispersed activities in the value chain
- Taxes imposed or incentives provided (or both) by various governments.

Every one of these costs is a function of not only location and scale but also how the company is organized and managed.

The more advanced a company's capabilities at cross-border integration are, the more sharply it will be able to reduce the costs of coordination, supply chain logistics, and misalignment. Nonetheless, these costs will never be zero and must be taken into account in assessing the size of the benefits that might accrue from using China or India as global hubs for any particular activity.

As an example of total cost analysis, consider the case of one of the world's largest consulting and IT services companies with a major business process outsourcing (BPO) hub in India. In a 2007 interview, a senior executive of this company identified the following as the three major elements of costs in his business:

- Infrastructure, such as buildings, utilities, and travel
- Technology, such as fiber optics and satellite-based communication links between the operations in India and other client and intracorporate locations worldwide
- Employee benefits and salaries

The first two elements of cost, infrastructure and technology, accounted for about 55 percent of total cost. These costs were relatively stable over time, although technology costs were declining and infrastructure costs were going up marginally because of inflation but with a downward pressure due to increasing economies of scale. The third element of cost, employees, accounted for 45 percent of total cost and was increasing at a 15 percent annual rate. Yet as he noted, the average total compensation of a BPO employee was about $7,500 in India versus about $45,000 in the United States. Thus, if salaries in India grew at a 15 percent annual rate ($1,225 per year over the next twelve months) and those in the United States grew at a 5 percent annual rate (i.e., $2,250 per year over the next twelve months), the absolute cost gap between the United States and India would still increase rather than decline over time.

Minimize Risk. The third major factor in deciding whether and how to leverage China and India as platforms for global advantage pertains to the impact of the different options on various types of risk: political risks, currency risks, intellectual property risks, natural hazards, and others. Depending on the activity and type of risk to which the company may be exposed, following are some examples of how companies can minimize their vulnerability:

- In order to reduce their exposure to policy and currency risks, many companies with major production centers in China are adopting a "China + 1" or "China + 2" strategy. Thus, the manufacturing base in China remains the primary production hub, and the company builds additional production hubs in locations such as Southeast Asia and India.

- In order to reduce their exposure to supply chain risks, an increasing number of companies are pursuing a dual-shore strategy, whereby every customer is served from two locations: one based in China or India and one based close to the customer.

- In order to reduce their exposure to intellectual property risks, many companies disaggregate the overall technology or product development project into subprojects and disperse responsibility for different subprojects across different locations and even different countries. Thus, deliberate (or, involuntary) leakage of intellectual property from any single location would cause only minimal damage to the company.

These are illustrative examples of how a company can minimize its exposure to various types of risk while still being able to leverage China and India for global advantage.

Insource Versus Outsource?

In August 2007, Eli Lilly & Co., the U.S.-headquartered pharmaceutical giant, announced that it had signed a research contract with Chi-Med, a China-based contract research company. As part of this contract, Lilly would hand over to Chi-Med a portfolio of synthetic compounds that may contain within them the potential to develop drugs to treat cancer and inflammatory diseases. Chi-Med would be responsible for preclinical research. Lilly would provide continuing support to Chi-Med as well as pay an upfront fee plus at least $20 million for any compound that emerges from this partnership. After the initial discovery by Chi-Med, Lilly will take over the potential drug candidates for clinical trials and clearance through the U.S. Food and Drug Administration. Chi-Med would also get a share of any royalties or profits that Lilly may earn from a drug that becomes commercially successful.[12]

It is easy to understand why Lilly would choose China for drug discovery research. Qualified researchers for this type of work in China cost about one-quarter of their counterparts in the United States or Europe. Also, the supply of talent is large and easily scalable. However, instead of contracting the work to Chi-Med, Lilly could have chosen to set up its own drug discovery center in China. Yet it did not. Thus, the question arises: What logic should guide companies such as Lilly in deciding whether they should set up their own global hub in China or India, or both, or rely on an outsourcing arrangement with an independent organization?

Another example is Portal Player, the Silicon Valley–based company that supplied the brains for the original Apple iPod. Portal Player set up its own R&D center in Hyderabad, India. Engineers based in Silicon Valley and Hyderabad collaborated around the clock to develop the microprocessor, satisfy an extremely demanding customer, and in the process help make history. What logic should guide a company (such as Portal Player) in figuring out whether an in-house R&D center in India was the smarter approach, or whether they would have been better off subcontracting the research to an India-based company such as Wipro, which has a thriving business in contract R&D? Did Portal Player succeed because of insourcing in India, or despite it?

Our own analysis, backed up by the logic of transaction cost economics,[13] leads us to put forward two major factors that should drive companies to decide whether to insource or outsource global hub operations in China or India: modular decomposability and economies of scale and scope.

Modular Decomposability. The more easily, cleanly, and without controversy a task can be decomposed into two or more parts, the more modular the subtasks become. A high degree of modularity permits two independent companies to take ownership of the separate tasks, write enforceable contracts that define the commercial relationship between them, and minimize the likelihood of wasteful friction. At the other extreme, a lack of modularity would make it almost impossible for two independent companies to agree on which is responsible for what. In such a case, what is required is joint ownership and, thus, an insourcing approach. Going back to the Lilly and Chi-Med example, note that the interface between preclinical research and clinical research is highly modular. Thus, outsourcing was a viable option for Lilly. In contrast, in the Portal Player example, the need for around-the-clock collaboration between the Silicon Valley and Hyderabad teams implied that a clean decomposition of the overall R&D project into two parts was infeasible. Thus, insourcing emerged as the only viable option.

Economies of Scale and Scope. In cases where the modular decomposability of the overall task is high, both insourcing and outsourcing are viable options. In such a context, economies of scale and scope should determine the choice between the two. In the Lilly case, Chi-Med has already built a large-scale preclinical research operation in China that performs contract research for several of the world's largest pharmaceutical companies. In contrast, while Lilly enjoys economies of scale in preclinical research in other locations, this is not the case for it in China. Thus, relying on a contractual relationship with Chi-Med enables Lilly to tap into the Chi-Med's greater scale and scope within China. This reasoning also leads us to predict that as Lilly expands the scale and scope of its drug discovery activities in China, it is more likely to set up an in-house research organization within the country.

The importance of scale and scope economies is illustrated also by a study from McKinsey & Co. and NASSCOM, an India-based industry association of software and service providers. According to this study, captive (that is, insourced) back office service operations are on average more expensive than outsourced operations, without any compensating advantages in terms of either better-quality work or lower staff turnover.[14] This is so because independent companies that provide outsourced back office services to several clients are generally much larger and thus more likely to enjoy economies of scale and scope than a captive operation with only one customer, its parent company. Economies of scale and scope manifest themselves not only in the form of lower cost but also in the form of better-quality work because a larger organization is able to attract better talent, provide more attractive career options, and build core competencies around its activity domain.

Building Local Capabilities

For any activity in the value chain, a direct corollary of the decision to locate a global hub in China or India is that the capabilities at this hub must meet or beat all four criteria: quality, responsiveness, total cost, and risk. This statement applies to every type of activity: a global research center, a global production base, a global marketing hub, or a global call center. As depicted in Figure 4.3, building the needed capabilities at a global hub will always require an optimal blend of global processes, global talent, and global resources with local processes, local talent, and local resources.

Because of huge variations across industries, company strategies, and specific activities, there can be no universal answer to

Figure 4.3. Building a Global Hub

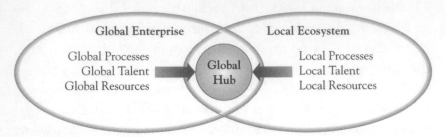

the question of what mix of global and local would be optimal for a particular global hub. The answer must be derived separately in each case. It is possible, however, to advance a set of universal guidelines that can be used to frame the analysis and discussions that lead to deriving the appropriate answer:

1. The creation of a global hub (or the transformation of an existing local operation into a global hub) must be driven by a clear mandate from the top leadership, including the corporate CEO.

2. The executive directly responsible for building the capabilities and resources at the global hub should be a believer in the idea and should have internal conviction that the local talent to be recruited for the hub will be capable of serving the global needs of the enterprise as well as or better than any other locations.

3. The senior leadership team of the hub, including the executive directly responsible for building it, must be deeply and simultaneously embedded in both ecosystems: the local ecosystem within the host country as well as the global ecosystem of the parent enterprise.

4. In building the global hub, the goal should be to accumulate the needed resources and capabilities as rapidly as possible while ensuring that the hub internalizes global processes and global standards.

5. As the resources and capabilities are being built, there should be a clear and well-communicated expectation that the hub is expected not just to implement the existing best practices of the enterprise but also emerge as a source of new leading-edge ideas for the global enterprise.

The case of how Accenture, the consulting and technology services giant, developed its global delivery capabilities in India provides an excellent example of how to build a global hub that can help the enterprise leverage the talent, cost, and innovation potential of India (or, similarly, China) for global advantage. Accenture entered India in 1987, and for the next fourteen years, its operations there consisted largely of a small consulting base targeted at the domestic Indian market. The turning point came in 2001 when Karl-Heinz Floether, a German executive who headed Accenture's worldwide Financial Services business and was also a member of the board of directors, sent one of his senior executives, Keith Haviland, to India with a mandate to start building an offshore group there. Haviland, a British citizen, reported directly to Floether and had built Financial Services group's existing delivery center in London. In short, Haviland started with a mandate from the very top and knew how to build a global delivery center. As Floether recalled:

> In 1999, I became group chief executive of the Financial Services operating group. . . . All around us, the market and industry and economic landscape were changing dramatically. . . . The global economy was in a huge downturn after the dot-com bust. . . . Cost reduction had become a top priority for all of our clients. . . . [Also] the availability of high-bandwidth network connections started to intensify competition from India-based companies. . . . So, I remember calling Keith Haviland and Sid [Khanna, managing director for India], who both worked for me in Financial Services. I told them to set up an offshore center in India to initially serve our Financial Services clients.[15]

Haviland co-opted some of his experienced colleagues from the United Kingdom and United States, and the team relocated to India. Within a few months, they had recruited the first two hundred staff members. At that point, Floether visited Haviland and his team. He also visited the campuses of some of the major Indian competitors, as well as other companies, including GE, Philips, and British Airways. The visit convinced Floether that he had seriously underestimated the quality and scale of the talent base available in India, as well as the competitive threat from Indian companies. At this point, he asked Haviland to pull out all stops and hire as fast as possible.

At the corporate level, Floether was also successful in making the case that India-based global delivery was going to be crucial not just for the Financial Services group but for every other operating group within Accenture. Soon after, the delivery centers in India were transferred from Financial Services to the company's Systems Integration and Technology organization, a global capability-centric organization which served all operating groups.

In a discussion on the various decisions and actions that helped ensure a successful and aggressive ramp-up of the delivery capabilities in India, Keith Haviland recalled the following as having played a particularly important role:[16]

- There was a clear mandate from the very top: first Karl-Heinz Floether and, shortly after, the board of directors.

- The senior leadership viewed the establishment of a major global delivery center in India as a long-term strategic commitment rather than a short-term experiment. This enabled Haviland and his team to recruit senior managers (many of them expatriate Indians) from existing Accenture operations in other locations who would return to India and lead the charge. The long-term commitment also made it easier for Accenture to recruit seasoned executives from competitors within India.

- From the early days, Haviland and his colleagues insisted that notwithstanding explosive growth, the Indian operations must adhere to Accenture's high-performance delivery model: the company's standard ways of doing things, standard methods and practices, standard measurement approaches, and so forth. Insistence on standard Accenture processes eliminated the need for reinvention and made rapid expansion easier.

- The founding team paid particular attention to ensuring that there would be no compromise in the standards for recruitment. In the early days, key human resource managers from London played a direct role in interviewing candidates.

- With backing from senior leaders, Haviland and his team started channeling client work to India. Two early clients were J. P. Morgan Chase and DuPont. Capitalizing on the company's excellent relationship with both clients, the leadership in the United States persuaded executives in these two companies to start experimenting with service delivery out of India. In the first stage, a team of software developers was sent on a short-term assignment from Bangalore to Chicago to work on projects for these clients. In the second stage, this team moved back to Bangalore and continued delivering services from there. Over time, these proactive efforts to start channeling client work to India helped ensure that the hubs in India were building not just human capacity but also proven delivery capability.

- As part of its corporate processes, Accenture implemented programs to assess external and internal customer satisfaction. The delivery teams in India were assessed regularly on their ability to satisfy external as well as internal clients on a worldwide basis.

- The delivery centers in India were pushed aggressively to achieve global credentials such as the Capability Maturity Model (CMM) Level 5, CMMi Level 5, ISO27001, BS7799, SAS70 Type II, and others. These credentials not only ensured that the hubs were developing required world-class capabilities but also eliminated any concerns that external clients or other units within Accenture may have about relying on India-based delivery centers.

Over time, as the momentum has fed on itself, Accenture's head count in India has grown from fewer than three hundred in 2001 to over thirty-five thousand by 2007. India is now the largest Accenture country in the world, with some of the strongest technology and consulting capabilities in the global enterprise. Several of the company's senior executives (such as Sandeep Arora, Lead-Delivery Centers for Technology in India; P. G. Raghuraman, Lead-Delivery Centers for BPO in India; and Harsh Manglik, chairman and managing director, Accenture India) are now based in India. It is widely believed that over the coming years, the parent company will derive many of its global leaders from its India-based operations.

Another example from a relatively smaller company in a different industry illustrates that while the details will always be context specific, the guidelines regarding how to build the required capabilities at a global hub in India or China are quite universal. Pacific Trade International (PTI) is a $100 million revenue home decor products company, headquartered in the United States. Founded in 1994 by David Wang and Mei Xu, PTI serves a blue-chip roster of retailers, such as Target, J.C. Penney, and IKEA. Its operations are based in three locations: the United States (design, marketing and sales), China (design and manufacturing), and Vietnam (manufacturing). PTI's two primary business units are Chesapeake Bay Candles, which focuses on decorative candles, and Blissliving, which focuses on home furnishing products such as beddings and decorative pillows. We take a closer look here at Blissliving, the newer of the two business units.

Launched in 2005, Blissliving operates two design centers: one based at corporate headquarters in Maryland and the other in Hangzhou, China. The Hangzhou design center is co-located with the production facilities. This co-location plays a critical role in helping accelerate speed of product development, ensuring that production technologies keep up with design requirements, and permitting greater degree of customization. Here is the sequence of steps that Blissliving followed in building the needed design capabilities to support its rapid global expansion.

1. The company hired two young French designers, fresh out of design schools in France, who would move to Hangzhou for a one- to two-year assignment. It also hired five local designers in China. The charge to the French designers was to train their Chinese colleagues rather than to lead the design work.

2. Simultaneously, the company hired a product manager and two designers in the United States. All three came with prior experience working with Chinese manufacturers.

3. As depicted in Table 4.4 the company followed a deliberate and systematic approach to build the needed mindsets and design capabilities at the hub in Hangzhou. As this table indicates, in the first season, the U.S. team executed all of the key steps in the design process. However, with each subsequent season, the responsibilities became distributed between the U.S. and the Chinese teams, with the latter taking on an increasing share of the responsibility.

4. By the end of six seasons, the China-based team had developed the ability to lead and execute the entire work for a collection.

Blissliving now has two design teams, one based in the United States and the other in China, each able to execute a complete design project on a global basis. The expanded dual capacity has become a significant asset to the company in expanding the scope of offerings for various markets around the globe. Mei Xu, PTI's

Table 4.4. Cultivation of Product Design and Development Capabilities at PTI's Design Hub in China

Activity	Spring 2006	Fall 2006	Spring 2007	Fall 2007	Spring 2008
1. Conduct market and trend research (visiting retailers, attending international trade shows)	Done by the U.S. team	Done by the U.S. team	Done by the U.S. team	Jointly done by the U.S and China team members	Jointly done by the U.S and China team members
2. Define themes and stories (for example, an ecofriendly collection for spring 2008)	Done by the U.S. team	Done by the U.S. team	Done by the U.S. team	Done by the China team with feedback and approval from the U.S. team	Done by the China team with feedback and approval from the U.S. team
3. Develop the trend board (a visual representation of a particular theme)	Done by the U.S. team	Done by the U.S. team	Done by the China team with feedback and approval from the U.S. team	Done by the China team independently	Done by the China team independently
4. Design the core pieces in the collection (for example, the duvet cover)	Done by the U.S. team	Done by the China team with feedback and approval from the U.S. team	Done by the China team independently	Done by the China team independently	Done by the China team independently
5. Design peripheral and accessory pieces (for example, pillow covers)	Done by the China team with feedback and approval from the U.S. team	Done by the China team independently	Done by the China team independently	Done by the China team independently	Done by the China team independently

president, explained the philosophy that guided the buildup of design capabilities in China:

> Building design capability in China required confidence, patience, and investment. In the beginning, it may appear to be a waste of effort because the design work coming from Hangzhou had to be revised again and again. So, we had to cultivate the design aesthetics and sensibility of the Chinese designers. However, we knew that they have the innate capability and also a burning desire to learn. We also knew that, to retain good talent, you have to give people responsibility for creative work rather than just technical execution of the details. In the long term, this investment will pay off hugely since Blissliving's design capabilities are now stronger compared with our U.S. as well as Chinese competitors."[17]

Ensuring Global Integration

In addition to building the necessary capabilities at a designated global hub, an equally important task is to ensure that these capabilities will be responsive to and serve the needs of other units and external clients worldwide. As depicted in Figure 4.4, effective and efficient integration requires a combination of hard and soft linkages.

The hard integrators serve as the foundation. They provide the enabling mechanisms for integration to occur. At the same

Figure 4.4. Linking Mechanisms to Integrate a Global Hub with Other Units of the Global Enterprise

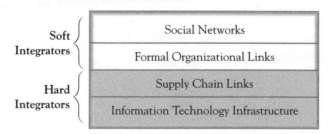

time, how these mechanisms are used (and whether they are used or abused) depends on people. Thus, the soft integrators play an equally important but complementary role to the hard integrators.

Information Technology Infrastructure. Given the rapidly growing power, increasing user friendliness, and declining cost of technology, we take it as given that it is better for companies to err on the side of over- rather than underinvestment in information and communications technologies. Companies such as IBM and Accenture, which can handle the IT needs of any global enterprise on an outsourced basis, are making access to a sophisticated IT infrastructure easier and less expensive. Without getting into the technical details of what would constitute sound decisions regarding IT infrastructure, we advocate the following:

- It is critical to have a common IT architecture (such as e-mail systems and databases) across the entire global network. No amount of sophistication in soft integrators can overcome the challenges that would be created by an inability to access real-time reliable data effortlessly.

- Companies should maximize the intracompany deployment and use of Web 2.0 technologies such as Wikipedia, Facebook, blogs, idea markets, and the like. These mechanisms permit large numbers of people to collaborate with each other easily, voluntarily, and inexpensively.

- Companies should constantly strive to increase the bandwidth of available communication links. A leading example today is Cisco's TelePresence, which permits near lifelike high-fidelity video communication between geographically dispersed individuals. The cost of high-bandwidth communication continues to decline dramatically.

Supply Chain Links. The goal of any well-designed and well-functioning supply chain system must be to ensure forward and backward visibility (into critical information such as demand forecasts, pending orders, available supplies, and production forecasts), responsiveness to fluctuations on both the demand and the supply sides, and, of course, efficiency on a total cost basis. As value chains become more finely disaggregated and companies rely on a larger number of production centers (as well as a larger number of external suppliers), the importance of forward and backward visibility rises. This is so because extended value chains increase the number of points where defects (such as lead in the paint used on a small part of a toy) can enter the production network and cause catastrophic failure later.

A senior executive at Nokia Corporation highlighted the importance of an effective and efficient supply chain management system in helping the company realize the competitive advantage being created in the company's R&D labs:

> We believe that at any point in time, we have at most a few weeks' advantage in product technology and design over our toughest competitors. It is important for us to make sure that this advantage at the R&D stage gets reflected in advantage at the retail store. That depends, however, on the effectiveness and efficiency of our supply chain logistics. A lousy supply chain system, which is, say, three weeks too slow can eat up much of the advantage that we may have created at the R&D stage, The customer cares only for the advantage that we can demonstrate in the retail store and later when the product is in use, not for what happens in R&D labs.

Formal Organizational Links. Formal organizational links include a variety of mechanisms. We look at three of the more important ones: reporting relationships, incentive systems, and budget allocation processes. In these areas, organizational decisions should be driven by a bias to induce integration of the hub with the rest of the global enterprise. A global hub that is poorly responsive to the needs of peer units in other countries becomes a deadweight rather than a source of competitive advantage.

With respect to reporting relationships, the central question pertains to whether the hub should report to the country manager locally within China or India or globally to the worldwide activity or business unit leader. Our perspective on this question is clear. While there will always be multidimensional matrix-type linkages, the primary reporting relationship of the global hub should be to the worldwide activity or business unit leader. A case in point is Microsoft's research operations in Beijing. True, the R&D center is located in China. However, as a global hub, its customer base includes Microsoft worldwide, not just Microsoft China. Thus, the correct decision about reporting relationships is to have the head of R&D in Beijing report directly to the head of worldwide R&D in Redmond, Washington, while maintaining a dotted-line relationship to other units in China, including the president of Microsoft China.

Another illustrative example is Accenture, which has multiple global hubs in India: a global hub for delivery of BPO services, a global hub for the delivery of technology services, and a global research center. The leaders of each of these global hubs report (as they should) directly and respectively to the worldwide leader for BPO services, the worldwide leader for technology services, and the worldwide head of research. Based in India, they have a close working relationship with each other and draw on support and guidance from the chairman of Accenture India. However, these local linkages represent lateral rather than hierarchical relationships.

As a third example, GE's John F. Welch Technology Centre in Bangalore belongs to and reports directly to the worldwide head of GE Research. It has close lateral linkages with other GE units in India. However, as a global R&D center, it gets its marching orders from the head of global research rather than the head of GE India.

With respect to incentive systems, key decision makers at the global hub must have a stake not just in managing internal activities at the hub but also in ensuring that these activities lead to commercial success by peer units in other countries. An effective way to build this responsiveness is to decompose the incentives for hub leaders into two parts: one part driven by functional excellence in how the hub is managed and the other driven by the financial results of the product lines and business units that depend on this hub.

An illustrative example is the Shanghai-based design hub for the Blissliving product line at PTI. An ideal incentive system for the designers in Shanghai would be as follows: an annual salary increase that is a function of labor market conditions in Shanghai as well as the designers' technical capabilities at their core task of design *and* an internal royalty-type bonus determined on the basis of the revenues generated by the products designed by them. Such a two-part incentive system is likely to ensure that the designers value both design excellence and market responsiveness.

Finally, the role of budget allocation processes in ensuring that a hub would be responsive to the needs of peer units in the rest of the global network is illustrated well by GE's technology center in Bangalore. This center gets half of its annual budget directly from corporate headquarters. These funds are allocated on the basis of beliefs regarding core technologies that would be of long-term and broad-based importance to most of the company's businesses. The other half of the budget comes from contracts signed between GE Research and the business divisions. This part of the budget automatically ensures that the technology center has to be responsive to the needs of the business divisions.

Social Networks. As we know from everyday experience, the effectiveness and efficiency of interaction between any two individuals are functions of not just technology links and formal organizational relationships, but also whether the people involved know each other as human beings and whether they like and trust each other. A considerable body of research has confirmed that social networks play a major role in fostering business relationships within the enterprise as well as across interfirm boundaries. Interpersonal familiarity and trust play a particularly important role in whether people are willing to share nonroutine information and their own judgments about the real story behind the hard numbers. While these observations are universally true across all cultures, the importance of social networks is even more important in the case of global hubs based in China and India. In both cultures, interpersonal relationships are known to play a significantly greater role than in Western societies. In short, the global enterprise must do its utmost to maximize the likelihood that the interaction between, say, a marketing manager sitting in Atlanta in the United States and a production head sitting in Hangzhou, China, will be between "John" and "Qiang" who know each other personally and can interact on a first-name basis rather than between "Mr. Smith" and "Mr. Wang" who see each other largely as occupants of formal organizational roles.

Social networks can be fostered through multiple channels. Some of the more common channels are periodic in-person visits to each other's locations (which should be designed to also include social interactions outside of the work environment), collaborations in cross-border business teams, joint participation in management development programs, and, in the case of high-potential employees, cross-country job rotations that foster professional development while also building social networks.

Managing Internal Politics

Notwithstanding economic rationality, the creation of global hubs (for R&D, production, back office services—you name it) is often fraught with internal struggles within the company for resources, jobs, decision-making power, and prestige.

A company's operations in China or India often start by producing for the local market or by offshoring low-end commodity tasks such as labor-intensive assembly or back office operations.

In these early stages, the China- or India-based activities may rightly be viewed by people within the company (including senior management) as relatively peripheral to the company's core. However, a major transformation in mindsets, allocation of key resources, and distribution of internal power becomes essential if the China or India operations are to shift from the periphery to the core. This shift may happen in one or both of two ways: a major scale-up in the magnitude of the China- or India-based low-cost operations or a growing reliance on China and India for high-end knowledge-intensive activities such as research, product development, and business model innovation. Scale begets power. Knowledge too begets power.

Making operations in China or India core to the company's global competitive advantage need not necessarily be a zero-sum game. Whether it is depends on two factors: the company's growth rate and the speed with which it needs to build up China- or India-based capabilities. For a rapidly growing company such as Google, the buildup of R&D activities in China and India can easily and accurately be portrayed as a non-zero-sum enhancement of the company's capabilities. In contrast, for a relatively mature company such as IBM, it is much harder to avoid the perception that the buildup in, say, India will not substitute for current capabilities in, say, the United States or Europe. Speed of buildup also plays a role in that a slower buildup of China- or India-based capabilities may allow senior management to deal with the fallout in existing operations through normal attrition such as retirements and turnover. On the other hand, a rapid buildup may make layoffs in existing locations necessary.

Regardless of whether a buildup of China- or India-based capabilities will affect jobs in existing locations, it is clear that as these two countries become more central to a company's global competitiveness, a shift must occur in the structure of power over key resources and decisions. We have yet to come across a company where this shift in resources and decision-making power took place without direct and enthusiastic support from

the company's CEO along with one or more of his or her colleagues on the corporate executive committee. If the CEO lacks
the conviction that China and India are core to the company's
future competitive advantage, the rest of the organization is
bound to remain frozen in protecting the status quo. Even when
the CEO has the conviction and the courage to act, he or she
will often need to rely on a powerful senior colleague to lead
the charge. The histories of how GE, Microsoft, and IBM built
global competence centers in China or India, or both, illustrate
the powerful role that enthusiastic support from the CEO can
play in this process.

GE's John F. Welch Technology Centre (JFWTC) in
Bangalore is now the largest of the company's four global R&D
centers: Niskayuna, New York (staff size: 1,500), Shanghai (staff
size: 1,500), Munich (staff size: 100), and JFWTC, Bangalore
(staff size: 4,000). The story leading up to the establishment of
JFWTC began in the mid-1990s when R. A. Mashelkar, then
director-general of India's Council for Scientific and Industrial
Research (CSIR), approached GE to inquire about any problems
that the country's national laboratories could work on. GE's plastics business gave CSIR some of its tough technological problems. Within a year, the National Chemical Laboratory came
back with a solution to one of the problems that GE Plastics had
worked on for years. At that point, Gary Rogers, president of the
plastics business, reported that given this talent, he would like to
set up a plastics R&D center in India. Jack Welch, who knew the
plastics business inside out, responded by arguing that if this reasoning was valid for plastics, it ought to be valid for the whole of
GE.[18] In 1999, the John F. Welch Technology Centre was born.
Welch attended the opening ceremony and noted, "India is a
developing country, but it is a developed country as regards its
superb scientific infrastructure. It is for this reason that we wish
to shift a part of GE's development effort to India."[19]

Microsoft's research center in Beijing, Microsoft Research Asia
(MSRA) is the largest research center outside Redmond in the

company's global R&D network, which also includes research labs in San Francisco, Silicon Valley, Cambridge (United Kingdom), and Bangalore. The center opened in 1998. Barely six years later, in a 2004 article, MIT's *Technology Review* magazine hailed MSRA as one of the hottest computer labs in the world.[20] According to a detailed history of Microsoft's trajectory in China, the leading champion behind the setting up of the China research operations was Nathan Myhrvold, group vice president and chief technology officer, who reported directly to Bill Gates. As Myhrvold would later recall, "Bill was quite in favor of it. That was the wonderful thing about what I did at Microsoft—Bill was very supportive and understood the value of making long-term investments. And so that's what we set out to do."[21] In a company such as Microsoft, it is hard to imagine much opposition for an initiative whose champions included Bill Gates and Nathan Myhrvold.

Consider now the case of IBM, whose staff in India soared from fewer than ten thousand in 2004 to over seventy thousand in 2007 and is still adding over ten thousand people a year. Sam Palmisano, who took over as CEO in 2002, knew the services business thoroughly, having served as president of this business for several years under his predecessor, Lou Gerstner. Thus, Palmisano knew firsthand what was happening in the worldwide services business and the rapidly growing threat that Indian IT companies would pose to IBM and other incumbents. He did not need to be persuaded that IBM in India must become as large as or larger than the Indian IT companies, and he became the lead champion behind the transformation. As part of helping IBM's stakeholders think differently about the new reality, Palmisano has used every occasion that he can to promulgate the concept of an integrated global enterprise. As he noted in a 2006 speech at INSEAD, the French business school:

> A globally integrated company looks very different. This is an
> enterprise that shapes its strategy, management and operations in
> a truly global way. It locates operations and functions anywhere

in the world based on the right cost, the right skills, and the right business environment. And it integrates those operations horizontally and globally. . . .

If you accept the principle that when everything is connected, work moves . . . then the burning question for companies, for nations, and for individuals is: What will cause work to move to me? On what basis will I differentiate and compete? Economics? Expertise? Openness? . . .

This is a big question, and I can't tell you how many CEOs, heads of state and academic leaders are grappling with it. After a good deal of soul-searching at my own company, we've decided. We've decided to compete on the basis of expertise and openness, and we are moving from a multinational to a globally integrated model just as fast as we can. . . . .

This is not easy to do. I can tell you that people develop an emotional attachment to businesses—and ways of doing business—that have been very successful and profitable in the past. But if you want to differentiate yourself and compete in this globally integrated environment, you have to be willing to change, to re-invent yourself, to innovate. And you have to be willing to tolerate the naysayers, at least for a while. . . . .

Already we have moved our global procurement mission to China, global services delivery to India, and many of the services that support our external and internal Web sites to places like Brazil and Ireland. These people are not leading teams focused on China or India or Brazil or Ireland. They are leading integrated global operations.[22]

As these cases illustrate, enthusiastic and explicit support from the very top is critical if the company is to leverage China and India as platforms for global advantage. Without such support, these two countries are likely to be treated largely as an "$n + 2$" phenomenon, two additional markets to go after, rather than as transformational for the whole enterprise.

Conclusion

As we noted in the opening chapter of this book, China and India represent four stories: rapidly growing megamarkets, platforms for global cost reduction, platforms for global innovation, and springboards for the emergence of new fearsome competitors. In this chapter, we have analyzed the second and third of these four stories, looked at the factors that make China and India meaningful platforms for global advantage, and put forward a road map for what a global enterprise must do to capture these advantages. Which of the four stories will be more critical at any point in time is likely to vary across industries as well as over time. Thus, the wise approach for any company is to pursue a multitrack strategy for these two economies.

GE provides a case in point. It entered India in the 1980s with the goal of looking for market opportunities in businesses such as lighting, appliances, power generation, and medical systems. However, the company discovered that the market opportunities in India at that time were pitifully small. At the same time, it discovered huge opportunities to leverage India's IT and R&D talent for its global businesses. GE built an immense IT services operation in India as well as the Bangalore-based John F. Welch Technology Centre. The market opportunities in India have taken off, and GE is now aiming for $8 billion to $10 billion revenue from India by 2010. We believe that GE's multitrack mindset has universal relevance for other companies regardless of industry, country of origin, or company size.

5

COMPETING WITH DRAGONS AND TIGERS ON THE GLOBAL STAGE

India and China are a tsunami about to overwhelm us.[1]

—*Curtis R. Carlson, president and CEO,*
Stanford Research Institute

During the past fifty years, Boeing Corporation has been the single largest exporter from the United States. The aircraft industry is important not only for its size but also for being one of the most technologically intensive, capital-intensive, and scale-intensive industries. The barriers to entry into this industry are extremely high—in fact, higher than into other high-tech sectors such as computing, telecommunications, and pharmaceuticals. It took the combined might of all of the rich European countries, over several decades, to create Airbus, the first viable competitor to Boeing.

Think now about which companies are likely to keep Boeing executives awake at night in another ten years. Clearly Airbus will remain one of the major competitors. But Airbus is a devil they know and understand. What may really keep them awake is Commercial Aircraft Corporation of China (CACC), a state-owned enterprise from China created in May 2008 by merging the commercial aircraft operations of two other existing state-owned enterprises, AVIC 1 and AVIC 2. The Chinese government has publicly stated its goal to make China a competitor in the global jumbo jet market by 2020. CACC's predecessor, AVIC 1, has already announced that it will be launching the maiden flight of ARJ21, a passenger aircraft with seventy to one hundred seats during the next twelve months.

Consider now another industry that has been and continues to be crucial to the fortunes of virtually every major industrial economy: automobiles. At the January 2008 Detroit Auto Show, one of the most important auto shows in the world, the talk of the town was not General Motors, Ford, Toyota, Renault-Nissan, or Daimler but a "new" company from a "new" country: Tata Motors from India. Tata had just introduced the least expensive car in the world, the Nano, with a starting price of twenty-five hundred dollars. At the other end of the spectrum, within the same month, Tata Motors had also emerged as the front-runner to close a deal with Ford Motor Company to acquire Jaguar and Land Rover, two iconic, upscale, and highly global British brands.

CACC and Tata Motors represent just the tip of the iceberg in the global restructuring underway in several of the most important industries in the world. In this chapter on the rise of Chinese dragons and Indian tigers, we examine the strategy implications of these developments for established multinationals, as well as the dragons and the tigers themselves. More specifically, we address these questions:

- How similar or different is the rise of global champions from China and India today compared with that from Japan and South Korea between 1970 and 2000?
- How globally fungible are the home country advantages of today's emerging market champions?
- What are the relative advantages and disadvantages of emerging global champions from China versus those from India?
- How serious a threat do the emerging global champions pose to incumbent multinational corporations (MNCs) from developed countries?

- What is the best strategy for established incumbents to neutralize the threat from emerging global champions?
- What weaknesses will the global champions from emerging markets need to overcome if they wish to survive as successful players on the global stage?
- How might they best overcome these weaknesses?

Strategic Logic and the Emergence of Global Champions

We begin with a conceptual discussion of the factors that enable new players to emerge on the global stage and challenge the established positions of incumbents. Our core premise is that the rise of the dragons and tigers is neither a universal nor a random phenomenon. It is not universal in the sense that not every company (not even every large company) from China and India will be able to grow into a significant global competitor. At the same time, it is not random in that one can systematically lay out the factors that will distinguish a firm that becomes a global leader from one that remains just a wannabe.

As depicted in Figure 5.1, three dominant factors determine the likelihood that a company from any country, developed or emerging, will end up as a global force within its industry: the country effect, the industry effect, and the company effect.

Country Effect

In the early stages of globalization, the only place where a company has any significant operations is its home country. Thus, it is critical that the company be able to leverage country-specific comparative advantages as it spreads its wings abroad. Without these advantages, the aspiring globalizer runs the risk of being little more than all hat and no horse.

**Figure 5.1 Factors That Drive the Emergence
of Global Champions**

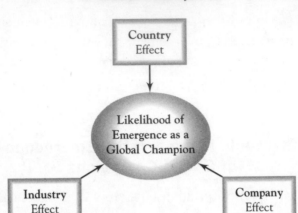

Country-specific advantages can be of many different types.
We highlight some of the most prominent ones:[2]

- *Labor costs.* Much lower labor costs for both blue- and
  white-collar work in their home countries have proven to
  be a major source of global advantage for companies such
  as China's Chery Auto, a car company, and India's Suzlon
  Energy, a wind turbine manufacturer.

- *Cost of raw materials and other inputs.* For Tata Steel, which
  acquired the much larger Anglo-Dutch Corus in 2006,
  access to India's low-cost iron ore has been a major source
  of competitive advantage as it becomes a global player.
  Similarly, access to abundant and lower-cost feedstock was
  the major advantage that Saudi Arabia's Sabic (Saudi Basic
  Industries Corp.) leveraged when it purchased GE's plastics
  business for $11 billion in 2007.

- *Cost of capital.* Abundance of capital in China and the oil-
  rich nations has made it much easier for state-owned or state-
  supported companies in these countries to access capital at a

much lower cost than would be feasible for companies based in the United States, United Kingdom, or India.

- *Talent pool*. Access to a large, well-educated, and relatively lower-cost talent pool has been a major source of global advantage for technology-intensive companies such as China's Huawei (in telecommunications equipment) and India's Infosys (in IT services).

- *Domestic scale*. A megasized domestic market is one of the primary reasons that a sizable number of companies based in the United States, Japan, and Germany have historically dominated their industries worldwide. A large domestic market gives the globalizing company home-grown scale economies that it can leverage against competitors in other markets. The large and rapidly growing size of the domestic markets within China and India is now playing a similar role for the dragons and the tigers.

- *Innovation*. A country's unique characteristics can serve as a driver of leading-edge innovation by companies embedded there. Think about why Japanese companies became world leaders in manufacturing innovations such as just-in-time and total quality management. Given Japan's high population density and thus expensive real estate, the cost of operating a U.S.-style plant would have been prohibitive. In order to survive and succeed even in the domestic market, companies such as Toyota had to invent new approaches to manufacturing that dramatically reduced the need to devote factory space to any task other than direct production. Once created, these innovations served as global rather than merely local advantages. Companies such as Tata Motors and Bharti Airtel are playing an analogous game. Since the per capita buying power of the Indian customer is extremely low, these companies and many others like them are pushing the envelope to create and deliver products and services that are ultra-low-cost. The resulting innovations in technology, product and service design, operations, and even the entire business model are likely to be highly fungible across borders.

- *Public policy.* Country effects can take the form of public policy that encourages and facilitates exports and foreign direct investment by domestic firms. The role of public policy is particularly evident in China, where the national government has pursued an explicit "go global" policy in recent years. As vice minister of commerce Ma Xiuhong noted in her remarks at a conference in 2006, "The Chinese government supports those domestic companies with the strength to invest in the rest of the world to jointly develop business with their international counterparts."[3] President Hu Jintao even included a reference to the importance of "go global" strategies in his report to the Seventeenth Party Congress in October 2007. Some of the planks in this policy include direct exhortation to state-owned enterprises, a helping hand by the Export-Import Bank of China in financing project outlays by foreign customers, coinvestment by China Investment Corporation (a sovereign wealth fund), and encouragement to state-owned enterprises to set up overseas economic and trade cooperation zones in countries and regions with a favorable investment climate.

Despite the major role that country effects can play in giving local players a foundation for global advantage, it is important to remember two other facts. One is that these advantages are equally available to almost all domestic companies within a China, an India, or a Brazil. Yet not every domestic company becomes a global champion. Thus, other factors, such as industry and company effects, also play a critical role. Second, in this era of open borders and a globally integrated world economy, most of the country-specific advantages are available not just to domestic companies but also to those from abroad. IBM has built almost as large a staff in India as the Indian IT giants. Thus, whether country effects become a source of competitive advantage depends also on the company's ability to internalize them.

Industry Effect

Industries differ in the extent to which the strengths from one country can be leveraged across other countries:

- *Economies of global scale.* In some industries (such as semiconductors and mobile phones), global scale in R&D, sourcing, or operations is very important. In others (such as nursing homes), what matters is local, not global, scale.

- *Economies of global scope.* In some industries (such as supply chain management software), most customers are multinational companies that prefer suppliers with the capability to provide the needed products and services on a worldwide basis. In others (such as food retailing), virtually all customers are local, and they place no value on whether the supplier is global.

- *Economies of global delivery.* In some industries (such as athletic shoes and call centers), goods and services can be produced in the most cost-efficient locations and distributed or delivered worldwide at a relatively low cost. In others (such as restaurants or home repair services), the product or service must be produced locally, near the customer.

These three factors—economies of global scale, economies of global scope, and economies of global delivery—drive some industries to become very globally integrated (examples are semiconductors, mobile phones, and remotely deliverable IT services), for some others to remain multidomestic (housing construction, food retailing, and consumer banking, for example), and for the rest to fall somewhere in between (such as Internet retailing and legal services).

Whether an industry is of the globally integrated or the multidomestic type has a major bearing on the likelihood that an emerging global player will be successful in realizing its aspirations. In a multidomestic industry, it is extremely hard (although not impossible) for an aspiring global champion to leverage its home-based advantage into other markets. Thus, established players in other countries have little to fear from such new entrants. Even a giant such as Wal-Mart faced miserable failures in Germany and South Korea precisely because of industry structure. Given the inherently multidomestic structure of the discount retailing industry, the local market leaders in Germany and South Korea could easily defeat Wal-Mart.

But if the industry in which you play is globally integrated, then you must treat aspiring global players with much greater seriousness. If they are not kept subdued when they are young, the risk is high that they will be able to globalize at a rapid rate and become even tougher to battle later. Interestingly, however, for the established multinational, globally integrated industries also offer an important advantage. It is precisely in such industries that the established multinational can leverage its global capabilities to apply tough competitive pressure on the aspiring globalizer in the latter's home market.

Consider the case of Nokia versus domestic competitors in China's mobile phone market. By every measure, the mobile phone industry is global. Thus, the bulk of the worldwide market has long been shared by a small number of global players—primarily Nokia, Samsung, Sony Ericsson, and Motorola. In 2003–2004, within the Chinese market, which had already become the world's largest, the global players came under serious attack from domestic challengers such as TCL and Ningbo Bird. Within short order, the domestic champions had captured over 51 percent of China's mobile phone market. To its enormous credit, Nokia decoded the developing scenario accurately and responded with all its might against the Chinese challengers. Among other moves, Nokia's actions included the introduction of much cheaper cell phone models and a rapid expansion in its distribution system. By 2007, the combined market share of the Chinese players had been reduced to 25 percent and was declining.

In short, the Chinese dragons, the Indian tigers, and the established multinationals must never forget that industry structure matters and must be factored into the design of strategic moves.

Company Effect

Today Infosys in IT services and Haier in home appliances are well-known and highly respected names within their industries worldwide. As of May 1, 2008, Infosys's market capitalization stood at $26 billion, second only to that of IBM in the worldwide IT services industry. Haier was the fourth largest home appliance manufacturer in the world, with not just the leading position in China but also rapidly rising market shares in other large markets, such as the United States, Europe, and India.

In understanding how Infosys and Haier became what they are, it is important to note that the explanation goes well beyond country and industry effects. In the mid-1980s, Infosys was just one of several hundred tiny IT services companies based in India. In 1991, ten years after its founding, the company's revenues were less than $2 million, and its market value was estimated to be only about $1.5 million. Similarly, in 1984, Haier, known at that time as the Qingdao Refrigerator Factory, was one of several hundred appliance manufacturers in China. Moreover, it was teetering on the verge of bankruptcy, and Zhang Ruimin, the newly appointed director, was the fourth boss in one year.

Why did Infosys leave most other Indian IT companies in the dust and emerge as the global giant that it is today? Why did Haier emerge from the ruins not merely to survive but to become one of China's most respected global companies? The answer lies in what we call the "company effect": the company-specific core capabilities, mindset, and organizational culture that distinguish the emerging champion from its peers within the home country. Leaders such as N. R. Narayana Murthy at Infosys and Zhang Ruimin at Haier were relentless in their passion to transform their companies into world-class organizations. Consider first the rise of Infosys.

In 1991, the Indian government initiated economic liberalization, and multinationals such as IBM began planning to reenter India. Many observers predicted that Infosys was basically "as good as dead." They doubted that it could withstand the expected war for talent, the company's key asset. Infosys's response was brilliant and highly atypical. Although the company did not need the cash, its leaders decided to do an initial public offering (IPO) and used the capital to build a world-class campus (one that would rival that of Microsoft or IBM in the United States) in what was still Third World Bangalore. They also decided that Infosys salaries would be in the top 85 to 90 percent of the companies in its peer group. Also critical, Infosys became one of the first companies in India to issue stock options to all employees. A top engineer from one of the Indian Institutes of Technology could now see that he or she had a better chance of becoming a millionaire at Infosys than at IBM.

As the U.S. government started to reduce the number of visas that could be granted to foreign workers doing projects in the United States, Infosys became one of the first companies in India to develop global delivery capabilities whereby the work could be done in Bangalore and exported from there instead of having to be done at the customer site in the United States. In order to assure customers that quality standards would continue to be met, Infosys became one of the first companies in India to receive ISO 9000 certification.

In the mid-1990s, rather than bow to intense pricing pressure from GE, which accounted for 40 percent of its revenues, Infosys's leaders decided instead to let GE go. They also vowed to significantly improve the company's marketing capabilities so that it would never again be so dependent on any one customer.

In 1998, Infosys became the first Indian company to achieve CMM-Level 4 certification from Carnegie-Mellon's Software Engineering Institute (SEI). In 2000, it again became the first Indian company to achieve CMM-Level 5 certification, the highest awarded by SEI. Until then, only forty companies in the world had achieved CMM-Level 5 certification.

In 1999, Infosys became the first Indian company to undertake an IPO on a U.S.-based stock exchange. Like the IPO in India in the early 1990s, this IPO also was done not just for financial but also strategic reasons. The company's leaders believed that an IPO on NASDAQ would help build name recognition and credibility with the chief information officers and CEOs of major U.S. corporations, all potential clients. By now, the company had arrived.

Consider now the rise of Haier. Just a few months after becoming the CEO in 1984, Zhang Ruimin pulled seventy-six newly built refrigerators from the production line, gathered all workers outside the factory, and asked them to join him in destroying these defective products. Such an act was unheard of in China and was highly symbolic. Many of the defects were minor, and each refrigerator would have sold for four times the average annual salary of a worker. The message hit home: the company would no longer produce substandard products. The CEO was convinced that better-quality products would command a higher price, even in the then very poor China. By 1988, Haier was widely regarded as the producer of the best-quality refrigerators in China. Although the company charged a premium price, its market share was growing. Haier's track record on all fronts—product quality, brand image, profitability, and cash flow—made it the obvious leader in consolidating the fragmented white goods industry in China.

Haier also entered into strategic alliances with several leading multinationals to build technological capabilities in product design and manufacturing. The alliances included a technology licensing agreement with Germany's Liebherr, imports of production technology from Denmark's Derby and Japan's Sanyo, and joint ventures with Japan's Mitsubishi and Italy's Merloni. As Zhang Ruimin explained the logic behind these moves, "First we observe and digest. Then we imitate. In the end, we understand it well enough to design it independently."

Haier became a pioneer in market segmentation and product innovation to meet the unique needs of different segments. The discovery that rural customers were using Haier washing machines to clean vegetables and sweet potatoes led the company to redesign its machines for rural customers so that they would no longer get clogged with mud. At the other end of the market, Haier introduced a tiny machine for customers in Shanghai. This machine could clean just a single change of clothes and was a hit with customers who lived in a hot and humid city and in tiny apartments.

Haier cultivated a culture of delighting customers with the quality of its after-sales service. Tales of its dedication to customer service were legendary, and many observers regarded Haier as the leader in after-sales service across China.

As is clear, these capabilities (a mania for product quality, a disciplined approach to building technological capabilities, an obsession with market responsiveness and product innovation, and a commitment to after-sales service) became the defining features of Haier. They had little to do with the fact that Haier was a Chinese company or that it was an appliance manufacturer. Zhang Ruimin and his team built these capabilities because they wanted Haier to become a world-class company, whether in China or outside China. This obsession with building world-class capabilities paid off handsomely as Haier ventured into markets outside China, especially in highly competitive markets such as the United States and Europe, where established incumbents ruled supreme and entry barriers were relatively high.

To sum up, the country-specific advantages of China and India provide significant potential opportunity for many of their home-grown companies to become global champions. However, this potential is likely to become a reality only for companies that figure out how to build leading-edge core capabilities in a systematic manner. Even then, we are much more likely to see global champions from China and India in industries whose underlying economics make them globally integrated than in those that are destined to remain largely multidomestic.

The Rise of Dragons and Tigers

We now delve deeper into the factors that are fueling the rise of the Chinese dragons and the Indian tigers. In particular, we expand on three observations:

- The emergence of global champions from China and India is taking place at a much faster pace than was the case with their predecessors from Japan and South Korea.
- To date, Indian companies have been more aggressive than their Chinese counterparts in globalizing through acquisition.
- Notwithstanding their strengths, aspiring globalizers from China and India face considerable challenges in realizing their ambitions.

Rapid Pace of Global Expansion

The emergence of global champions from China and India is taking place at a much faster pace than was the case with Toyota, Sony, Samsung, and LG from Japan and South Korea one generation ago. The faster pace is due almost entirely to the fact that the new global players are much more acquisition driven than was the case with their Japanese and South Korean predecessors. In 2007, the value of outbound deals from China was about $30 billion, 60 percent higher than in 2006 and larger than the

$25 billion value of inbound deals. For India, the value of 2007 outbound deals totaled over $35 billion, five times that of 2006, and larger than the $32 billion value of inbound deals.[4]

A primary driver of the trend toward globalization through acquisition is that capital markets, both public and private, are much more global now than in the 1970s and 1980s. Despite the subprime crisis engulfing much of the world economy in 2008, if the business logic makes sense, it is not very difficult for an aspiring globalizer to secure debt or equity financing to fund a cross-border acquisition. By way of example, look at Tata Motors's deal with Ford to buy the Jaguar and Land Rover brands, plants, and intellectual property rights. Tata signed the deal for $2.3 billion in March 2008, to be financed largely through loans from a consortium of Indian and overseas banks. The acquisition became final on June 2, 2008.

The aggressive pace of today's globalizers is also being fueled by other complementary trends. The market for companies is much more liquid today than was the case two decades ago. Importantly too, so is the market for senior executive talent. Thus, as the Chinese and Indian companies globalize, they are able to recruit seasoned veterans (including returnee Chinese and Indians) from the established multinationals in the United States and Europe to guide their global expansion moves:

- At Tata Group, the Group Corporate Centre, the apex body comprising nine senior executives, includes Alan Rosling as an executive director. Rosling is a British citizen whose background includes a Harvard M.B.A., serving as special advisor to the British prime minister, and senior executive positions with the Jardine Matheson Group. Other foreign nationals within the senior ranks of the Tata Group are Raymond Bickson, an American who is CEO of the Indian Hotels Company, and Trevor Bull, managing director of Tata AIG Life Insurance.

- The CEO of Jet Airways, India's largest airline and a rapidly expanding global player, is Wolfgang Prock-Schauer, an Austrian national. Prock-Schauer had previously served as an executive vice president with Austrian Airlines and chairman of the Star Alliance Management Board.

- At Chery Automobile, the executive in charge of international business is Zhang Lin, a Chinese national who obtained a Ph.D. in engineering from the University of Michigan and served as a senior executive with Chrysler from 1995 to 2003 before returning to China to join Chery.

- In June 2006, Shanghai Automotive Industry Corporation (SAIC), China's largest automaker, hired Phil Murtaugh as an executive vice president in charge of overseas operations. Prior to this role, Murtaugh had served as the chairman of General Motors China and negotiated the joint venture relationship between GM and SAIC. Although Murtaugh left SAIC in September 2007 to become the head of Chrysler's Asian operations, it appears by all accounts that his tenure at SAIC was viewed as mutually productive.

It is true that Japanese companies such as Nissan and Sony currently have non-Japanese CEOs. Nissan's CEO is Carlos Ghosn, a Frenchman who was born in Brazil to Lebanese parents. And Sony's CEO is Howard Stringer, a U.S. citizen who was born in Wales. It is important to note, however, that Japanese companies are bringing in seasoned Western executives in order to help revive troubled companies. In contrast, a growing number of Chinese and Indian companies are recruiting seasoned veterans from the outside at a much earlier stage in the expectation that these veterans can help steer them wisely on the path to globalization.

Chinese Dragons Versus Indian Tigers

Notwithstanding major similarities in the emergence of tigers and dragons from India and China, there also are important differences. The first major difference pertains to the fact that on average, Chinese companies are far ahead of India in globalization through exports of manufactured goods. In turn, Indian companies are far ahead of China in globalization through exports of remotely deliverable services. These differences derive directly from the historically differing strengths of the two economies.

The second difference pertains to the fact that a much larger number of Chinese (as compared with Indian) companies are emerging as global giants in the supply of equipment and project management services for infrastructure projects such as the construction of highways, electric power plants, and ports. Having built more infrastructure over the past fifteen years than has ever happened in any other country in the world, Chinese companies bring well-developed and much lower-cost capabilities to these tasks. Take, for example, the construction of hydroelectric dams. China is home to almost half of the world's forty-five thousand biggest dams. Chinese companies such as Gezhouba Co., an engineering firm, and Sinohydro Corp., a dam builder, have recently won multibillion-dollar orders for dam projects in other developing countries. Often these projects are financed by the Export-Import Bank of China, a state-owned enterprise.[5]

Another example is State Grid Corp., a state-owned enterprise that owns provincial and regional transmission companies within China. It is the largest power company in the world, with 1.5 million employees and 2006 revenues of $116 billion. In December 2007, State Grid and two host country partners signed a twenty-five-year deal to manage Philippines' power grid for $3.95 billion. According to Sun Jinping, head of the company's international division, "We have experienced power shortages, but we have proven technology which can be used for upgrading the network. This is very valuable in a market like the Philippines. They are now experiencing very fast demand. They need this kind of experience."[6]

The third major difference pertains to the much stronger capabilities of Indian companies (relative to their Chinese counterparts) at playing the cross-border acquisition game, especially when it comes to making large acquisitions in developed countries. Obviously there are exceptions, such as Lenovo's purchase of IBM's PC business in 2005. However, as a general statement, it is valid to claim that Indian companies are far ahead of their Chinese peers at making large cross-border acquisitions and integrating them successfully. Let us look at the reasons.

The two key requirements for success in globalizing through the mergers-and-acquisitions (M&A) mode are strong financial skills (to do the deal on the right terms) and strong post-merger integration skills (to make the deal work). In general, emerging global champions from India have an edge over their Chinese counterparts on both dimensions. Given an abundance of capital in China and a well-recognized propensity on the part of China's state-owned enterprises to put national policy goals ahead of shareholder value maximization, Chinese corporate leaders are still at a relatively early stage in developing world-class finance skills. In contrast, Indian business leaders are probably at the leading edge on this dimension. Indian business leaders also have an edge in postmerger integration skills. China's is a command-and-control economy embedded in a culture that respects hierarchy. In addition, China is a relatively homogeneous society in terms of race, religion (or lack of it), and language. In contrast, India is a ferociously democratic country with one of the largest intracountry diversities in the world on almost any dimension that matters. Thus, the cultural DNA of Indian business leaders makes them more adept at horizontal integration and managing horizontal organizations than is currently the case with most Chinese business leaders. Finally, Indian corporate leaders have the well-known advantage of fluency in English so crucial to cross-border integration.

In globalizing through acquisition of companies in the developed economies (especially the United States), another advantage that Indian companies appear to enjoy pertains to the significantly lower political sensitivity of acquisitions by companies from India relative to those from China. The reasons are multifaceted and perhaps rooted in the similarities or differences in the cultures, political systems, and dominant languages among various countries. Any sizable bid (say, above $1 billion in deal size) by a Chinese company to acquire a controlling stake in a U.S. company would almost certainly be a front-page story in the *Wall Street Journal* and is likely to invite negative comments from U.S. politicians. In contrast, even large acquisitions by companies from India are treated by the media and the politicians as relatively routine commercial events. A recent case is an agreement announced by India's Essar Steel to buy the U.S.-based Esmark, a steel producer and distributor, for $1.1 billion in cash. It was a relatively small news item on page B5 of the *Wall Street Journal*.[7]

Chinese companies are responding to their relative disadvantage at playing the cross-border M&A game by adopting a learning mode. In concrete terms, this is reflected in the willingness of Chinese companies to take a minority stake rather than outright control. Recent examples include a $5.6 billion investment by the Industrial and Commercial Bank of China to acquire a 20 percent stake in South Africa's Standard Bank; a $2.7 billion investment by Ping An Insurance to acquire a 4.18 percent stake in Fortis, a Belgium-based banking and insurance company; and a $14.05 billion investment by a partnership between China Aluminum and Aluminum Corporation of America to acquire a 12 percent stake in Rio Tinto, an Anglo-Australian mining company.

We anticipate that as China and India continue to grow and develop more diversified strength, there will be convergence in the strengths and weaknesses of the dragons and the tigers. In the meantime, globalizers from both economies have a lot of learning to do. Considerable opportunities also exist for entrepreneurs who can figure out how to combine an abundance of capital in the Middle East with an abundance of manufacturing capabilities in China and an abundance of organizational and managerial capabilities in India.

Challenges for the Dragons and Tigers

For the emerging global champions from China and India, the most salient common challenge pertains to the accumulation and upgrading of capabilities in all key elements of the value chain: (1) product and process technologies; (2) sourcing, production, and supply chain processes that can deliver high-quality products and services on a consistent basis; (3) accessing distribution channels in foreign markets; and (4) establishing credibility and trust with potential customers in far-away lands. What the dragons and the tigers bring to the table is access to vast pools of scientific and engineering talent, the ability to produce goods and services at a low cost, burning ambition, and the ability to move with speed. However, most of them lack the stock of scientific and technical knowledge, organizational discipline, market credibility, and brand image that established companies such as IBM, Procter & Gamble, and Caterpillar have built over decades. These weaknesses can be overcome partly through acquisitions and partly through a process of learning from the ground up—as is being demonstrated by companies such as Tata Motors, Lenovo, Huawei, Suzlon Energy, and Chery Auto. However, accumulating new capabilities is never an automatic and easy process. It takes time and requires humility coupled with determination. Box 5.1 details the systematic and disciplined manner in which India's Suzlon and China's Chery have attempted to build as well as acquire the needed capabilities. As these cases also illustrate, this task is far from over.

A second common challenge pertains to the risk of hubris getting the better of cold analysis and sound judgment. As it is, hubris is a common malady in M&A deals (witness the complete failure of the DaimlerChrysler merger). In the case of emerging champions from China and India, the risk of hubris is greater. The roots of hubris lie in an abundance of external adulation. That is not too far from the reality for China and India today.

Box 5.1: Capability Accumulation at India's Suzlon and China's Chery

The Rise of Suzlon Energy

By the end of 2007, Suzlon Energy was the world's fifth largest wind turbine manufacturer with R&D centers in India, Germany, Belgium, and Netherlands; manufacturing operations in India, China, Belgium, Germany, the United States, and Australia; and customers in most of the world's major markets. For 2007, the company recorded revenues of about $1.4 billion.

Suzlon's roots go back to 1994 when it was a polyester yarn manufacturer in western India that faced chronic shortages of power. Tulsi Tanti, the CEO, purchased two small-capacity wind turbine generators from Vestas, a European company, to address this problem. However, the equipment suppliers appeared not particularly interested in installation and after-sales maintenance and service. Sensing an opportunity, Tanti decided to make wind turbines his main business and exited from the yarn operations. In the late 1990s, Suzlon signed a deal with Sudwind Energy GmbH, a small German company, to sell its turbines in India. Eventually Sudwind went bankrupt, and Suzlon hired its engineers to set up an R&D center in Germany. Also, in the late 1990s, Suzlon acquired AE-Rotor Techniek BV, a bankrupt Dutch company, to design rotor blades. In 2003, the company started exporting low-power wind turbines to the United States and other markets. In 2005, it undertook an IPO in India.

The rapid ramp-up to become a global powerhouse began in 2005 with the acquisition of Hansen Transmissions, a Belgium-based gearbox maker for wind turbines. Along with rotor blades, the gearbox is one of the most technology-intensive and critical components in a wind turbine. By all accounts, Suzlon's decision to acquire Hansen and how it managed this company after the acquisition was brilliant. The acquisition price of 371 million euros was financed by internal cash flow and corporate debt from Barclays and Deutsche Bank. At the time of the acquisition,

Hansen's order book was full for two years, with supply commitments to Suzlon's competitors Vestas and Siemens.

Within a hundred days of the acquisition, Tanti laid out his five-year vision for Hansen: (1) expand gearbox production capacity from 3.2 to 15 gigawatts; (2) establish production centers in four low-cost countries including China and India; (3) increase revenues at a 40 percent annual rate; and (4) increase earnings before income, depreciation, taxes, and amortization from 12 to 15 percent of revenues to 25 percent. Within eighteen months, Hansen was well on its way to achieving these targets. Tanti appointed Ivan Brems, a Hansen veteran, as the acquired company's new CEO and, in order to assure Hansen's customers, created a new supervisory board of independent directors. Production capacity had been increased to 6.6 gigawatts. Construction was under way to build a 3 gigawatt plant in China and a 5 gigawatt plant in India. Suzlon also started injecting India's frugal engineering skills into Hansen. In another important move, in December 2006, Tanti decided to take Hansen public again, this time on the London Stock Exchange. The IPO raised $440 million to finance expansion of Hansen's production capacity. Although Suzlon's stake had been diluted to 73 percent, within a span of eighteen months, Tanti had increased the value of Suzlon's original investment of 371 million euros to five times that amount.

Tanti made his next major move in May 2007 when Suzlon beat out France's Areva to acquire Germany's REpower Systems, a high-power wind turbine maker. It paid a little over 400 million euros for a 33.85 percent stake in REpower. However, Suzlon also signed voting pool agreements with two of REpower's other main shareholders, France's Areva and Portugal's Martifer, to gain control over 87.1 percent of voting rights. In exchange for ceding voting rights over its 30 percent stake to Suzlon, Areva obtained the right to sell its stake to Suzlon at market price after one year; Suzlon also agreed to use Areva as its preferred supplier for transmission and distribution infrastructure. Similarly, Martifer ceded voting rights

(Continued)

over its 23 percent stake to Suzlon in exchange for its right to sell this stake to Suzlon after two years at a preagreed price. As of early 2008, Suzlon was in a waiting mode with respect to its ability to access REpower's technology for high-power wind turbines. Under German law, until Suzlon has voting rights over all outstanding shares, it and REpower must continue to deal with each other at arm's length.

The Rise of Chery Automobile

Chery Automobile was founded as a provincial state-owned enterprise in China's Anhui province in 1997. Its first car, produced on December 18, 1999, represented something of a milestone in Chinese manufacturing history: it was the first car produced by a totally Chinese-owned and -managed company. Over the ten years since then, Chery has continued to maintain an independent streak. In 2007, the company sold 381,000 cars, making it China's fourth-largest passenger vehicle manufacturer. Among the major Chinese auto companies, Chery was the only player that had not yet entered into a joint venture agreement with a foreign car company. According to our interviews with Dr. Zhang Lin, head of Chery's international business activities, this independence was one reason that Chery had become the most aggressive globalizer in China's auto industry. The total sales figure of 381,000 cars for 2007 included 119,800 cars sold in overseas markets, making Chery the number one auto exporter from China.

Chery has been relentless in building its technological and design capabilities through both mechanisms: learning from others' experience and its own internal efforts. Its CEO brought twelve years' experience managing the plant that assembled Jetta at the FAW-Volkswagen joint venture. When Volkswagen centralized its R&D operations in China, Chery hired many of the technical staff who were offered early retirement. The company also acquired a stake in a design company founded by a team of experienced designers who had worked for a joint venture between China's Dongfeng and France's Citroen and spent time at Citroen's operations in France. Zeng and Williamson noted in their analysis of Chery: "In total, Chery has twenty foreign experts on its full-time research staff and dozens more foreign retirees on consulting contracts working on improvements at every stage of its assembly lines. The result: an unmatched capability to deliver innovative designs that extend its product variety while keeping costs low."*

As of early 2008, Chery was still on a learning curve with respect to building cars that would meet the safety standards in developed country markets. Thus, to date, the company's exports have been confined to emerging markets such as Syria, Iran, Egypt, Turkey, Malaysia, Indonesia, Ukraine, Russia, Argentina, and Chile. However, it seemed clear that Chery was moving up in its capability to serve more demanding customers in developed markets. In November 2006, Chery signed an agreement to sell 100,00 engines annually to Italy's Fiat Group. A few months later, in July 2007, Chery signed an agreement with Chrysler to supply compact cars that would be sold globally by Chrysler under the Dodge brand. In August 2007, Chery's one-millionth car rolled off the assembly line.

*M. Zeng and P. J. Williamson, *Dragons at Your Door* (Boston: Harvard Business School Press, 2007), p. 164.

The possibility of hubris clouding sound judgment is illustrated well by the case of China's TCL Multimedia, a consumer electronics firm. In 2002, TCL was rated as one of China's largest industrial enterprises, and Li DongSheng was being feted as a hero by the media not just within but also outside China. The troubles started in 2003 when TCL acquired Thomson SA's television business and Alcatel's mobile handset business. Both acquisitions were weak businesses with products and technologies that were becoming rapidly obsolete. In essence, they were misguided acquisitions. Lack of capabilities at postmerger integration made a bad situation worse. As *China*

International Business observed in an analysis of TCL's woes in December 2006:

> Li himself has confessed that . . . [the] mistakes . . . [included] lack of capital, underestimation of the difficulty of the take-over, a lack of international talent reserves and the low speed of reintegration. The most fundamental error, Li says, is the company's blind optimism and eagerness for quick results. . . . Seen in a positive light, what TCL has suffered helps dramatise the gap between top-notch Chinese entrepreneurs and global players. "Sometimes it is very difficult to make accurate predictions beforehand. You have to jump into it if you really want to know it," says Li.[8]

By 2006, TCL was struggling for survival. The TCL saga has served as an expensive but highly valuable lesson not just for its own leaders but for other aspiring dragons and tigers.

A third common challenge pertains to the brand image that China and India still have in much of the developed economies. By and large, in most people's minds, the image continues to be one of "low cost" rather than "high quality," "luxury," or "world class." Notwithstanding its first-rate leadership and organizational capabilities, the Tata Group faced this challenge in its moves to acquire Jaguar and Land Rover from Ford, as well as a stake in Orient-Express, a New York Stock Exchange–listed luxury hotel and cruise firm. In December 2007, Ken Gorin, chairman of the Jaguar Business Operations Council, a U.S.-based dealer group, told the *Wall Street Journal*, "I don't believe the US public is ready for ownership out of India for a luxury-car brand such as Jaguar. . . . I believe it would severely throw a tremendous cast of doubt over the viability of the brand." Along similar lines, a few days later, the media reported that Paul White, CEO of Orient-Express, had written a letter to R. K. Krishna Kumar, the vice chairman of Indian Hotels, a Tata subsidiary, noting that "any association of our luxury brands and properties with your brands and properties would result in a reduction of our brands and of our business and would likely lead to erosion."[9]

In our judgment, it is only a matter of time (perhaps less than five years) before Indian and Chinese companies learn how to overcome these challenges. Look back to Toyota in the 1980s. In 1980, the Western world appeared far from ready to embrace a luxury car from Japan. By the early 1990s, media reports indicated that Bill Gates had been spotted driving in a Lexus.

Strategic Implications for Established Multinationals

The structure of most industries has changed dramatically over the past twenty years. Given the accelerating pace of change, it is inevitable that in most industries, structural change over the next ten years will be at least as large as that over the previous twenty. The ongoing technological upheaval will be one of the drivers of this change. The rise of new global players from the emerging economies will be another.

In 2000, the top five global players in virtually every industry were companies that had their roots in the developed economies of the United States, Europe, Japan, and, in some cases, South Korea. By 2025, it is not unlikely that two out of the five biggest companies in every industry may be from China, India, or one of the other big emerging markets, such as Brazil, Russia, or Mexico. Not every aspiring globalizer from the emerging economies will succeed in realizing its ambitions. But it is certain that many of them will. Similarly, not every company that is an established leader today will stumble and get swallowed. But it also is certain that many of them will.

What should you and your team do to increase the odds that your company is one of the leaders in its industry by the time 2025 rolls in? We discuss four complementary strategic moves: (1) neutralize the dragons' and tigers' home court advantage, (2) join forces with the dragons and tigers, (3) leverage the power of China+India, and (4) protect your competitive position in markets outside China and India.

Neutralize the Dragons' and Tigers' Home Court Advantage

The starting point for battling the dragons and tigers on the world stage is to figure out how best to neutralize the country-specific advantages that they enjoy. In essence, this requires competing with the Indian or Chinese global players by becoming an insider in these economies. If executed well, such a strategy can help established multinationals close the gap between their cost structure and ability to innovate in relation to that of the Indian or Chinese globalizers. And offering stiffer competition to the emerging dragons and tigers on their home turf can help contain the latter's profit margins, cash flow, and thus aggressiveness on the global stage. Dell is pursuing this strategy against Lenovo in the PC business. Similarly, IBM and Accenture have pursued this strategy exceptionally well in taking on the challenge from Indian players such as Tata Consulting, Infosys, and Wipro in the global IT services industry.

Lenovo's purchase of IBM's PC business in May 2005 immediately made it the number three PC company in the world and potentially a major threat to Dell's (and similarly Hewlett-Packard's) positions globally. Lenovo enjoyed several advantages. It had a low-cost manufacturing base in China that could be particularly important in laptops, where shipping costs as a proportion of total costs are much lower than in the case of desktops. Lenovo also enjoyed a dominant position in China, the world's largest and fastest-growing PC market; this gave the company significant economies of scale. Shortly after the acquisition, Lenovo hired William Amelio, Dell's Asia chief, to be its new CEO. Dell has responded by becoming fiercely aggressive against Lenovo in the Chinese market. It has beefed up its R&D and manufacturing capabilities in China, introduced ultra-low-cost models designed and manufactured in China, and signed agreements with major Chinese retailers such as Gome and Suning to sell Dell PCs through over a thousand retail outlets in urban and rapidly growing rural markets.

In 2001, IBM's India-based operations were tiny, with a staff of only about four thousand people. In contrast, Indian IT services companies were on a roll, with growth rates exceeding 50 percent a year. Indian companies had proven their technical skills with inoculating multinational firms' computer networks against the Y2K bug. Also, their capabilities were moving up in sophistication at a rapid rate. Furthermore, given weak economic conditions in the United States and Europe, it was clear that an increasing number of IBM's current and future clients would be looking to Indian companies to help reduce their cost structures. IBM started ramping up its India-based operations in full seriousness around 2004. During that year, it signed a $750 million outsourcing contract with Bharti Tele-Ventures (now called Bharti Airtel), India's leading mobile operator. It also acquired Daksh eServices, an Indian company providing business process outsourcing services. This became the start of seeing India not just as a market but also as the emerging center of gravity for IBM's services business globally.

In 2004, IBM started expanding its India-based global delivery capabilities aggressively. The head count in India grew to 38,500 (by the end of 2005), 53,000 (by the end of 2006), and 70,000 (by the end of 2007). In mid-2006, Amitabh Ray, head of IBM's global delivery operations in India, felt confident enough to predict, "Three years from now, we'll definitely be the largest IT services company from India."[10] It appeared likely that by 2009, IBM's head count in India would exceed 100,000, accounting for nearly 30 percent of the company's global workforce. By almost every measure, IBM had transformed its services business into an integrated global enterprise with India as the center of gravity within a short span of five years.

Accenture serves as another good example of an established multinational that concluded that the best way to compete with the rising IT giants from India was to neutralize their India-specific advantages (while still being able to leverage its own global capabilities and customer relationships). At the end of 2000, Accenture's head count in India was a mere two hundred. The transformation started during 2001–2003 when the corporate leadership team committed itself to the idea of building Accenture India into the company's leading hub for the delivery of global services. The head count grew rapidly from five hundred (in 2002) to thirty-three hundred (in 2003) to ten thousand (in 2004) to sixteen thousand (in 2005) to twenty-three thousand (in 2006) and to thirty-five thousand (in 2007). As Karl-Heinz Floether, group chief executive for systems integration, technology, and delivery and the leading champion behind this transformation, observed in an interview in October 2007:

> What company of our size and success in its current business model could attempt to accomplish such extraordinary change and stay at the top of its industry and outperform the competition? We sent leaders from around the world to India—many of whom are of Indian origin—to help build a world-class capability from zero to 35,000 people in only five years. And now, we are filling top leadership roles around Accenture with many of those Indian leaders. . . . Today, we have a world-class operation in India. Our growth rate exceeds that of our Indian competitors.[11]

Join Forces with the Dragons and Tigers

Other than small toehold acquisitions, the strategies of Dell, IBM, and Accenture to fight fire with fire featured an aggressive but organic buildup of their capabilities and operations within China and India. An alternative approach to accomplish the same goal is to join forces with the dragons and tigers by acquiring or aligning with one or more of these home-grown guerrillas.

The main advantage of a "join forces" strategy is speed, as it can potentially make the established multinational an immediate insider. As such, this strategy is much more appropriate for multinationals that are late and need to play a catch-up game. This strategy can also be appropriate in cases where the mindset required to build the China- or India-based capabilities is radically different from the prevailing mindset of the established multinational. Electronic Data Systems (EDS) and Renault-Nissan provide interesting examples.

In early 2006, EDS found itself severely lagging behind IBM and Accenture in building India-based global delivery capabilities. At that time, EDS's head count in India was only about three thousand as compared with nearly forty thousand for IBM and nearly twenty thousand for Accenture. Given the speed with which IBM and Accenture, as well as the major Indian competitors, were ramping up their capabilities in India, EDS concluded that acquisition was the smarter route for it to try to close the gap. In June 2006, the company paid $380 million in cash to acquire a majority stake in MphasiS BFL Limited, a rapidly growing middle-sized applications and business process outsourcing services company based in Bangalore. This acquisition immediately gave EDS access to eleven thousand India-based employees skilled in advanced applications development, emerging technologies, and services for business process outsourcing and customer relations management. Equally important, it gave the company a much stronger India-based platform for more rapid expansion over the next five years.

There is every reason to conclude that EDS has done an effective job in integrating MphasiS. Jerry Rao, the cofounder of MphasiS and its CEO at the time of the EDS acquisition, is still affiliated with the company. As of early 2008, Rao was chairman of EDS's Asia-Pacific Advisory Board as well as vice president and general manager for EDS India Operations. In an interesting development, EDS's success in ramping up its Indian operations appears to have made it a particularly attractive acquisition target for Hewlett-Packard, a deal that was completed in August 2008. The acquisition of EDS is a major plank in Hewlett-Packard's renewed efforts to compete more forcefully with IBM in IT services.

Renault and Nissan, the French and Japanese auto companies with equity holdings in each other and a common CEO, also illustrate the strategy of joining forces with local players to take on the emerging dragons and tigers. Tata Motors's debut of a twenty-five-hundred-dollar car (the Nano) in January 2008 indicated that the low- and middle-price segments of the auto markets around the world (including in Europe and the United States) would very likely be under attack from India-based companies within five years. As recently as mid-2007, even Japanese auto executives had proclaimed that it was impossible to deliver a car that would meet safety and emission standards for that price. Yet Tata Motors did it. The Nano was a vivid illustration of Indian companies' growing capabilities in frugal engineering: designing products and services that would be functional and yet ultra low cost to produce and deliver. As Wolf-Hennig Scheider, a senior executive at the German company Robert Bosch (which supplied engine technology for the Tata Nano), noted, "Low-price vehicles are not vehicles of inferior quality equipped with the most basic components. They are inexpensive technical solutions produced using state-of-the-art components."[12]

There appears no reason to discount the possibility that within less than five years, a souped-up Nano meeting European safety, emission, and reliability standards could be in dealer showrooms in London, Paris, Milan, or Berlin at a price 25 to 30 percent below the least expensive European car. Carlos Ghosn, the combative and highly revered CEO of Renault and Nissan, appears to have concluded that fire must be met with fire. As he noted, "The challenge is to build a low-cost car that makes money. . . . And if Tata can do it, we can do it."[13] He has also concluded that it would be extremely difficult for Renault to overcome this challenge on its own: "They understand frugal engineering, which is something we aren't as good at in Europe or Japan."[14] By early 2008, Renault and Nissan were in serious discussions with India's Bajaj Auto to set up a three-way joint venture to produce an ultra-low-cost car first for the Indian market and later for export worldwide.

Despite the advantages of speed and access to already established local capabilities, the "joining forces" strategy comes with challenges. An acquisition can be costly and, if not integrated effectively, can prove to be a disastrous distraction. Similarly, a strategic alliance poses the challenge of aligning the vision, the goals, and the disparate capabilities of different companies. Given his track record at managing the alliance between Renault and Nissan, Carlos Ghosn has demonstrated that it can be done. However, considerable research indicates that strategic alliances between companies within the same industry (particularly when the "allies" have the potential to become global competitors) are risky and highly prone to conflicts and eventual dissolution.[15]

Leverage the Combined Power of China and India

The idea here is to pursue an integrated China+India strategy. Notwithstanding the rapidly growing economic integration between China and India, given the history of a brief war in 1962 and unsettled border disputes, there remains a certain degree of political tension between the two countries. Political leaders in both countries have expressed optimism that these disputes will eventually be resolved harmoniously. Yet any such resolution is still a few years away. Also, until they start working together and discover how much they have in common, most Chinese managers understand little about India, just as most Indian managers understand little about China. Thus, for at least the next five years, companies headquartered in countries outside China or India are likely to have an easier time pursuing an integrated China+India strategy than would generally be the case with emerging players from within China or India. In short, established MNCs may have considerable opportunity to leverage China+India to do battle with Chinese companies within China and globally, as well as the opportunity to leverage China+India to do battle with Indian companies within India and globally.

Cisco Systems provides a good example of a concerted attempt to pursue a China+India strategy to take on Chinese challengers such as Huawei Technologies in China, India, and globally. Founded in 1984 at Stanford University, Cisco is the undisputed global leader in networking solutions. As we noted in Chapter Two, it reported revenues of $35 billion in 2007, up 22 percent from 2006. Depending on market segment, Cisco's competitors included Juniper Networks, Nortel, Alcatel-Lucent, Nokia, Microsoft, and most significant, Huawei, a privately owned company with strong backing from the Chinese government.

Among its traditional competitors, Huawei was perhaps Cisco's toughest challenger. It was already a large company, with 2007 revenues of $16 billion, up 45 percent from 2006. At current rates of growth, Huawei's revenues could catch up with Cisco's within less than five years. Huawei was also a very global company, deriving 72 percent of revenues from outside China, and it had set up R&D centers in several locations, including Bangalore, Silicon Valley, Texas, Stockholm, and Moscow. Huawei enjoyed several sources of competitive advantage, notably:

- The ability to deploy almost half of its seventy thousand employees on R&D since, on a per person basis, Huawei's engineers cost only about 20 to 25 percent of their peers in the United States or western Europe.

- An early-mover advantage in leveraging the software engineering capabilities of India to complement its own hardware engineering capabilities in China; Huawei's largest software R&D center outside China was located in Bangalore with a staff of over fifteen hundred.

- A sourcing and production base in China, and thus much lower costs for the manufacture and assembly of its equipment.

- A passion for customer support. Our interviews with several of Huawei's customers and competitors uniformly yielded the observation that Huawei was almost maniacal in responding urgently to customers' queries and problems with a high degree of on-site engineering support.

- A gung-ho action-oriented and army-like culture that reflected the founder's background as an officer for the People's Liberation Army.

- An alignment between its lower-cost offerings and the rapidly growing needs of customers in emerging markets.

- Access to low cost and preferred financing from China's state-owned banks.

Huawei's strategic goals and trajectory seemed perfectly aligned with the government's explicitly stated policy to help Chinese companies emerge as global champions, especially in technology-intensive sectors.

Cisco's response to the challenge from Huawei has been to pursue a China+India strategy with a vengeance. In November 2007, Cisco announced a five-year $16 billion initiative for China that included ramped-up procurement from China, venture capital investment in China, the establishment of Cisco Networking Academies with a particular focus on central and western provinces being targeted by the government for accelerated development, an equity stake in and strategic alliance with the business-to-business player Alibaba.com, and plans to help China develop green technologies and its IT services sector. At the same time, Cisco has assigned a complementary role to its base in India. In December 2006, John Chambers announced it was setting up a second global headquarters in Bangalore. Wim Elfrink, executive vice president for global services, took on a second title, chief globalization officer, and relocated to India. The India initiatives also included a rapid ramp-up in Cisco's R&D staff there to about ten thousand people within three years. Importantly too, Chambers announced that within three years, 20 percent of Cisco's top leadership talent would be relocated to Bangalore and would carry out their global responsibilities from there. The Bangalore campus also makes it much easier for Cisco to work closely with all of the world's major IT services companies (including IBM and Accenture) because Bangalore is the global hub for them too. Most importantly perhaps, relocating a sizable proportion of global leaders to Bangalore makes it much more likely that Cisco will be able to understand the needs of customers in emerging markets more accurately, more comprehensively, and more proactively.

Protect Competitive Position in Markets Outside China and India

Finally, competing with the dragons and the tigers on the world stage also requires that the established multinational defend its position outside China and India—not just in other emerging markets but also in the developed markets of North America, Europe, and Asia. Notwithstanding their large size, China and India are not (and even fifty years from now, will not be) the only megamarkets in the world. China's population is about one-fifth that of the entire world and is likely to remain at roughly that level for the foreseeable future. Thus, even when China becomes richer and its per capita income catches up with that of the other countries, its GDP will still be only about 20 percent of world GDP. Also, as China becomes richer, its economy will become a mature, slower-growing economy. In short, even fifty years from now, it is a reasonable bet that 75 to 80 percent of the global demand for most products and services will be outside China. True, there will be some products and services where

China may account for a disproportionately high percentage of global demand. If so, then these high figures will be balanced by lower percentages in some other products and services. The same calculations apply to India.

Thus, if you are the leader of a company such as Boeing, Dell, or Cisco, you can take some comfort in the fact that over both the short and long terms, a dragon or a tiger would find it difficult to have privileged home country access to anything more than 20 percent of global demand. The remaining 80 percent will be outside the home market and will be up for grabs by whichever company is smarter at building and managing a globally integrated enterprise that is able to internalize the differentiated comparative advantages of various locations. There is no reason that the established multinational should cede any of this market to an aspiring global champion from China or India.

Of course, the strategies discussed earlier (neutralizing the home country advantages of the dragons and the tigers and leveraging the complementary strengths of China+India) are likely to play a critical role in helping the established multinational defend its competitive position in markets outside China and India. However, in its historical markets, the established multinational should also have other advantages that it could leverage, such as established relationships with distribution channels and customers, superior understanding of customer needs, and products, services, and solutions that are more tailored to local market requirements.

Conclusion

Over the next ten years, the global structure of most industries will undergo greater change than in the previous twenty. Reflecting this change, we predict that the list of the world's largest five hundred companies in 2020 will include a much more even mix of players from the United States, Europe, Japan, India, and China, as well as other large, emerging economies.

Not every established multinational of 2008 will make it from here to there. Some will get swallowed up by the rising dragons and tigers. At the same time, not every aspiring globalizer from China or India will succeed in realizing its ambitions. Some will stumble and wither away or get acquired by their compatriots or foreign multinationals. On either side (established multinational, or aspiring dragon or tiger), the odds will favor companies whose leaders combine an entrepreneurial orientation, a bias toward acting as if the future is already here, and sound analysis along the lines discussed in this chapter.

6

THE WAR FOR TALENT

Dealing with Scarcity in the Midst of Plenty

Trespassers will be recruited.

Sign on the walls of a software company in India

Finding people [in China] is easy. Finding the right
people is harder.[1]

Andy Cosslett, CEO, InterContinental Hotels Group

Between them, China and India account for 40 percent of the
world's population and about the same proportion of its workforce. The size of the labor force is not just large but has been
growing at a rapid rate. In 1990, the total number of working-
age people (those fifteen to sixty-four years of age) was 768 million in China and 501 million in India. By 2005, China's figure
had grown to 929 million and India's to 703 million.[2] The number of college graduates has gone up even more dramatically.
China produces over 5 million college graduates a year, more
than four times as many as ten years ago, and India produces
about 3 million college graduates, three times as many as in the
1990s.

Yet every survey and every interview with every executive
in both China and India paints a picture of massive scarcity.
Consider, for example, a recent report from three U.S. chambers of commerce in China. Finding, training, and retaining
top managers was rated by 37 percent of the 324 companies in
their survey as the number one operational challenge, ahead of

other issues such as corruption or piracy.[3] J. Norwell Coquillard, chairman of the American Chamber of Commerce in Shanghai, observed: "Demand for skilled, qualified staff still outstrips supply, and this key operating constraint shows no sign of easing in the near term."[4] In India, Nasscom, the National Association of Software and Services Companies, has estimated that by 2010, its industry would face a shortage of a half-million professionals. At any of the top five business schools in India, the entire class of graduating M.B.A.s is placed in less than four hours, a tiny fraction of the time that this process requires at the Harvard Business School. A growing number of CEOs, such as Sunil Bharti Mittal, chairman and managing director of Airtel, India's largest mobile operator, acknowledge publicly that it is often "cheaper to import managers" from the United States or Europe than to hire locally.[5]

In this chapter, we begin by looking at why there exists this scarcity in the midst of plenty in China and India. We then put forward guidelines about what a company might do to increase its odds at winning the ongoing brutal war for talent.

The War for Talent in China

The talent crunch in China is particularly severe at the senior management level, in certain industries such as financial services, in certain function areas such as accounting, and on the east coast.

Over the past five years, several discontinuous changes in the structure and dynamics of China's economy have sharply escalated the demand for managers. First, there has been a radical broadening in the China-focused agendas of multinational corporations (MNCs). Until even three to four years back, most MNCs viewed China primarily from the lens of low-cost manufacturing for export back to other markets. While low-cost manufacturing remains an important story, an increasing number of MNCs now view capturing the China market at least as, if not more, important. Companies such as IBM, GE, Cisco, and Microsoft have pulled out virtually all stops in their efforts to increase revenues from China by at least 30 percent a year, that is, three times the GDP growth rate. Add to that a growing recognition that notwithstanding concerns regarding intellectual property rights, China provides one of the world's two largest pools of science and engineering talent and that too at a fraction of costs in rich countries. Thus, China (along with India) has also become one of the two most important destinations for new R&D centers.[6] As MNCs intensify their efforts to go after market opportunities and talent in China, they are forced also to redouble their efforts to localize senior management. The need for local knowledge is far more critical when trying to capture local market opportunities and recruit and retain local talent than if the agenda is confined to assembly and export. According to *China Daily*, mainland-born executives made up only 3 percent of MNCs' senior teams in 1995. By 2005, the figure had gone up to 35 percent and was rising.[7]

Second, the Chinese government has embarked on an aggressive policy of consolidating, professionalizing, and at least partly privatizing state-owned enterprises (SOEs). Add to this an official "go global" campaign aimed at the larger SOEs and championed by the very top leadership, including President Hu Jintao and Premier Wen Jiabao. Larger, publicly listed, and more professionally managed companies with a mandate to pursue aggressive global expansion need a different breed of managers than the SOEs of yesterday did. According to a 2005 McKinsey & Co. report, globalizing Chinese companies will need seventy-five thousand senior managers by 2015 to 2020 against today's figure of only about three thousand to five thousand.[8]

Third, a growing number of domestic private sector companies are growing in size, going public, and poaching seasoned executives from established MNCs with both fat paychecks and sizable stock options. For example, David Wei, until November 2006 the president of B&Q China, a subsidiary of the British

DIY retailer Kingfisher, is now president of Alibaba.com, China's and, by some measures, the world's largest business-to-business auction company, which had a successful listing on the Hong Kong Stock Exchange recently. Similarly, Jun Tang, formerly president of Microsoft China, is now the head of Shanda Interactive Entertainment. As part of the move, Jun received 2.66 million options that could eventually be worth more than $100 million.[9] Given these developments, it is hardly a surprise that MNCs in China report a 30 to 40 percent turnover in senior executive positions.

In the financial services sector, private savings in China exceed $2 trillion. Given a lack of investment options and a stock market that was going nowhere (but down) until the end of 2005, virtually all of these funds were kept in bank accounts. Since then, liquidity on the Shanghai and Shenzhen stock exchanges has increased dramatically. Also, at the end of 2007, the Shanghai Stock Exchange composite index stood at above 5000 versus around 1150 at the end of 2005. The net result has been a flood of money pouring into China's capital markets. Assets managed by funds grew from $40 billion in 2005 to around $450 billion by the end of 2007. The implications of this growth on the demand for financial analysts, fund managers, and securities brokers are obvious.

Every segment of the financial services sector has seen similarly explosive growth. For example, as part of its World Trade Organization accession agreement, the Chinese government has begun to open up the banking sector to foreign banks. As a result, companies such as HSBC, Standard Chartered, Bank of East Asia, and Citigroup have been increasing their China staff by 30 percent or more annually. They need experienced staff who are also bilingual. It is impossible to develop these capabilities overnight.

In terms of functional skills, the shortage of accountants is particularly acute. Before the start of market reforms, the accounting system in China was based largely on Soviet-era fund-based accounting and was designed to inform state planners how the funds were being used and whether production quotas were being met. Western accounting concepts such as assets, liabilities, cash flow, profit margins, and return on investment were largely alien. Even today, almost thirty years after the start of market reforms, concepts such as bad debt provisions, asset impairment, and market-to-market accounting are still in the process of being understood and implemented.

In 1985, accounting standards based on international norms were established for the joint ventures that were beginning to be set up. In 1992, the Ministry of Finance issued a new set of standards for domestic companies. Known as the Accounting Standards for Business Enterprises, these were based on International Accounting Standards and adapted to local conditions. However, as a World Bank report noted, despite these reforms, the quality of domestic financial statements was insufficient for most international users.[10] In 2001, with backing from the World Bank, former premier Zhu Rongji helped set up the China National Accounting Institute, a boot camp for executives and accountants serving in the country's economic departments and state-owned companies. The institute currently trains about twenty-five thousand people a year.[11] At the opening ceremony, Premier Zhu called corruption cases covered by false accounting a "tumor" on China's economic order.

More recently, on February 5, 2006, the Ministry of Finance published a new set of accounting and auditing standards based on the International Financial Reporting Standard. The ministry also ruled that all companies listed on the Shanghai and Shenzhen stock exchanges must start complying with the new standards by January 1, 2007. Yet in an economy that is about one-quarter the size of the United States at market exchange rates (and about two-thirds as large when adjusted for purchasing power parity), the Chinese Institute of Certified Public Accountants has only 140,000 members. To make matters worse, only half of these are known to practice accounting.

If China were to have as many certified public accountants (CPAs) as the United Kingdom does on a per capita basis, it would need an estimated 5.3 million of them! While it is debatable whether any economy needs as many CPAs on a per capita basis as the United Kingdom, a widely held belief is that China needs at least 300,000. By some estimates, the country does have a large number of accountants: about 13 million. However, there is considerable question as to how knowledgeable many of them are about proper accounting standards.

China also faces a supply-side challenge rooted in its education system. Given a de facto prevalence of the "stuffed duck" syndrome (the more information you can stuff into the student, the better), there continues to be an excessive emphasis on rote memorization, imparting only theoretical knowledge rather than a balance between theory and application, and individual work rather than teamwork. Education is focused narrowly around passing the final examinations rather than internalization and application. This is true across virtually all disciplines, including professional ones such as engineering and business. Thus, graduates emerge with poorly developed skills at taking initiative, problem solving, and teamwork. Add to that an ongoing weakness in the English language. Despite a serious national campaign to improve English language skills, even in major cities such as Beijing and Shanghai, graduating students' English language skills continue to be extremely weak—barely passable in terms of speaking and understanding spoken English and thoroughly inadequate in terms of writing. In tier 2 and tier 3 cities, English language capabilities are even weaker. These characteristics imply that companies, especially MNCs, must be prepared to invest in additional training and development before the fresh recruits become fully productive.

During recent years, a growing proportion of Chinese professionals who had gone abroad for further studies have been returning to China (see Table 6.1). These returnees, often called

Table 6.1 Brain Drain Versus Brain Circulation (000s)

	2002	2003	2004	2005	2006
Number of Chinese students who went abroad during the year	125	117	115	119	134
Number who returned to China during the year	18	20	25	35	42

Source: *China Statistical Yearbook 2006*.

haigui, or "sea turtles," have played an increasingly important role in helping the Chinese economy, especially in jobs that require strong English language capability, bicultural skills, and deep understanding of how Western companies are managed. At the senior levels, Zhang Lin, the executive in charge of international business for Chery Automobile, is an excellent example. He went to the United States for a doctorate in engineering at the University of Michigan and then served as an executive with Chrysler for almost ten years before returning to China. Returnees have also played a visible role as the founders of some of China's high-technology start-ups—for example, Robin Li, the cofounder of Baidu, the leading Internet search provider in China, and Ge Li, the cofounder of Wuxi PharmaTech, the leading company from China in outsourced R&D for customers in pharmaceuticals, biotechnology, and medical devices. Robin Li earned a master's in computer science from the State University of New York at Buffalo and worked for Infoseek, a Silicon Valley start-up before returning to China. Ge Li earned a Ph.D. at Columbia University and was a member of the start-up team for a U.S.-based company before returning to China.

Notwithstanding the returnees' extremely important contributions to the Chinese economy, their numbers are small, so this phenomenon can do little more than have a marginal impact on the ongoing war for talent in China.

The War for Talent in India

The crunch for professional talent in India, which started becoming particularly severe around 2003–2004, has several contributing factors.

First, about five years ago, India's IT services sector started to acquire bulk. As the larger Indian companies (such as TCS, Infosys, and Wipro) have continued to grow at their historical 30 to 40 percent annual rate, each of them is now adding over ten thousand (more recently, over twenty thousand) professionals a year rather than just a few thousand. For example, in March 2002, Infosys Technologies employed fewer than eleven thousand people; as of mid-2008, the figure stood at over ninety thousand. In addition, some of the major international players have woken up and decided to take on the Indian players at their own game. Between 2003 and 2008, IBM and Accenture alone added over 100,000 professionals to their employee base in India. There have also been large expansions by the tier 2 and tier 3 Indian players, as well as other MNCs such as Microsoft, EDS, Capgemini, SAP, Oracle, GE, and Cognizant. True, India is a large country. However, whereas migration from the rural areas can increase the supply of unskilled labor rapidly, growing the supply of professionals is much stickier and takes longer. Aside from concerns over quality, even aggressive entry and ramp-up by private educational institutions also takes time to bear fruit. Thus, India's IT services industry has been soaking up science and engineering graduates from all fields—not just information technology, computer science, and electrical engineering. Companies in other industries have been left scrambling. As the head of HR at one of India's largest motorcycle manufacturers noted to us, "Visiting any of the top-tier engineering institutions was like going to the beach after a tsunami. There was nobody left." A running joke in one of the mining and metals companies is that it has become impossible for them to recruit engineers at India's mining schools because all of them get lured away by the IT sector for data mining tasks.

Second, around 2003–2004, India's economy started to go into overdrive, exhibiting a steady growth rate of not 6 to 7 percent a year but over 8 to 9 percent a year. Notwithstanding the branding value of the IT industry in helping India acquire an image of smart techies, it is a niche industry that accounts for only 5 percent of the country's GDP. Thus, the bulk of the growth rate in GDP over the past five years has come from two sources: the manufacturing sector, including industries such as steel, cement, autos, consumer goods, chemicals, paper, and infrastructure, and non-IT service sectors, such as financial services and transportation. Just as in China, a booming economy has meant rapid growth in real estate prices, the stock market indexes, the rate of savings and investment, and the consumption of a whole variety of goods and services: cars, health care, telecommunications, banking, consumer durables, and travel for business and tourism, among others. The Bombay Stock Exchange composite index (the Sensex) ended the year 2005 at just below 10,000. It closed 2007 at above 20,000. In short, over the past five years, India's IT sector has been taking in ever larger chunks of the country's science and engineering pool at the same time as the rest of the economy has started to grow rapidly and needs this talent.

Third, given a restructuring underway in many industries, major shortages have begun to appear even for positions that require training and skills in fields other than science and engineering. Retailing and construction are good examples. India today has the world's largest unorganized retail sector: a retail sector populated by small mom-and-pop operators. However, a retailing revolution has now kicked in and is in high gear. By some estimates, this industry alone is likely to need 2.5 million employees by 2010 whose tasks will be very different from those performed in a tiny family-owned shop. This workforce needs to be created and groomed from scratch. In construction, India's infrastructure today is where China's was in the early 1990s. Just as China's infrastructure boom started in earnest in 1995, India's is starting now, with the government planning to invest about $100 billion per year, or 9 percent of the GDP. This means that a company such as DLF, India's largest real estate developer, needs to hire an additional twenty thousand to twenty-five thousand semiskilled construction workers every year. Notwithstanding the large supply of labor in India, what the rapidly growing industries need is millions of workers who are not just willing but also professionally trained in tasks such as laying bricks, cutting and bending metal pipes and pieces, and carpentry.

Fourth, paralleling the story in China, MNCs have expanded the scope of their strategic agendas for India. India remains an attractive place for offshore IT and back-office work. However, it is now also a robust market that can be ignored only at the peril of corporate survival. For example, GE has targeted $10 billion in revenues from India by 2010, and companies such as Hyundai and Suzuki have made India the sole global hub for the production and worldwide export of subcompact cars. After China, India has also become the second most attractive location for the establishment of new R&D centers.[12] Finally, even as Chinese companies are on a rampage to go global, Indian companies have been outdoing their Chinese peers in acquiring major European and American companies such as the U.K.-based steel giant Corus and the auto marquees Jaguar and Land Rover, Germany-based wind turbine manufacturer REpower Systems, and the U.S.-based Novelis, the world leader in aluminum rolling and recycling. Given their fluency in the English language, much deeper and longer exposure to Western management ideas, a lifelong experience with private sector companies, financial and accounting savvy, and much greater ease at working horizontally across cultures, Indian managers have also been in high demand for regional (Asia-Pacific, emerging markets) as well as global positions in a growing number of non-Indian MNCs, including those from China.

Finally, as in China, the vast majority (estimated to be as high as three-quarters) of Indian college graduates suffer from a "last-mile unemployability" problem.[13] True, they are likely to be reasonably good at English—although with a thick accent. However, they are also likely to have focused too much on passing examinations rather than internalized learning and too much on theory rather than a balance of theory and application. They are also likely to lack skills at effective communication and professional comportment. These are remediable problems. However, without investment in the required training and development, the potential of this talent remains just that: a potential. As the *International Herald Tribune* noted rather astutely,

> The job market for Indian college graduates is split cleanly in two. With a robust handshake, a placeless accent and a confident walk, you can get a $300-a-month gig at Citibank or Microsoft. With a limp handshake, a thick accent and meek posture, you might peddle credit cards door to door for $2 a day. India was once divided chiefly by caste. But it is today divided just as starkly between those with the skills sought by the new economy of call centers and software houses, and those ensnared in the old economy by a lack of skills.[14]

Like their Chinese peers, returnee Indians have helped ease the talent crunch in highly important but niche roles, especially at senior levels in companies such as Accenture and IBM and as technology entrepreneurs and venture capitalists. As examples on the corporate side, look at people such as Harsh Manglik, chairman of Accenture India, and Inderpreet Thukral, vice president for strategy and business development at IBM India. Manglik graduated from the Indian Institute of Technology in 1970, earned an M.B.A. from Carnegie-Mellon, and spent over twenty-five years in leadership positions with IBM and Symantec before returning to lead Accenture's operations in India. Inderpreet Thukral graduated from India's University of Roorkee, earned a Ph.D. from Rensselaer Polytechnic Institute, and spent several years with IBM Global Services before returning to India to lead the strategy and business development function there. On the venture capital side, Vani Kola provides a typical and illustrious example. Kola earned an undergraduate degree in engineering from India's Osmania University, obtained a master's from Arizona State, and cofounded two software companies in Silicon Valley, RightWorks Corporation and Nth Orbit, before returning to India as a cofounder of NEA-IndoUS Ventures.

To sum up, although the total labor pool in India is large and is being aided by a growing pool of returnee Indians, major pockets of scarcity exist in virtually all professions.

Winning the War for Talent

Given the intensity of the war for talent, it is virtually impossible for any company to shield itself completely from the labor market reality. In particular, companies have little choice about staying in line with the market in terms of total compensation. Aside from compensation, however, companies do have the ability to influence the rate of attrition. In an industry or job function where the average turnover may be 20 percent, it matters greatly whether the turnover in a company is 10 percent or 30 percent. In a market with high turnover, it also matters greatly how effective and efficient a company is in managing the recruitment process. Thus, in this discussion, we take it as a given that companies generally have to be market competitive regarding compensation and focus on other variables in the HR value chain.

As depicted in Figure 6.1, our road map for winning the war for talent focuses on four domains: treating HR as a strategic function, smart recruitment, smart training and development, and smart retention. We discuss each of these in turn.

HR as a Strategic Function

There are at least three reasons why the human resources (HR) function must be regarded as more strategic in China and India

Figure 6.1 Action Domains for Winning the War for Talent

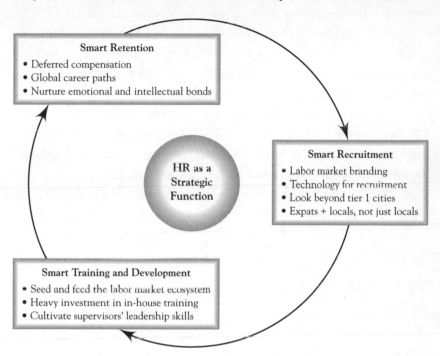

Smart Retention
- Deferred compensation
- Global career paths
- Nurture emotional and intellectual bonds

HR as a Strategic Function

Smart Recruitment
- Labor market branding
- Technology for recruitment
- Look beyond tier 1 cities
- Expats + locals, not just locals

Smart Training and Development
- Seed and feed the labor market ecosystem
- Heavy investment in in-house training
- Cultivate supervisors' leadership skills

than in most other countries. First, HR is likely to be dealing with much larger numbers and far more rapid growth. In its entire history, IBM had never added seventy thousand people to its rolls in five years as it has had to do in India. Second, these labor markets have very high turnover, which makes the HR function both more important but also more challenging. Third, given rapid growth and high turnover, the ratio of new employees to the existing employee base is likely much larger in China and India than in most other countries. Thus, the need for effective and efficient training and development is likely to be much greater.

Every company talks about HR as a strategic function; however, talk is not the same thing as reality. Two of India's leading companies that do understand this have leaders whose convictions are reflected in their actions. One is Infosys, India's second largest IT services company. In 2006, T. V. Mohandas Pai, voluntarily championed a move from his very successful role as the company's CFO to become the head of HR. In the IT services industry, human resources are far more critical than financial ones. Thus, in agreeing with Pai and reassigning him to manage HR, the company's leaders were making sure that they acted in line with business reality. Another company is the Aditya Birla Group, a $28 billion revenue diversified industrial giant that has been one of the leading globalizers from India. Dr. Santrupt Misra, the company's head of HR, is widely regarded as the right-hand man of the company's chairman, Kumar Mangalam Birla. Unlike most other HR executives, Misra is also a member of the company's board of directors.

Smart Recruitment

In the area of recruitment, a company can potentially create an advantage for itself in four domains: labor market branding, leveraging technology for recruitment, looking beyond tier 1 to consider tier 2 and 3 cities as possible locations for the company's operations, and ensuring that the local leadership team includes both local nationals and expatriates rather than just all local nationals or all expatriates.

Invest in Labor Market Branding. It is entirely conceivable that the mightiest of global companies may still be relatively small players in China or India. Toyota, the world's largest automaker, is not the largest auto company in either China or India. Similarly Wal-Mart, the world's largest retailer, is not the largest retailer (or even the largest foreign retailer) in China, and it is just entering India. Thus, business leaders need to remember that their company's existing brand value may not necessarily carry over from current markets into China or India. Also, brand value in the market for products and services is quite different for brand value in the market for talent. Even if a company has a highly visible product or service brand, it may still require tailored actions for labor market branding. Google in India provides an interesting example of the value of this branding. Landing a job at Google is known to be a plus in helping the young engineer, male or female, become a much more attractive catch in the market where the employer's visibility and job title are often as important as salary.

Accenture in India illustrates how ideas from product and service marketing can also be applied to labor markets. The company engages in fine segmentation of the labor market in order to develop a tailored strategy for each segment. The segmentation helps it plan campus visits and determine the specifics of its labor market campaign, including how much to spend and what messages to communicate to potential recruits through ads in movie theaters and coffee houses, sponsorship of rock concerts, and other channels. As with product and service marketing, Accenture also conducts research after the campaign to assess labor market brand awareness, brand attractiveness, and the like.

As part of labor market branding, here are some additional questions to ask: How often does the CEO visit China and India? How often is she or he interviewed by the local media? And how often do local managers visit college campuses, give talks, and serve as guest speakers?

Leverage Technology for Recruitment. Technology can serve as a potential basis for competitive advantage when the number of people to be recruited is large and the targeted individuals are technologically savvy. Both conditions apply in the case of large companies, such as IBM, Infosys, and Huawei, that need to hire thousands of technical graduates each year. In a typical year, Infosys, for example, receives over 1 million résumés. The company requires that the résumés be submitted online. Automated filtering whittles the number down to about 160,000. These applicants are notified by automated e-mail and invited to take an online test. This reduces the pool to about 80,000 applicants, who are then interviewed to determine which 20,000 to 25,000 or so should get the actual job offers.

When a company is dealing with such large numbers, its recruitment technologies are crucial. As in other contexts, however, a specific company's technology may be more or less effective and efficient than its competitors', thereby making a difference to competitive advantage. The power of technology can be leveraged not just to make the hiring process more effective and efficient, but also in the entire recruitment value chain: building awareness, giving targeted individuals a virtual peek into the company, and so forth.

Look Beyond Tier 1 Cities. The war for talent is most brutal in hot spots such as Bangalore and Shanghai. Tier 1 cities generally have the best infrastructure and the largest pool of qualified individuals. At the same time, however, they also feature the toughest competition for talent, the highest salaries, and the highest turnover rates. Thus, companies should give serious consideration to tier 2 (and possibly also tier 3) cities. Even in a highly developed tier 2 city, such as Dalian in China, salaries for professionals can be 30 to 50 percent lower than in Shanghai.

The case of how Intel made a successful move to central China illustrates well the advantages of looking beyond tier 1 locations. It also illustrates that capturing these advantages may require the company to nurture the local ecosystem from which it will draw the required talent. In 2003, Intel decided to set up its newest Chinese factory not in Shanghai, where its previous research and production operations were based, but in Chengdu, the capital of Sichuan province in central China. On the plus side, labor costs in Chengdu were 30 percent lower than in Shanghai, and the local government was happy to provide tax incentives. On the minus side, the region did not have a single high-tech factory, and Intel executives were concerned that other local companies were unlikely to be the best training grounds for their prospective workforce.

For the Chengdu plant, which would focus on labor-intensive assembly and test operations, Intel decided to "train most of its workers from scratch, including hiring fresh college graduates for 70% of its non-hourly positions, compared with 30% in all other locations."[15] In order to nurture the labor market ecosystem from which Intel would be hiring, the company's personnel visited local universities and vocational schools. They assessed professors and curricula and added courses on semiconductor physics and factory processes. Intel also bought the textbooks for some of the local schools. In an interesting example of partnership between Intel and local universities, a professor at the local University of Electronic Science and Technology of China even built a small factory in the classroom where students could practice assembly line operations and have their actions recorded and dissected for feedback and improvement. After recruitment, all employees were sent to existing factories in Shanghai, Malaysia, and Philippines for further training and acculturation. The acculturation included helping the new workers internalize Intel's culture of constructive confrontation by noting that the criticism focused on the problem rather than the person. Once the plant was up and running, it was benchmarked routinely against other plants in the company's global network. In 2006, the company was completing work on its second plant in Chengdu. In 2007, Intel announced that it would build a major chip set plant in Dalian, another tier 2 city, located on China's northeastern coast.

Hire a Mix of Expatriates and Locals. At the senior executive levels in China and India, salary differences between expatriates and local nationals have all but vanished. For this as well as other reasons, we believe that companies should prefer to build senior-level teams with a mix of expatriates and local nationals rather than go all the way toward complete localization (or, as is less often the case, a reliance on just expatriates). Preference for a hybrid team is likely to yield at least four benefits. First, it will ease the recruitment challenge by enabling the company to draw from a larger pool. Second, it will help integrate the activities in China and India with the rest of the global network. Given the growing importance of these two countries as platforms for worldwide competitive advantage, complete localization of senior management will run the risk of isolating these operations rather than integrating them more deeply into the global enterprise. Third, creating a hybrid team is likely to help accelerate the transfer of the company's core systems, processes, and values to China and India. Finally, including some expatriates on the senior management team is likely to help these executives develop a deeper understanding of the cultures, economies, and ground-level realities of China and India; they will take this knowledge back when they return home.

A hybrid senior team of expatriates and local nationals must ensure that the team includes the needed mix of capabilities and will function as a cohesive group that can make the right decisions at high speed, not an easy task. In China, we have come across far too many examples where an expatriate country manager recruited a senior team member from within China largely on the basis of good English language skills and good interpersonal chemistry—only to realize later that in terms of needed functional skills and relationships, the individual was basically useless. The reverse can also happen: smart, highly competent, and well-connected local nationals may be critical members of the local team; however, they may wonder why the China or India subsidiary needs an expatriate whom they regard as less competent and more expensive (if not in terms of salary, then in terms of the usual expatriate allowances such as housing and tuition benefits).

As part of recruitment and talent management, it is also important to make sure that there is an equally active reverse flow of executives. Thus, fast-track managers from China and

India must form an important part of the company's global talent pool to be deployed as expatriates to other countries, including other major global hubs.

Smart Training and Development

We put forward three guidelines with respect to training and development: nurture the labor market ecosystem within China and India, invest more heavily than the corporate average in in-house training, and cultivate supervisors' leadership skills.

Nurture the Labor Market Ecosystem. The brutal war for talent in China and India exists precisely because the supply of people with the required capabilities has not gone up at the same pace as the demand for them. Facing such a situation, a company has two options. It can take a reactive stance by waiting for the supply side to catch up and, in the meantime, poaching from competitors. Or it can take a proactive stance that is, seed and feed the ecosystem of colleges and universities that play the most central role in creating the needed supply. We believe that this proactive approach should be the preferred one for most medium to large enterprises. Nurturing the ecosystem is not free. However, a primary reliance on poaching from competitors may be even more expensive.

India's Pantaloon Retail provides a good example of how a company can proactively nurture the labor market ecosystem. Pantaloon Retail is India's largest retailer and is expanding at the rate of one new outlet per week. Organized retail is still a relatively new phenomenon in India; thus, retail companies face the massive problem of how to hire and train thousands of people every month—people who will view retailing as a "cool" sector to work in and who will be passionate and skilled enough to provide customers with the desired shopping experience. No other company faces this problem at a bigger scale than Pantaloon.

In 2003, Kishore Biyani, the company's managing director, started tackling the problem by establishing partnerships with a number of regional business schools such as the Welingkar Institute of Management (Mumbai), Indian Institute of Social Welfare and Business Management (Kolkata), and Chennai Business School (Chennai). Pantaloon helps shape the curriculum for a two-year master's degree in retail management and sends its senior staff as visiting faculty to help students understand the practical side of organized retailing. The company also sends about sixty of its own employees each year as students in these programs. Every employee who has been with the company for one year is eligible to apply. Screening and selection from this pool are done by an external vendor. For the employees, it is an excellent proposition. They get a two-year sabbatical and a master's degree, while the company pays their salaries as well as tuition fees. The eleven collaborating schools in this ecosystem graduate about seven hundred candidates each year. Pantaloon takes back its own cohort of sixty employees and hires about a hundred of the new graduates. The decision to hire only some of the graduates is deliberate: it enables Pantaloon to nurture a much larger number of retail management programs at business schools spread throughout India. Also, notes Sanjay Jog, the company's head of HR, "The courses will lose their credibility if we take the entire batch of students. We want other retailers to pick up candidates from our partnering institutes as well."[16] Pantaloon managers believe that this program, coupled with other initiatives, has played a major role in keeping its middle management attrition rate at 4 percent, a fraction of the industry average of 20 to 25 percent. For frontline staff also, the company's attrition rate is 8 percent, down from 12 percent four years back.

As a similar example from China, consider the case of IHG (InterContinental Hotels Group). IHG is the largest international hotel operator in China, considerably bigger than competitors such as Wyndham, Marriott, Hilton, or Starwood, and it is expanding rapidly within China. According to Andy Cosslett, the company's CEO, the biggest challenge is finding the right people. To help address the challenge, IHG has signed collaborative agreements with ten local schools that run hotel management programs. The company sponsors a special academy in these schools. Students who join the academy participate in IHG-tailored programs, where they learn about the company and its systems and processes. This enables these students to join IHG right after graduation. As Cosslett noted in a 2008 interview with *China Daily*, "We are supporting, training and sponsoring them and will hopefully get some of them overseas."[17]

Invest Heavily in In-House Training. In-house training serves as a critical complement to nurturing the external ecosystem. Last-mile unemployability is one of the major reasons for the scarcity of supply in China and India. There is no shortage of college graduates. However, most of them emerge with an abundance of theoretical knowledge but a paucity of skills at application, teamwork, and effective communication. China (more so than India) has the additional challenge of an education system and a culture that encourages obedience rather than speaking one's mind. These are all remediable weaknesses. However, they do require investment by the company in training and development. In many cases, such investment may be necessary also to impart company-specific technical skills and to help the new employees understand and internalize the company's values and norms of behavior.

Depending on the context, investment in training and development can range from the simple and inexpensive at one extreme to the complex and much more expensive (but still essential) at the other. An example of the simple and inexpensive kind is Cisco Systems's R&D center in Shanghai, established in 2005. By 2007, the center had grown to over five hundred researchers with an average age of twenty-seven. Jan Gronski, the center's managing director, recruited Chris Dong, his number two, from another company in China. Barring this and a few other exceptions, Gronski and Dong's strategy has been to hire talented but inexperienced researchers straight from universities rather than poach from competition. They have opened Cisco Clubs at three universities in China, which give students a chance to work with Cisco engineers. Gronski and Dong also run a management seminar every Thursday that addresses simple but essential behavioral skills such as how to share openly what is on your mind, how to make decisions, and how to make presentations. As Gronski noted, "I call it management kindergarten class."[18]

The Infosys Global Education Centre provides an example of the other extreme. Opened in 2005 in Mysore, a city about ninety miles from Bangalore in southern India, the center occupies 335 acres and is one of the world's largest corporate training centers. At the completion of an expansion phase currently under way, it will have 10,300 residential rooms, 500 faculty rooms, and the capacity to train over 13,000 professionals simultaneously. Often described as a "combination of Disney World, Club Med, and a modern American university,"[19] the center includes a bowling alley, a hair salon, an infinity pool, India's largest gym, a world-class cricket field, a 24/7 library, and a geodesic dome with three movie theaters. Its mission is to train the company's new recruits not just from universities within India but from every one of the company's geographies including the United States, Europe, and China. Infosys's recruitment philosophy is to hire for learnability rather than sheer technical skills. The company has long believed that it can turn most smart graduates into software engineers regardless of their academic background. A typical fourteen-week training program costs Infosys about five thousand dollars per person. Like the company's headquarters campus in Bangalore, the center is designed not just to achieve a serious intellectual agenda but also to leave a lasting psychological impact: a message that everything about Infosys is first rate and that the Infosys brand stands for the very best quality in the world.

While much of the training focuses on technical skills, part of the time is devoted to the development of soft skills such as interpersonal communication, team building, and body language. N. R. Narayana Murthy, the company's chairman and chief mentor, described the logic behind the investment in this center:

> Our industry, which is primarily based on good quality talent, has to ensure that the quality of the raw material, people, is very high. So, right from the beginning, we have realised that good quality human resources is a strategic resource for us. One of the biggest challenges before any company is scalability. How do you scale up in terms of numbers without losing quality, productivity, response time, value system and focus on cost control. So our Global Education Centre is a classical example of enhancing scalability.[20]

Invest in Supervisors' Leadership Skills. It is a well-accepted fact that how an employee is treated by the immediate supervisor plays a vital role in determining how motivated the person will be and how long he or she will stay with the organization. Given the scarcity of supply over demand, most companies in China and India find that people need to be promoted to supervisory positions at a younger age and with fewer years of experience than would generally be the case in the United States, Europe, or Japan. This reality demands that companies should invest in cultivating leadership skills among people who have been promoted to supervisory positions and will be managing others. The payoffs from this investment are likely to be large.

Smart Retention

Retaining the talent that you have worked diligently to hire depends on several factors, including whom you hire, how you hire, and what investment you make in their training and further development. We focus here on several additional measures targeted more directly at retention: deferred compensation policies, global career paths, and cultivation of deeper intellectual and emotional bonds between the individual and the company.

Offer Deferred Compensation Policies. Deferred compensation policies tie part of compensation directly to length of stay with the company. Depending on the specifics of the situation, deferred compensation can be designed in one or more of several ways: stock options that vest over time, subsidized loans for the purchase of a car or an apartment, and retention bonds. As an example of how retention bonds can be designed, consider the case of a U.S.-headquartered industrial products company that is one of the leaders in its industry worldwide. The company has a sizable presence in China in manufacturing, marketing, and sales. As the Shanghai-based director of HR for Asia-Pacific explained to us:

> We do a fair bit of management training. The programs can last anywhere from three to four weeks to even six months in some cases. For a three- to four-week program, taking into account the direct costs of training, hotel and travel expenses, and lost salary, it may cost us about twenty thousand dollars. I have a policy that if we send somebody for training abroad, the person must sign a two-year bond. If they leave before the two-year period, they must pay the company back what it cost us to send them for training. Also, if somebody does not want to sign a bond, then we will not invest in training them. In addition to this training-related bond, we have also signed two-year or three-year retention bonds with several of our key managers. If they stay through the bond period, they get a sizable bonus, which can be as high as 50 percent of annual salary.

Develop Global Career Paths. When they are thinking rationally (often but not always true), most smart professionals attach greater importance to long-term career success than short-term compensation. Through its policies, an MNC can help direct the attention of its high-potential staff members in China and India away from the local labor market and toward a global career path within the multinational enterprise. As is obvious, this requires that the MNC develop a systematic and highly visible program of treating its professionals within these two economies as not just local but also regional and global resources.

Depending on the business and the individual, globalization of the career path can be accomplished in either of two ways: assigning the individual to a posting in another country or keeping the individual within the home country (China or India) and changing the responsibility from a local to a regional or a global one. For example, at Goodyear, the U.S.-headquartered tire company, the managing director for the company's business in Turkey is an expatriate from India. Sriram Mangudi, Asia-Pacific head of HR for Timken, the U.S.-headquartered giant in bearings and related products, is an example of the latter. Mangudi joined Timken's operations in India. He remains based in Bangalore, but his HR responsibilities have recently been upgraded to cover the region rather than just India.

Nurture Emotional and Intellectual Bonds. Emotional and intellectual bonds refer to noneconomic ties that bind an employee to the organization. Emotional ties are a function of whether the employee views the company as a caring organization that is sensitive and responsive to the broader needs of not just himself or herself but also the society to which the individual belongs. Intellectual bonds are a function of whether the employee understands, agrees with, and likes the company's strategic direction and the opportunities that it provides for professional development. Following are some of the factors that can nurture emotional bonds:

- Is your company a fun place to work?
- Is your company as sensitive to local holidays and festivals such as Diwali (in India) or the Spring Festival (in China) as it is to, say, Christmas and New Year's Day?

- Does your company build a sense of community within its local organization, or do people remain purely as individual employees with no emotional ties to each other?

- Does your company go above and beyond its contractual responsibilities in times of personal emergency and distress for an employee?

- Does your company's agenda within China and India include making a contribution to the country's social needs, or is the agenda solely economic?

- Does your company see China and India as its permanent homes, or is it acting merely as a "foreign tourist" or "foreign trader"?

- In times of national emergency, such as the May 2008 Wenchuan earthquake in China, does your company respond with genuine caring, or is its response viewed as largely perfunctory?

Examples of factors that drive intellectual bonding include the following:

- Does your company share its vision and strategy for the global market (and the role that China or India plays in this strategy) with the employee base in these two countries, or do your employees operate largely in the dark with no sense for the bigger picture?

- Do your employees in China and India agree with and like the company's vision and strategy?

- Do the employees view your company as an organization that will help them acquire important and highly valued skills and capabilities, or do they view their current tasks as just a job to earn a living?

- Are the employees proud of the fact that they work for your company?

These are illustrative rather than comprehensive lists of factors that are likely to matter in cultivating emotional and intellectual bonds. Such bonds will not reduce the necessity of keeping compensation structure competitive with market conditions. However, they will almost certainly have a notable impact on how productive the employees are, how effective they are in drawing new talent to the company, and the company's attrition rate within China and India. The economic impact of advantages in these areas could well swamp any disadvantages from rising compensation levels.

Conclusion

Throughout history, rapid economic growth in every industry and every geographical region has always been a double-edged sword: vast opportunities but also brutal competition at both ends of the value chain: on the output side, where companies fight the battle for customers, and on the input side, where companies fight the battle for physical resources and people. As is widely and openly acknowledged, people are a company's greatest asset. However, for the same reasons, it is equally true, although rarely stated publicly, that people can also be a company's greatest liability. Which side of the balance sheet people belong to depends very much on how effective a company is at recruiting the right talent, nurturing it, and keeping it dedicated to building the company rather than moving on to its competitors. Given the scarcity of professional talent, this task is particularly challenging in China and India. In this chapter, we have looked at why and where the major pockets of scarcity lie in these two economies and proposed guidelines for improving the odds of winning the ongoing war for talent.

7

GLOBAL ENTERPRISE 2020

China and India are likely to fundamentally
reorganize the way production and trade are
conducted.[1]

—*Jeffrey E. Garten, former dean,*
Yale School of Management

The central thesis of this book has been that we are in the middle
of a fundamental transformation in the structure of the economic,
social, and political landscape around us. With each passing day,
the global economy is becoming increasingly multipolar and ever
more integrated. Consider the following:

- In recent years, over 50 percent of the growth in world GDP
  has come from emerging markets. China's GDP is expected
  to become the world's largest by around 2030 and India's the
  world's second largest by around 2045.

- In 2007, for the first time in history, the total deal size of
  emerging-into-developed economies was estimated to have
  exceeded that of developed-into-emerging economies. The
  hunted are fast becoming the hunters, and it is no longer
  obvious as to who may be the predator and who the prey.

- Emerging economies are becoming the fount of some radical
  innovations such as a three-thousand-dollar car, a three-
  hundred-dollar laptop, and a thirty-dollar cell phone. Bharti
  Airtel, India's leading cell phone operator, provides nationwide cell phone services at two cents per minute and yet has
  some of the highest profit margins in the world and a market
  capitalization of over $30 billion.

- In 2007, China was the third largest producer of motor vehicles in the world after Japan and the United States. It is expected to become the world's largest by 2015. During the eight years from 1999 to 2007, China accounted for 42 percent of the worldwide growth in the production of motor vehicles. According to Goldman Sachs, the total number of cars on the roads in China and India could rise from 30 million today to 750 million by 2040.

Most CEOs (and their senior colleagues) are well aware that the world's economic center of gravity is shifting from the developed to the emerging economies, in particular, China and India. Notwithstanding this general awareness, very few truly grasp the magnitude and pace of change and the multifaceted nature of the new reality. Fewer still have figured out what these developments mean for the future architecture of their company.

As with all other turning points, not every enterprise will make it from here to there. Established multinationals face a particularly acute competitive threat from new global players that have radically different capabilities, radically different mindsets, and radically different notions of speed, combined with easy access to global capital and global talent. In this chapter, we pull together the conclusions from our analysis and outline what the features of a global enterprise must be if it is to emerge as one of the winners ten years from now.

Analytical Building Blocks

There are four building blocks to our analysis: (1) rethinking global strategy, (2) rethinking innovation, (3) rethinking organization, and (4) globalization of the corporate mindset (see Figure 7.1). We accord a central role to corporate mindset because the cognitive biases of the senior leaders have a decisive impact on resource allocation and corporate direction.

Figure 7.1 Global Enterprise 2020: Analytical Building Blocks

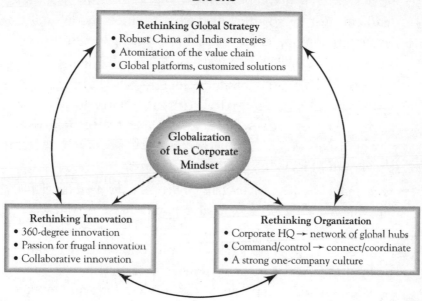

We analyze each of these building blocks in turn. Our underlying premise is that a company's global strategy, its approach to innovation, its organizational structure and processes, and the mindset of its senior leadership must always stay slightly ahead of changes in the external environment. It is when companies lead environmental shifts (and are coplayers in making them happen) that they are more likely to emerge as the rule changers and the new champions. Others run the risk of becoming roadkill.

Rethinking Global Strategy

The new global reality demands a zero-based rethinking of the answers to three of the most central questions pertaining to global strategy:

- *What market position must we achieve and sustain within our industry on a worldwide basis?* Embedded in this broader question are subquestions such as: What should we deem to be our strategic markets? What target opportunities in these markets must we go after? And what business models must we design and implement to realize these opportunities?

- *How should we globalize our resource base?* For any resource (research laboratories, production centers, sales units, and so forth), globalization refers to the number and choice of locations where resources will be based. Decisions regarding the global dispersion of a company's resources flow directly from the design of its value chain architecture.

- *How should we manage the tension between the need for global integration and the need for local responsiveness?* At one extreme, the choice may be to offer a globally standard mix of products and services (for example, commercial aircraft by Boeing). At the other extreme, the choice may be to offer locally tailored products and services for every market (for example, ice cream by Unilever).

These questions lead to the following three imperatives for the rethinking of global strategy.

Robust (Not Surface-Skimming) China and India Strategies

By our estimates, less than one-tenth of the world's five hundred largest companies have even close to a robust strategy for either China or India, let alone both. By *robust strategy*, we mean a strategy that is fundamentally market driven (What do the customers in China and India need?) rather than product driven (How can we sell our current products and services in China and India?).

Consider the case of a Fortune 500 company in the services industry with over $10 billion in 2007 revenues. It derives over 75 percent of its revenues from the United States and Canada. Yet by most estimates, over 80 percent of the market for this company's products and services is outside North America. While the

U.S. market is largely mature, that in emerging markets (especially China and India) is growing at over 20 percent a year. When senior executives at this company analyze the global market, the question they ask is, "How large is the market for our U.S.-based products and services, especially those that provide the bulk of our revenues and profits?" What they overlook is that in their industry, much of the market opportunity in China and India is for ultra-low-cost products and services that must be conceived, designed, and manufactured within these markets. Cloning or mere adaptation of U.S.-based products and services does little more than skim the surface of the vast opportunities in these emerging epicenters.

Contrast this with the approach that Deere & Co. took. A few years back, Deere's Agricultural Equipment division initiated a complete redesign of its strategy for India and other emerging markets. Previously Deere had viewed India predominantly from the lens of its existing U.S.-based products: large, technologically advanced, and very expensive machines designed for large American farms. Not surprisingly, executives had concluded that the market for their products in India was very small and had assigned India a relatively peripheral role in the company's global strategy.

Our discussions with a senior-level strategy group focused on two central questions: (1) How does Deere define its business: as a supplier of "large 100+ horsepower tractors" or as a supplier of "agricultural equipment"? (2) How large is the current and future market for agricultural equipment in India that may be smaller in size and horsepower and may not look anything like the company's machines for the U.S. and other developed markets? Discussions around these questions revealed that the company's global strategy had been driven too much by a product-centric mindset and not enough by a market-centric mindset. These discussions also led to Deere's decision to upgrade its engineering center in India and give the Indian subsidiary the needed autonomy and resources to design and manufacture products for the Indian as well as other emerging markets. Since then, Deere's India-made tractors (the 5003 series) have proved to be popular with farmers in India and other emerging markets. To its surprise, Deere has discovered that these small, very basic, low-horsepower, highly maneuverable, and inexpensive tractors (with a starting price of $14,400) are proving to be popular as well with hobby farmers in the United States.[2]

The markets in China and India are not just large and rapidly growing but also radically different from those in the developed countries. Selling the same or defeatured versions of existing products and services does little more than skim the surface of the market opportunities. The winning corporation of tomorrow needs instead a robust strategy that stays within the bounds of the company's business domain ("beverages" for Coca-Cola, "hospitality" for Marriott, and "agricultural equipment" for Deere) but is market rather than product driven.

Atomization of the Value Chain

Go back only about thirty years, and for most firms, global expansion meant a clear choice between either of two strategies: export from home (as Toyota, Sony, and IBM did) or produce locally to sell locally within each foreign market (as Procter & Gamble and Unilever did). The former strategy made sense if scale economies were very high and tariff and transportation costs low relative to total costs. In such cases, virtually all elements of the value chain were concentrated in the home country. The latter strategy made sense when scale economies were low and tariff and transportation costs prohibitively high. In such cases, virtually the entire value chain was replicated in each market. Either way, other than sourcing of raw materials and distribution of finished goods, virtually all elements of the value chain were colocated in the same country and often on the same corporate campus.

Today's reality is vastly different. For a Hong Kong–based apparel supplier, fulfilling an order for a U.S. or European retailer can mean that the fabric may be woven in China, the fastenings may be sourced from South Korea, and the actual sewing may be done in Guatemala or Vietnam. A PC company can now source hardware and software components from twenty countries, conduct assembly operations in five countries, and sell the finished laptops in over two hundred countries. A physician in Boston can order an MRI scan on a patient after midnight and, if needed, have a highly experienced radiologist based in Bangalore send back a reading of the image within minutes. An architectural firm based in New York can do the overall design for a building in Manhattan and have the engineering details of the piping, plumbing, and electrical wiring drawn up by a subsidiary in Shanghai.

This trend toward atomization of the value chain will continue and become more finely grained. Communications technologies are rapidly becoming more user friendly and less expensive. Next-generation communications technologies are almost certain to bring high-fidelity video telephony to the mobile phone rather than just a laptop. These developments will make it increasingly crucial for companies to push the envelope in terms of an increasingly finer disaggregation of the value chain and an optimization of the choice of locations for individual activities, subactivities, and even sub-subactivities. Also, as the relative competitiveness of locations shifts over time, companies will need to be increasingly flexible in shifting the operational base of specific activities. William Amelio, Lenovo's CEO, has termed this approach to running the company *worldsourcing*. Amelio is right on the mark. An ever greater commitment to worldsourcing will be one of the defining features of tomorrow's global corporation.

Global Platforms, Customized Solutions

Some of the earliest literature on globalization argued that the future would belong to companies that offered globally standardized products. The assumption was that the world is moving toward a converging commonality and that a strategy of global standardization would enable the company to deliver advanced, functional, reliable, and low-priced products.[3]

We disagree completely and predict that the end game in glo-balization will be extreme customization, not extreme standard-ization. Ask any serious observer (the World Bank, International Monetary Fund, or Goldman Sachs) to define *globalization* and the answer will be that globalization refers to integration across countries.[4] Integration is a fundamentally different concept from homogenization. As we look ahead, the world economy will be far more integrated than it is today. At the same time, people will demand and be able to buy, at reasonable prices, more, not less, customized products and solutions than we do today.

The Left Foot Company based in Helsinki, Finland, provides an interesting example of the shape of things to come. As the company notes on its Web site, "You can get a pair of made-to-measure left® shoes, manufactured from high quality materials that you have selected, delivered to your door. Once your feet have been scanned at a left®foot company outlet and you have signed in to our system you can order new shoes via our web pages." The company is headquartered in Helsinki, relies on assistance from a shoe design firm based in Italy, sources the scan-ner from Germany, has a factory in Estonia, and sells through affiliated stores in several European countries, as well as Japan, Hong Kong, and Malaysia. This approach to selling customized shoes would be impossible without the combined power of tech-nology and globalization.

Our prediction regarding extreme customization as the future reality rests on two premises. First, heterogeneity within and across countries (in buying power, cultural norms, hab-its, language, climate, body shape and size—you name it) will remain an enduring feature of humanity for many decades to come. Even as buying powers converge across countries, given the side effects of capitalism, large income and wealth disparities within countries will remain a permanent feature of virtually all societies. Aside from buying power, look also at the cultural reality of societies. With each passing day, the United States, Europe, India, and China are becoming more (not less) multi-cultural with a growing number of subcultures.

Figure 7.2. How Technology Reduces the Cost of Customization

Absolute cost reduction because of more comprehensive optimization of location

Flattening of the curve because of better ability at (and reduced costs of) customizing

Cost per Unit

Extent of Customization

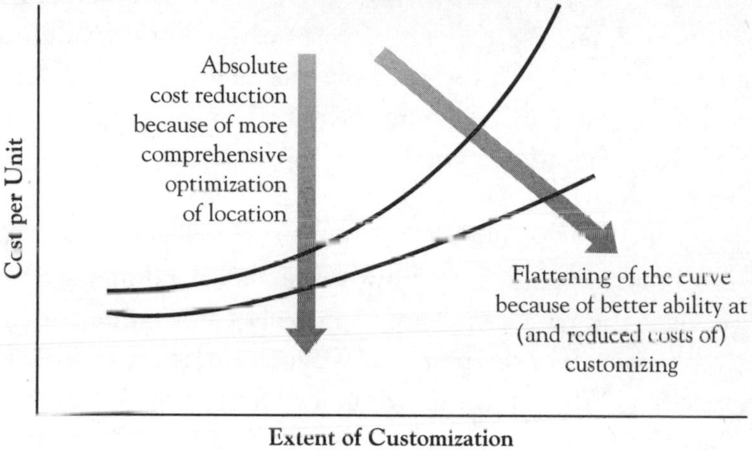

Second, as illustrated by the Left Foot Company (and depicted in Figure 7.2), developments in information, communications, and manufacturing technologies are rapidly reducing the cost of customization. This is already evident in the ability of individuals to customize—at near zero cost—the PC they buy, the first Web page they see, and the news they get. Over the next decade, it will start becoming evident in other goods and services, such as the medicines they take, the books they read, the clothes they wear, and the cars they drive.

Large emerging markets such as China and India are not just very different from those in the United States and Europe, they are also vast and internally diverse. There is no such thing as an average Chinese consumer or an average Indian consumer. Thus, the winning corporation of tomorrow will have to be a master at the art and science of fine segmentation and mass customization. Technologies and platforms are and will become increasingly global. In a seeming paradox, it is the very globalization of technologies and platforms that will enable companies to offer extremely customized and yet low-cost products, services, and solutions that will vary not just across individual customers but also from today to tomorrow.

Rethinking Innovation

Innovation is best defined as the "production or emergence of a new idea."[5] We use this term to stand for both an outcome (the new idea) and a process (how the new idea emerged). It is hard to imagine any issue more central to society than innovation. All adaptation, whether evolutionary or revolutionary, requires innovation.

Applying the imperative of innovation to innovation itself suggests that how companies must think about and manage innovation over the next ten years is unlikely to be similar to what they have done over the past ten. We focus on three of the major differences: (1) the rapidly growing need for pervasive innovation in all activities and at all levels of the organization; (2) the rapidly growing need for innovation that economizes on raw material and energy use, minimizes the environmental impact of the company's products and processes, and yields products and services that are ultra low cost; and (3) the rapidly growing need for companies to work across interfirm boundaries—that is, in collaboration with other firms—to develop new products, processes, and solutions.

360-Degree Innovation

At least three major forces are causing a steady decline in the half-life of technologies, products, services, processes, and even entire business models. The first is the ongoing march of technology, which continues to advance at an exponential rate. In 1990, if you wanted to buy a book, you had to walk to a brick-and-mortar store. By 2000, you could order one over the Internet, and it would be delivered to your home in three to five days. Today you can order it as an e-book and have it delivered instantaneously to your PC, PDA, or even a cell phone. Tomorrow, a book may be something entirely different from today's static product, which is updated, if at all, once every few years by the author. It may be a dynamic product where you and others like you serve not just as readers but also as ongoing cocreators of and even characters in the story. The impact of rapid technological advancement is evident all around us: in autos, pharmaceuticals, clothing, and even the lowly toothbrush.

The second force is the all-around transparency imposed by the Internet. A company's actions are becoming increasingly visible to almost every stakeholder—customers, competitors, suppliers, shareholders, employees, alliance partners, the community, governments, and social activists—in real time. A direct result has been that barriers to competitive imitation have rapidly gone down even as companies are now scrutinized and held more accountable by more stakeholders more frequently. Not surprisingly, the tenure of CEOs the world over is on a steady decline. As the Internet continues to become more powerful, the ability to hide will decline even more. The only salvation will be an accelerated pace of innovation.

The third force is the emergence of new competitors from nontraditional countries: competitors that bring different capabilities (such as significantly lower-cost structures and larger pools of R&D talent), are very ambitious, and are comfortable moving at great speed. The processes that have resulted in the emergence of such new champions (Cemex, SABMiller, ArcelorMittal, Tata Motors, Lenovo, and Huawei Technologies) are still in the early stages. As these processes gather momentum, we should see a cascading effect.

Given these trends, tomorrow's global enterprise will have to figure out how to make innovation an always-on and 360-degree pervasive activity. It will not be confined to the company's R&D labs. Even mundane activities such as cleaning the office floor and ensuring security at the office entrance will require a passion for innovation. Might we put carpets or vacuum systems at the entrance that remove well over 90 percent of the dirt from people's shoes as they enter the building? What newer technologies could we invent or acquire that reduce security risks while also cutting waiting times and making the entrance to the building a more pleasant experience? Given the pressure to save every penny and every ounce of raw material, asking questions such as these will need to become a central responsibility of not just people in the skunk works but everybody, including the janitor, the receptionist, and the sales representative.

A Passion for Frugal Innovation

By *frugal innovation*, we mean innovation that strives to create products, services, processes, and business models that are frugal on three counts: frugal use of raw materials, frugal impact on the environment, and extremely low cost. The rapid rise of emerging markets (with China and India as the central players) is once again the prime mover behind the critical need for all three types of frugality.

Take global warming. Two of the biggest contributors to global warming are emissions from cars and, perhaps surprisingly, buildings that need to be kept well lit and comfortable: cool in the summer and warm in the winter. Look now at the impact of China and India in these two areas. In 1999, motor vehicle production in China was barely 14 percent of that in the United States. By 2007, it had jumped to 82 percent. In 2007, China added more square meters of urban floor space than all of the developed countries combined. India is behind China by about ten to fifteen years, but it is following a similar path. As economic development in both countries spreads to the countryside, these trends are not likely to abate. In fact, the numbers will become much larger. No wonder, then, that the price of almost every commodity has risen sharply over the past ten years and that China and India have become two of the biggest contributors of greenhouse gases into the air that we breathe.

It is unlikely that for the sake of lifestyles in the developed world, China and India will decide to put brakes on their own growth. Instead, what we will witness is a rapid shift from products, services, and processes that are energy inefficient, raw material inefficient, and environmentally inefficient to those that are. Companies that take leadership on these fronts on a worldwide basis are likely to find it easier to preserve and increase their global market shares at the expense of those who spend their time lobbying governments to ease up.

Note also that over the next twenty years, the bulk of the absolute growth in market demand for most products and services will occur at the middle- and low-income levels in the big emerging markets. Winning these megamarkets will require that products and services also be ultra low cost. The Nano, the twenty-five-hundred-dollar car introduced by India's Tata Motors in January 2008, is a leading example of such frugal innovation.

A passion for frugal innovation will become increasingly essential not just for companies that sell consumer products and services but also for those that are purely in business-to-business domains such as Nokia Siemens Networks (NSN), Ericsson, and IBM. Bharti Airtel is the world's lowest-cost provider and India's market leader in cell phone services. Its ingenuity lay in devising a new business model for mobile telephony that relied heavily on outsourcing all network operations (to NSN and Ericsson) and all business support services (to IBM). For this business model to succeed, it was essential that companies such as NSN and Ericsson depart from their traditional practices and agree to get paid for network operations on a per minute basis rather than for selling and installing the equipment. In short, the Bharti Airtel model works because all of the players (NSN, Ericsson, IBM, and Bharti Airtel itself) are committed to frugal innovation.

Over the coming decade, companies such as GE, which must help hospitals in Beijing and Kolkata provide better care at a lower cost; Otis, which must provide lower-cost and more energy-efficient elevators and escalators for tomorrow's Mumbai; and Carrier, which must keep buildings in Guangzhou and New Delhi cool in the summer, will have no choice but to become ever more passionate about frugal innovation. Otherwise the market will move to companies that are.

Collaborative Innovation

The disaggregation of value chains coupled with greater outsourcing means that even as companies become more global and more diversified, they are becoming more focused regarding what they manage within their own boundaries. In short, companies are becoming embedded in ever larger interfirm networks. In 2003, P&G's revenues were only $43 billion. By 2007, barely four years and several acquisitions later, its revenues had grown to $76 billion. Thus, by 2007, P&G had a more diversified portfolio and deeper presence in more countries. Yet at the same time, P&G outsourced a greater percentage of its manufacturing operations and a greater percentage of its business support services.

The growth in outsourcing is being fueled by a combination of more intense competition plus developments in information technology. As companies become subject to the transparency brought about by the Internet and as barriers to imitation and new entry decline, companies find themselves facing more intense competition. Consequently, the penalties from internalizing any activity that somebody else can do better, cheaper, or faster have gone up. As a complementary development, the growing power of information technology is making it possible to accurately measure and effectively coordinate increasingly complex interfirm transactions.

The trend toward disaggregation will continue. Companies will find that the features, quality, performance, and price of their end products will depend increasingly on the decisions and actions of their business partners on all sides of the value chain. Thus, unless companies become masters at the art and science of collaborative innovation, they will find themselves playing just a commodity game within some other player's differentiated business system.

Disaggregation of the value chain is not the only factor that will make collaborative innovation increasingly important. Other factors are the rapid integration of multiple technologies into the same product, service, or process and a growing external market for proprietary intellectual property. Look at the integration of multiple technologies. Today's PC is not just a computing and office productivity device; it has also become a source of multimedia communication, information, and entertainment. Today's cars have largely become computers on wheels. Today's books need to be published and made accessible not just in paper-based formats but also in many different types of digital formats. And it may not be long before contact lenses may come embedded with medications so that those who use these lenses can both see better and become healthier in the process. As disparate technologies come together into a single product, service, or process, companies will find that no matter what their size, they do not have the mastery of all of the essential technological puzzles. Directly relevant innovation will increasingly take place outside the firm's boundaries or collaboratively at the interfaces between firms.

The final driver of the move toward reliance on external innovation is the emergence of increasingly sophisticated markets for proprietary intellectual property such as patents and trademarks. Intellectual Ventures is a company founded in 2000 by Nathan Myhrvold (until then, chief strategist and chief technology officer at Microsoft) and Edward Jung (until then, chief architect and advisor to the executive staff at Microsoft). It has emerged as one of the major players in creating a liquid market for patents that often remain buried and unused in corporate vaults.

Rethinking Organization

Every company's organization is an ecosystem that consists of complementary elements such as structure, processes, and culture that work together to drive the company's decisions and actions. We identify three of the most important ways in which tomorrow's global corporation will need to be different from that of today: (1) a reengineering of the company's worldwide corporate headquarters from a single location to a network of global hubs that are situated in a small number of carefully selected locations; (2) a shift in how the company is managed—from a command-and-control model to connect-and-coordinate model; and (3) an ever greater need to cultivate a strong one-company culture that provides the intellectual, social, and psychological glue to bind a geographically dispersed staff into a cohesive body.

Network of Global Hubs

Among the world's five hundred largest corporations, we regard Cisco Systems as one of the top five that are at the leading edge in trying to figure out what the global enterprise of tomorrow must look like. Here is what Wim Elfrink, chief globalization officer and executive vice president of Cisco Services, recently said about the impending "virtualization of the corporation":

> The tradeoff between the intimate but inefficient old-world organization and the hyper-efficient but impersonal modern organization is on the verge of extinction. Today, the increasing pervasiveness of broadband networks have facilitated the slicing and dispatching of corporate functions around the globe. . . . The ability to be both dispersed and close will encourage a transformation from today's typical client-server corporate model, in which a central headquarters is linked to various satellite offices, to more of a peer-to-peer network. This translates into an extraordinary cultural shift . . . and possibly from the very idea of a corporate headquarters.[6]

We agree entirely with Elfrink. Legacy notions of corporate headquarters will undergo a transformation over the next ten years. Even in the case of most U.S.-headquartered companies, where the historical home market will remain the world's largest for the next couple of decades, the locus of market opportunities and major functions will shift rapidly. Today the United States accounts for only 25 percent of the world's GDP, only 10 percent of growth in world GDP, and only 5 percent of the world's population. With each passing year, all three numbers are falling. Thus, for any company that wants to emerge or stay as one of its industry's global leaders ten years from now, it is imperative that the center of gravity of its marketing and sales efforts, its manufacturing operations, and even its R&D activities shift sharply to other countries. We do not suggest that the role of the United States will somehow cease to be unimportant. Far from it. We do believe, however, that even for today's so-called American companies, U.S. operations will have to be viewed not as the mother ship but as one of five to ten major global hubs. Similar transformations will be required of companies such as Toyota, Nissan, Siemens, and Daimler that we view today as "Japan-centric" or "Germany-centric." Companies that resist such transformation will do so at their own peril.

What will replace the old-fashioned mother ship based in Armonk, New York, or San Jose, California? Some observers have proposed that the new global architecture will consist of regional hubs (say, North America, South America, Asia, Europe, and so forth); in such an architecture, each regional hub would have all of the resources and decision-making power to manage all operations within its region. With due respect to the proponents of such a view, we disagree. The world economy is becoming not only increasingly multipolar but ever more globally integrated. IBM's procurement operations in China serve the company's global needs, not just those in Asia. Similarly, IBM's global delivery centers in India serve the needs of its clients worldwide and not just those in Asia. Microsoft's research center in Beijing is a global hub for the development of next-generation user interfaces for the global market and not just China. These are only a few of countless examples that will multiply over the coming ten years. The last thing that the global enterprise of tomorrow should do is to become a federation of regional fiefdoms.

Instead, what will be needed is the creation of a small number of global, not regional, hubs, each situated in a carefully selected location. Some of the central criteria for these locations will be (1) physical proximity to the global epicenter of that particular function or line of business; (2) attractive and safe living conditions for senior executives and their families, who will spend much of their time living in and working out of these global hubs; and (3) world-class connectivity in terms of both telecommunications infrastructure, as well as airports and flights so that the executives based at these hubs can stay connected with their peers as well as external partners in other locations with the least amount of wasted time and effort.

IBM, Nokia, Cisco, Lenovo, and Infosys provide some early examples of companies that are transforming the central corporate headquarters into a network of carefully dispersed global hubs. In October 2006, IBM moved the office of its chief procurement officer, John Paterson, to Shenzhen, China. The company noted in its announcement of the move:

> The decision . . . marks the first time the headquarters of an IBM corporate-wide organization has been located outside the U.S. This move illustrates a shift underway at IBM from a multinational corporation to a new model—a globally integrated enterprise. . . . In a multinational model, many functions of a corporation were replicated around the world—but each addressing only its local market. In a globally integrated enterprise, for the first time, a company's worldwide capability can be located wherever in the world it makes the most sense, based on the imperatives of economics, expertise and open environments.[7]

In the case of Nokia, the corporate headquarters and the CEO's office are in Helsinki. However, Richard Simonson, the chief financial officer, is based in New York City, one of the world's top two financial centers. Finally, take the case of Cisco. In December 2006, Wim Elfrink, executive vice president for Cisco Services, relocated to Bangalore, the world's epicenter for IT services. Although Elfrink is based in India, his responsibilities remain entirely global.

From Command-and-Control to Connect-and-Coordinate

How the emergence of the commercial Internet has transformed markets and enterprises has been well documented.[8] We focus here on how the more recent Web 2.0 technologies will reshape the way global enterprises are managed.

For corporations, Web 1.0 was mainly about making transactions more efficient. Companies could book an increasing proportion of orders over the Internet largely by customers themselves. Employees too could engage in a greater degree of self-service, particularly for routine matters such as checking the company's policy about annual vacations or keeping track of their stock options. And suppliers could engage in more real-time coordination between customer needs and their own production and logistics schedules.

In contrast, the thrust of Web 2.0 developments (such as online social networks, Wikipedia, podcasts, and blogs) is predominantly about collaboration. On top of these Web 2.0 innovations, recent years have also witnessed major developments in communications technologies. Examples on the consumer side include Skype and Yahoo Messenger, which permit zero-cost real-time audio-video communication between any two individuals in the world as long as they are connected to the Internet. Examples on the corporate side include technologies such as Cisco's TelePresence, which enables people to interact and collaborate with others in remote locations using life-size, high-definition video and audio with fidelity so high that one can almost "feel" the other person's presence.[9]

Given the pace of advances in communications technologies, it is hard to speculate what Web 3.0 and Web 4.0 technologies may look like. However, looking at the collaboration capabilities already unleashed by Web 2.0 technologies, it is clear that the global enterprise of tomorrow would have to be managed predominantly by a horizontal connect-and-coordinate model rather than a hierarchical command-and-control model. The impact of the new collaboration technologies is likely to be particularly profound on knowledge-intensive and creative tasks where coordination is not constrained by the delays currently inherent in the movement of physical goods.

Combining the growing power of collaboration technologies with the fact that knowledge workers are becoming almost like free agents who stay with any particular organization for increasingly shorter tenures (or may literally be free agents who sell their services on a contractual basis to any buyer) leads to some interesting insights. Could it be that as key knowledge workers become free agents, the competitive advantage of the enterprise will derive less from the individuals who "work for it" than from the technological and social mechanisms that the company deploys to transform individual knowledge and skills into a collaborative product, service, or solution?

A Strong One-Company Culture

As companies become geographically more dispersed, the need for tight integration across organizational subunits will increase rather than go down. No CEO ever wants to have things go out of control and let chaos reign. It is only when leaders are confident that the company will not fall apart that they are comfortable in pushing the envelope in creating a distributed organization with roots in many countries. GE, IBM, Cisco, P&G, and Nokia are some of the leading examples of how a global enterprise that is ready for tomorrow ought to be run. Each of these companies has a strong culture that defines what they believe in, who they are, and what makes them different from and superior to their competitors.

Building a strong one-company culture (one with widely shared and internalized core values, beliefs, and behavioral norms) does not mean a lack of diversity. P&G operates in almost every country and has a large portfolio of brands, none of them called P&G. Yet you could go to any corner of the P&G empire, and CEO Alan Lafley would hope that you should get the same answer to key questions such as what the job of a brand manager is, why we should win in the marketplace, what the two moments of truth are, and so forth.

The push for a strong corporate culture while operating in a world of enduring heterogeneity across national cultures requires deliberate and sophisticated decisions about what constitutes the "core" and what the "context" with regard to corporate culture. For example, as Toyota set up factories in the United States, it wisely concluded that most aspects of the manufacturing culture in its Japanese factories were a core part of its corporate culture and that the last thing it should do is to emulate the historical manufacturing culture of the U.S. auto industry. At the same time, it knew that it would be ridiculous to have each day in a San Antonio factory start with Shinto prayers. The four basic rules (pertaining to how people work, how people connect, how the production line is constructed, and how to improve) that guide Toyota's production system are part of the core.[10] What religion people believe in, what food they like to eat, or what language they speak are part of the context.

Cultivating a strong one-company culture requires paying attention to investing in corporate infrastructure: the communications and IT infrastructure, the HR infrastructure, the intellectual infrastructure, and the emotional infrastructure. A strong corporatewide communications and IT infrastructure ensures that people have easy access to and the ability to communicate with others within the enterprise. A strong HR infrastructure ensures that there are no glass ceilings and that anybody anywhere in the world has an equal chance for training, development, and career advancement. A strong intellectual infrastructure ensures that people share the same worldview, the same strategic priorities, and the same corporate lingo (which may be jargon to outsiders but enables people within the company to communicate with each other efficiently without loss of content). Finally, a strong emotional infrastructure ensures that people take pride in the global enterprise, identify with it, and are willing to engage in voluntary extra-role behavior that goes beyond what is minimally required by formally defined job specifications.

It is the reality of a strong infrastructure that makes it easy for a company such as P&G to appoint an Indian male as the general manager of its beauty care business in China without fear of failure or to take a high-end facial cream, SK-II, developed by its Japanese subsidiary and roll it out globally.

Globalization of the Corporate Mindset

The term *mindset* refers to the cognitive lenses through which people make sense of the world around them. To understand the power of mindsets, recall the following examples:

- In 1927, Harry M. Warner, the founder of Warner Bros., observed, "Who the hell wants to hear actors talk?"

- In 1943, Thomas Watson Sr., the architect and chairman of IBM, speculated, "I think there is a world market for maybe five computers."

- In 1977, Ken Olsen, chairman and founder of Digital Equipment, noted, "There is no reason for any individuals to have a computer in their home."[11]

- In 2003, Seth Godin, one of the foremost Internet marketing experts, observed that while Google provided a terrific search service, it was not the foundation for a great business.[12]

What is going on here? These are really smart people. The problem is that, like Harry Warner, they were looking at the future from the lens of the past. When movies were silent, actors were selected for how they looked and not how they spoke.

Thus, most of them had terrible voices. Harry Warner was right in asking why in hell anybody would want to hear them talk. What he overlooked, however, was that a new business model might emerge—one based on actors who not only looked good but also had great voices. Think now about whether you and your colleagues might similarly be looking at the global reality from the mental prison of past business models.

Companies and business leaders can be said to have a global mindset when they reflect two characteristics: an openness to and awareness of diversity across cultures and markets combined with a propensity and ability to integrate across this diversity. Becoming a prisoner of diversity is just as bad as being blind to it.

Most business leaders still view foreign markets as an add-on supplement to the domestic market. Very few have internalized the fact that even for U.S.-headquartered companies, 75 percent of the world's GDP is outside the United States and that emerging economies are growing three times as fast as the U.S. economy. Thus, it may well be more prudent to view opportunities outside the United States as more central to the company's future than those within the United States.

The primary explanation for why most companies lack global mindsets is that leaders with the power to shape the company's future direction are far removed psychologically, cognitively, and physically from the new epicenters of global change. The net result is that they rely primarily on information that is not merely several months old but that also has been filtered and processed to make it palatable—in other words, information that may well be useless or even misleading. Given the vastness, complexity, dynamism, and importance of China and India, there can be no substitute for gut-level judgment based on direct observation and deep immersion within these societies.

What steps must a company undertake in its moves to globalize the sensing and decision-making capabilities of the corporate leadership? The starting point in cultivating a global mindset is to deepen people's knowledge of major cultures and markets other than their own home country. The key here is to build knowledge that is deep rather than superficial. Deep knowledge comes not from short visits but from on-the-ground immersion over a longer period. It comes not from observation but from problem solving within the new culture. This requires that the career paths of fast-track employees must involve cross-border on-the-ground experience in at least a couple of the major economies. Of course, as you do that, it is crucial to make sure that the identification of fast-track employees is blind to nationality or cultural background.

Another mechanism to deepen knowledge of different cultures and markets is to rotate the locations of key meetings and, when a particular group meets in a location, to make sure that the agenda includes addressing not only the immediate task at hand but also learning from field experience, even if the experience is only for half a day.

Deeper learning of other cultures can also be fostered by building interpersonal networks that cut across borders. Deployment of technologies such as Facebook within the company is making it easier by the day. Evolution has programmed human beings into social animals. As each of us knows from personal experience, people like to interact with others, and they interact more frequently, more openly, and more helpfully with others whom they know and like. The idea here is not that the company should mandate the formation of cross-border interpersonal networks. Rather, what the company should do is eliminate every barrier that prevents such networks from emerging spontaneously on their own.

The final and perhaps most potent mechanism for cultivating a global mindset is to globalize the company's leadership architecture. On this issue, the first question to ask is, Where should the leaders come from? Having studied strategic leadership over the last twenty years, we have come to the firm belief that the best leaders are not those who are supposedly objective but those who are biased—with an important caveat that those biases reflect the reality of the future rather than that of the past. The best leaders are those who have a sense for where the future is headed and are passionate about this vision. Vision and passion reflect a biased view of the world, a bias that propels the company forward rather than holds it back. Some questions to ponder are: How many of the top three hundred people in your company today reflect a deep knowledge of geographics that represent your future markets and sources of your future talent pool? What about the executive committee? Also, what about the board of directors?

The second major question pertaining to globalization of the leadership architecture pertains to the question of where people with decision-making power should sit. In far too many companies, there is a gap of five to ten thousand miles between the location of major opportunities and the location of decision-making power. The typical outcome is that people in the field often find themselves banging their heads against a wall. Business leaders who spend most of their time in New York City, Tokyo, or Munich have a difficult time looking at the world from anything other than American, Japanese, or German eyes. If you are keen to transform your company into a next-generation global enterprise, you need to start figuring out why companies such as Cisco, IBM, and GE have started to relocate some of their most powerful executives to the new epicenters of the global economy. It is instructive to take note of a favorite expression of Cisco's Wim Elfrink: "You can't think out of the box while sitting in the box."[13]

In conclusion, the successful global corporation of tomorrow will be one that figures out how to take advantage of three realties: the rapid growth of emerging markets and the increasing multipolarity of the world economy; enduring cultural, political, and economic differences across countries and regions; and the rapidly growing integration of national economies. Organizationally, it will be managed as a globally integrated enterprise rather than as a federation of regional or national fiefdoms. And it will be led by business leaders who have global mindsets and are masters at building bridges rather than moats.

Notes

Preface

1. See A. Beebe and L. Cheng, "Winning in China's Mass Markets" (Armonk, N.Y.: IBM Institute for Business Value, 2007), p. 4.

Chapter One

1. V. Mallet, "The Rebalance of Power," *Financial Times*, Apr. 5, 2008, p. 7.
2. Quoted in "The Past, Imperfect," *Time*, July 15, 1996, p. 54.
3. See M. Palmer, "Motorola Trails Samsung in Global Market," *Financial Times*, Nov. 27, 2007.
4. See BearingPoint, "2005 Form 10-K Annual Report," p. 3.
5. See A. Maddison, *The World Economy: Historical Statistics* (Paris: Organization for Economic Cooperation and Development, 2003). Maddison is perhaps the most renowned scholar of world economic history and has published a series of books for the Organization for Economic Cooperation and Development on the changing structure of the world economy over the past two thousand years.
6. J. Llewellyn, R. Subbaraman, A. Newton, and S. Varma, "India: Everything to Play For," Lehman Brothers, Global Economics Paper, Oct. 2007; R. de Milliano, "India 2020: Rise of the Elephant," Rabobank Special Scenario Studies, Oct. 2020; D. Wilson and R. Purushothaman, "Dreaming

with BRICs: The Path to 2050," Goldman Sachs Global Economics Paper No. 99, Oct. 2003.

7. J. O'Neil, S. Lawson, and R. Purushothaman, "The BRICs and Global Markets: Cars, Crude, and Capital," Goldman Sachs Global Economics Paper No. 2004-09, Oct. 2004.

8. S. Tucker, "China and India Keep Building on Success," *Financial Times*, Dec. 18, 2006, p. 21.

9. "Construction Equipment Sector to Grow Five-Fold, Says McKinsey," *Economic Times*, Bangalore, Nov. 15, 2007, p. 19.

10. Authors' field interviews plus an IDC India survey as reported in A. Yee, "Soaring Salaries to Hit India IT Group Margins," *Financial Times*, Sept. 12, 2007, p. 18.

11. See V. Wadhwa, G. Gereffi, B. Rissing, and R. Ong, "Where the Engineers Are," *Issues in Science and Technology*, Spring 2007.

12. G. T. Huang, "The World's Hottest Computer Lab," *MIT Technology Review*, June 2004.

13. Quoted in R. Kirkland, "The Greatest Economic Boom Ever," *Fortune*, July 12, 2007.

14. See Asian Development Bank, "Inequality in Asia," Aug. 8, 2007.

15. "All Mouth and No Trousers," *Economist*, Mar. 29, 2007.

16. See R. Meredith, *The Elephant and the Dragon* (New York: Norton, 2007), p. 89.

17. See A. Chozick, "Nissan Races to Make Smaller, Cheaper Cars," *Wall Street Journal*, Oct. 22, 2007, p. A1.

Chapter Two

1. Knowledge@Wharton, Interview with HCL's Shiv Nadar, Sept. 27, 2006.

2. J. Welch and S. Welch, "The Welch Way: Choosing China or India," *BusinessWeek*, Mar. 19, 2007, p. 110.

3. See D. Wilson and R. Purushothaman, "Dreaming with BRICs: The Path to 2050," Goldman Sachs Global Economics Paper No. 99, Oct. 2003.

4. In 2004, the percentage of paved roads to total was 81 percent in China versus 47 percent in India; rail lines hauled five times as much goods tonnage in China as in India; and China's port container traffic was eighteen times that of India. See World Bank, *The World Development Indicators 2007* (Washington, D.C.: World Bank, 2007).

5. In 2006, China and India attracted $79 billion and $7 billion, respectively, in inbound foreign direct investment. See World Bank, *The World Development Indicators 2007*.

6. In March 2007, China enacted a new enterprise income tax law due to take effect on January 1, 2008. Under this law, the corporate tax rates would be equal for foreign as well as domestic enterprises. In effect, for domestic enterprises, the tax rates would come down from 33 percent to 25 percent; for foreign enterprises, they would go up from the previous average of 15 percent to 25 percent.

7. BP, *BP Statistical Review of World Energy 2007* (2007).

8. Abstracted from International Energy Agency and J. Spencer, "Why China Could Blame Its CO_2 on West," *Wall Street Journal*, Nov. 12, 2007, p. A2.

9. B. Einhorn, "Dell Raises Its Stake in India," *BusinessWeek*, June 18, 2007.

10. IDG News Service, "Lenovo Gets Ready for Big India Push," Sept. 30, 2005.

11. G. Fairclough and J. Spencer, "Dell's New PC Marks Global Push," *Wall Street Journal Europe*, Mar. 22, 2007, p. 6.

12. "The Ties That Bind," *BusinessWeek*, June 8, 2007.

13. See open letter to suppliers dated May 22, 2006, http://www-03.ibm.com/procurement/proweb.nsf/contentdocsbytitle/United+States~IBM+Procurement+headquarters+moving+to+Shenzhen+China?OpenDocument&Parent=Global1Procurement.

14. S. Bhattacharya, "China Calling," *Business Today*, Dec. 16, 2007, p. 245.

15. A. Qiu, "Dalian: China's Bangalore," *China International News*, May 2007, p. 49.
16. "Mahindra to Use Weak Dollar to Buy US Factories," *Economic Times*, Dec. 4, 2007.
17. R. Waters and C. Freeland, "View from the Top: William J. Amelio, Lenovo President and Chief Executive," *Financial Times*, Aug. 3, 2007, p. 8.
18. Authors' interview in Bangalore with Ravi Venkatesan, chairman, Microsoft India, Nov. 2007.
19. R. Sachitanand, "GE's Innovation Hub," *Business Today*, Apr. 6, 2008, p. 74.
20. AmCham Shanghai and Booz Allen Hamilton, "China Manufacturing Competitiveness 2007–2008," Mar. 2008.

Chapter Three

1. J. Doebele, "Standing Up to a Giant," *Forbes*, Apr. 25, 2005.
2. C. Nuttall, "EBay's Ambitions in China Suffer Setback," *Financial Times*, Dec. 19, 2006, p. 1.
3. Asian Development Bank, *Inequality in Asia*, 2007.
4. "The World's Billionaires," *Forbes*, Mar. 5, 2008.
5. F. Warner, "Going for Gold," *Forbes*, July 2, 2007.
6. J. Lu and Z. Tai, "EBay's Strategy in China: Alliance or Acquisition," Case HKU701, Asia Case Research Center, University of Hong Kong, 2007.
7. E. Bellman and C. Rohwedder, "Western Grocer Modernizes Passage to India's Markets," *Wall Street Journal*, Nov. 28, 2007, p. B1.
8. J. Leow, "In China, Add a Caterpillar to the Dog and Pony Show," *Wall Street Journal*, Dec. 10, 2007, p. B1.
9. E. Bellman, "In India, a Retailer Finds Key to Success Is Clutter," *Wall Street Journal*, Aug. 8, 2007, p. A1.
10. See Exhibit 2 in C. Holloway, "Flextronics: A Focus on Design Leads to India," Case Study OIT-45, Stanford Graduate School of Business, 2005.

11. See F. A. Martinez-Jerez and V. G. Narayanan, "Strategic Outsourcing at Bharti Airtel Limited," Case 9–107–003, Harvard Business School, 2006, p. 8.

12. E. Bellman, "In India, Rural Poor Are Key to Cellular Firm's Expansion," *Wall Street Journal*, Sept. 24, 2007, p. A1.

13. Authors' interviews with managers at B&Q China in July 2007. See also G. Desvaux and A. J. Ramsay, "Shaping China's Home-Improvement Market: An Interview with B&Q's CEO for Asia," *McKinsey Quarterly*, 2006.

14. Authors' interviews with Wim Elfrink, executive vice president, Cisco, in Bangalore, Feb. 2008, and with Jim Sherriff, chairman, Cisco China, Apr. 2008. See also Cisco, "Cisco Announces Next Stage of Corporate Strategy for China," press release, Apr. 16, 2008. As part of the Eleventh Five-Year Plan, China's Ministry of Commerce began implementing the Thousand-Hundred-Ten Talents Project in 2006. The aim of this five-year project was to foster the creation of one thousand Chinese companies that would be internationally qualified to be services providers on an outsourced basis, attract one hundred global companies to start outsourcing their services activities to China, and build ten cities into major services outsourcing hubs.

15. See A. Beebe and L. Cheng, "Winning in China's Mass Markets" (Armonk, N.Y.: IBM Institute for Business Value, 2007), p. 4.

16. The term *logical incrementalism* was coined by J. B. Quinn. See his book, *Strategies for Change: Logical Incrementalism* (Homewood, Ill.: Irwin, 1980).

Chapter Four

1. E. K. Sharma, "Chipping In," *Business Today*, Feb. 10, 2008, p. 58.

2. Based on interviews with senior managers at the John F. Welch Technology Centre, Bangalore, Nov. 2007.

3. A. Jack, "GSK to Spend $100m on R&D in China," *Financial Times*, Dec. 13, 2007, p. 20.

4. J. L. Lunsford, "Cessna's New Plane to Be Built in China," *Wall Street Journal*, Nov. 28, 2007, p. A14.

5. See V. Wadhwa, G. Gereffi, B. Rissing, and R. Ong, "Where the Engineers Are," *Issues in Science and Technology*, Spring 2007. The data in this article also indicate that China has a rapidly growing lead over both the United States and India in the production of Ph.D.s in engineering and technology. In 1995, China produced about two thousand Ph.D.s in engineering and technology versus about five hundred for India and seven thousand for the United States. In 2005, the numbers were over nine thousand for China, about eight thousand for the United States, and about one thousand for India.

6. Quoted in "Something New Under the Sun: A Special Report on Innovation," *Economist*, Oct. 13, 2007, p. 8.

7. D. Wilson, R. Purushothaman, and T. Fiotakis, "The BRICS and Global Market," Goldman Sachs, Global Economics Paper No. 118, Oct. 14, 2004.

8. "Something New Under the Sun," p. 8.

9. See also A. K. Gupta, V. Govindarajan, and H. Wang, *The Quest for Global Dominance*, 2nd ed. (San Francisco: Jossey-Bass, 2008), Chap. 4.

10. Abstracted from Boston Consulting Group, "Harnessing the Power of India," May 2006.

11. F. W. McFarlan, W. C. Kirby, and T. Y. Manty, "Li & Fung 2006," Case 9–301–077, Harvard Business School Publishing, May 2007.

12. J. Spencer, "Lilly, China Firm to Develop Drugs," *Wall Street Journal*, Aug. 21, 2007, p. A11.

13. See O. E. Williamson, *The Economic Institutions of Capitalism* (New York: Free Press, 1985).

14. J. Range, "Rethinking the India Back Office," *Wall Street Journal*, Feb. 11, 2008, p. A6.

15. Interview with Karl-Heinz Floether in *The India Story* (Accenture, Oct. 2007).
16. Authors' interview with Keith Haviland, Dec. 7, 2007.
17. Authors' interview with Mei Xu, president, Pacific Trade International, May 15, 2008.
18. Authors' interviews with senior managers at the John F. Welch Technology Centre, Bangalore, Nov. 2007.
19. Quoted by R. A. Mashelkar, former director-general of India's Council for Scientific and Industrial Research in R. A. Mashelkar, "Technology: Opportunity and Challenge," *Tribune*, Jan. 3–7, 2004.
20. G. T. Huang, "The World's Hottest Computer Lab," *Technology Review*, June 2004.
21. Quoted in R. Buderi and G. T. Huang, *Guanxi: Microsoft, China, and Bill Gates Plan to Win the Road Ahead* (New York: Simon & Schuster, 2006), p. 36.
22. S. J. Palmisano, "Leadership, Trust and the Globally Integrated Enterprise," remarks at INSEAD Business School, Fontainebleau, France, Oct. 3, 2006.

Chapter Five

1. Quoted in "A Special Report on Innovation," *Economist*, Oct. 13, 2007, p. 19.
2. For a detailed analysis of country-specific advantages, see M. E. Porter, "The Competitive Advantage of Nations," *Harvard Business Review*, May 1990.
3. Zheng Caixiong, "Vice-Minister Urges Domestic Firms to Go Global," *China Daily*, Aug. 8, 2006, p. 10.
4. S. Tucker, "China and India Begin to Deliver on M&A Promise," *Financial Times*, Dec. 20, 2007, p. 16.
5. S. Oster, "China: New Dam Builder for the World," *Wall Street Journal*, Dec. 28, 2007, p. B1.
6. R. McGregor, "China Power Group Offers Skills to Manila," *Financial Times*, Dec. 17, 2007, p. 6.

7. R. G. Matthews, "Essar Steel of India Set to Acquire Esmark," *Wall Street Journal*, May 1, 2008, p. B5.

8. W. Lixin, "TCL's Overseas Struggle," *China International Business*, Dec. 2006, p. 44.

9. Quoted in S. Robinson, "Is India Bad for Jaguar?" Time.com, Dec. 14, 2007.

10. Quoted in S. Sengupta, "IBM's Tryst with India," *BusinessWorld*, May 22, 2006.

11. Interview with Karl-Heinz Floether, in *The India Story* (Accenture, Oct. 2007).

12. G. Edmondson, "Renault's Race to Replace the Rickshaw," *BusinessWeek*, Nov. 2, 2007.

13. Edmondson, "Renault's Race to Replace the Rickshaw."

14. D. Kiley, "Ghosn Hits the Accelerator," *BusinessWeek*, May 12, 2008, p. 48.

15. J. H. Dyer, P. Kale, and H. Singh, "When to Ally and When to Acquire," *Harvard Business Review*, July-Aug. 2004.

Chapter Six

1. Wang Zhenghuang, "Hotel Chief Exec Sees More Room for Growth," *China Daily*, Mar. 4, 2008, p. 15.

2. World Bank, *Global Economic Prospects 2007* (Washington, D.C.: World Bank, 2007).

3. See "2008 White Paper: American Business in China" (Shanghai: American Chamber of Commerce, 2008).

4. See A. Batson, "Help Wanted: Top Managers in China," *Wall Street Journal*, Apr. 29, 2008, p. B4.

5. See J. Johnson, "More Westerners Take Top Posts in India as Locals' Pay Demands Soar," *Financial Times*, May 30, 2007, p. 1.

6. "2007 Global R&D Report," *R&D Magazine*, Battelle, Sept. 2006.

7. Li Weitao, "Local Executives Take Helm at Big Corporations," *China Daily*, Sept. 4, 2007.

8. D. Farrell and A. J. Grant, "China's Looming Talent Shortage," *McKinsey Quarterly*, no. 4, 2005.

9. Weitao, "Local Executives Take Helm at Big Corporations."

10. See R. Ball, A. Robin, and J. Shuang Wu, "Accounting in China" (Washington, D.C.: World Bank, 2001).

11. See B. Jopson, "Number-Crunchers Line Up for Boot Camp," *Financial Times*, Dec. 8, 2006, p. 8.

12. "2007 Global R&D Report," *R&D Magazine, Battelle*, Sept. 2006.

13. We first came across the brilliantly coined term *last-mile unemployability* in an April 2007 India Knowledge@Wharton interview with Manish Sabharwal, chairman of TeamLease, the biggest player in India's temporary staffing industry.

14. "India's College Graduates," *International Herald Tribune*, Nov. 7, 2006, http://www.iht.com/slideshows/2006/11/07/business/web.1107college.php.

15. E. Ramstad and Qin Juying, "Intel Uses China as Blueprint to Grow," *Wall Street Journal*, May 23, 2006.

16. D. Chatterjee, "School for Retailers," *Business Today*, Dec. 30, 2007, p. 60.

17. Zhenghuang, "Hotel Chief Exec Sees More Room for Growth," p. 15.

18. B. Einhorn, "The Shanghai Scramble," *BusinessWeek*, Aug. 20, 2007, p. 53.

19. J. Schlosser, "Harder Than Harvard," *Fortune*, Mar. 17, 2006.

20. S. Roy, "Infosys Builds a Realistic Dream," Rediff.com, July 16, 2005.

Chapter Seven

1. Quoted by W. Holstein in an interview with J. E. Garten, former dean of the Yale School of Management. See W. Holstein, "Only a Passing Grade," *Chief Executive Magazine*, June 2005.

2. J. Mero, "Global Innovation: John Deere's Farm Team," *Fortune*, Apr. 14, 2008, p. 119.

3. T. Leavitt, "The Globalization of Markets," *Harvard Business Review*, May 1983.

4. For an extensive discussion of globalization, see A. K. Gupta, V. Govindarajan, and H. Wang, *The Quest for Global Dominance*, 2nd ed. (San Francisco: Jossey-Bass, 2008), Chap. 1.

5. See A. K. Gupta, P. Tesluk, and M. S.Taylor, "Innovation at and Across Levels of Analysis," *Organization Science*, 2007, 18, 885–897.

6. See W. Elfrink, "Executive Perspective: Virtualizing the Corporation," *ThoughtLeaders, Cisco Systems*, 2008; also our personal discussions with Wim Elfrink in January and February 2008.

7. "IBM Shifts Global Procurement Headquarters to China," press release, IBM Corporation, Oct. 12, 2006.

8. See F. Cairncross, *The Death of Distance* (Boston: Harvard Business School Press, 1999), and "A Survey of Business and the Internet," *Economist*, June 26, 1999.

9. This assessment is based on our own experience at using TelePresence.

10. S. Spear and H. K. Bowen, "Decoding the DNA of the Toyota Production System," *Harvard Business Review*, Sept.-Oct. 1999.

11. All three quotes from "The Past, Imperfect," *Time*, July 15, 1996, p. 54.

12. Quoted in T. Eisenmann, S. Bakshi, S. Briens, and S. Singh, "Google Inc.," Case 9–804–141, Harvard Business School, 2004.

13. Authors' personal discussions with Wim Elfrink during January and February 2008.

The Authors

Anil K. Gupta is widely recognized as one of the world's leading experts on strategy and globalization. He is the Ralph J. Tyser Professor of Strategy and Organization and research director of the Center for International Business Education and Research at the Smith School of Business, University of Maryland at College Park. He received a doctorate from the Harvard Business School, an M.B.A. from the Indian Institute of Management at Ahmedabad, and a B.Tech. from the Indian Institute of Technology at Kanpur. Gupta also serves as chief adviser to the China India Institute, a research and consulting organization based in Bethesda, Maryland.

Gupta is the author, coauthor, or coeditor of over seventy papers and three previous books: *The Quest for Global Dominance* (Jossey-Bass, 2008), *Smart Globalization* (Jossey-Bass, 2003), and *Global Strategy and Organization* (John Wiley, 2003). *Financial Times* has published four of Gupta's papers in the Mastering Global Business series. The *Wall Street Journal* has published an invited full-page article by Gupta, "Getting China and India Right."

The recipient of numerous awards for excellence in research and teaching, Gupta has been recognized by *Business Week* as an Outstanding Faculty in its *Guide to the Best B-Schools*, inducted into the Academy of Management Journals' Hall of Fame, and ranked by *Management International Review* as one of the Top 20 North American Superstars for research in strategy and organization.

Gupta serves regularly as a keynote speaker at major conferences and corporate forums in the United States, Europe, China, and India. He has served as a consultant, adviser, or executive education faculty on strategy and globalization with some of the largest corporations in the world, including IBM, National Semiconductor, Marriott, First Data, Monsanto, ABB, Lockheed Martin, McGraw-Hill, Indian Oil, McCormick, TeliaSonera, Metso, UPM-Kymmene, Finnair, Cemex, Penoles, and the IRI Group.

Gupta is an elected member of the board of directors of Origene Technologies (a gene cloning company). He earlier served on the boards of directors of Omega Worldwide (NASDAQ, an asset management company), Vitalink Pharmaceutical Services (NYSE), NeoMagic Corporation (NASDAQ, a semiconductor company), and TiE-DC, the premier organization of entrepreneurs and venture capitalists dedicated to fostering entrepreneurship in the mid-Atlantic region. He is also a member of the board of advisers for Asia Silicon Valley Connection (San Mateo, California), RavGen (a Maryland-based biotechnology venture), and India Globalization Capital. In addition, he has been an adviser to the U.S.-India Business Council.

Gupta has also served as a visiting professor at Stanford University, Dartmouth College, Bocconi Business School (Milan, Italy), Helsinki University of Technology and Helsinki School of Economics and Business Administration (Finland), and IPMI (Jakarta, Indonesia). He has been quoted by the *Wall Street Journal*, *Washington Post*, *USA Today*, *China Daily*, *China Business News*, *China Entrepreneur*, *Economic Times*, *India Today*, *Times of India*, *Red Herring*, *ComputerWorld*, and *CIO Magazine*, as well as other leading media in the United States, China, India, Italy, and Finland.

Haiyan Wang is managing partner of China India Institute, a research and consulting organization with a focus on creating winning global strategies that leverage the transformational rise of China and India. She is responsible for overseeing the organization's strategic direction, research and consulting focus, and all program activities.

She is the coauthor of the highly praised book *The Quest for Global Dominance* (Jossey-Bass/Wiley, 2008). Her opinion pieces have appeared in top international media such as the *Wall Street Journal*, *Economic Times*, *China Daily*, *Times of India*, and *CEO Magazine*.

A native of China, Haiyan Wang has spent the past twenty years consulting for and managing multinational business operations in China and the United States in several industry sectors. Drawing on her broad international experience, she consults with clients and speaks at conferences on building and exploiting global presence, especially in China.

Haiyan Wang was among the first group of Chinese to study international business shortly after China embarked on economic reforms and opened its doors to the outside world. In the mid-1980s, she published several papers on China's foreign trade reform in Chinese journals such as *International Business* and *International Trade Tribune*.

In the late 1980s, Haiyan Wang worked for Minmetals, one of the twenty largest enterprises in China and a global Fortune 500 company. At Minmetals, she was responsible for importing steel to supply China's auto, petrochemical, and appliance industries.

In the United States, Haiyan Wang began her career working as a management consultant with Kepner-Tregoe, based in Princeton, New Jersey. She was responsible for facilitating strategic decision making, complex project management, and organizational process redesign. Her clients included some of the largest corporations in the United States and Asia, including Johnson & Johnson, Corning, Sprint, and the Singapore-based Far East Ship Yard.

Haiyan Wang also served as director of business development at E-Steel Corporation, a New York–based pioneer in the global steel industry e-marketplace. At E-Steel, she led the company's efforts to form partnerships between the company and top Chinese steel producers such as Baosteel.

Haiyan Wang also served as a senior marketing and operations executive at PTI Inc., a global manufacturer and wholesaler of home decor products with supply chain operations in the United States, China, and Vietnam. She helped to realign the company's strategic focus to service top retail chains such as Target, IKEA, Kohl's, and J.C. Penney.

Haiyan Wang received a bachelor's degree in economics from the Shanghai Institute of Foreign Trade and a master's degree in international business from the University of International Business and Economics in Beijing. She also holds an M.B.A. from the University of Maryland at College Park.

Index